THE AIMS OF REPRESENTATION
SUBJECT/TEXT/HISTORY

IRVINE STUDIES IN THE HUMANITIES
Robert Folkenflik, General Editor

Irvine Studies in the Humanities Volumes

Murray Krieger and Contemporary Critical Theory,
    Bruce Henricksen, ed.

The Aims of Representation: Subject/Text/History,
    Murray Krieger, ed.

THE AIMS
OF REPRESENTATION

SUBJECT/TEXT/HISTORY

edited, with an Introduction by
Murray Krieger

Columbia University Press
New York   1987

Library of Congress Cataloging-in-Publication Data

The Aims of representation.

Includes bibliographies.
1. Criticism. I. Krieger, Murray, 1923–
PN85.A36   1987   801'.95   86-33408
ISBN 0-231-06584-1

Columbia University Press
New York   Guildford, Surrey
Copyright © 1987 Columbia University Press
All rights reserved

Printed in the United States of America

Clothbound editions of Columbia University Press are Smyth-
sewn and printed on permanent and durable acid-free paper.

7-2-90

For Eugenio Donato
Theorist of memory

A NOTE ON THIS SERIES

This is the second in a series of volumes to be published by Columbia University Press on topics in the Humanities. This volume originated in lectures and colloquia organized by the Focused Research Program in Contemporary Critical Theory at the University of California, Irvine. I am grateful to Dean Terence D. Parsons of the School of Humanities, Dean Jaime Rodríguez of the Division of Graduate Research and Studies, and Executive Vice-Chancellor William J. Lillyman for their support. The members of the Program wish to acknowledge their debt to the late Eugenio Donato and Frank Lentricchia, their former colleagues, who in 1981 helped formulate the subject that led to this volume. For translating the Lyotard essay, I thank Cecile Lindsay. For help with a broad range of problems, I am indebted to the board of directors of Irvine Studies in the Humanities. Jean Symonds and Betty Terrell gave our group secretarial support. Finally, I would like to thank Paul A. Davis for his work as copy editor and for compiling the index. These volumes are published in conjunction with the Wellek Lectures, given annually at the University.

Robert Folkenflik, General Editor

THE CONTRIBUTORS

DAVID CARROLL is a professor of French at the University of California, Irvine, and currently director of the Focused Research Program in Contemporary Critical Theory. His published work includes a book entitled *The Subject in Question: The Languages of Theory and the Strategies of Fiction* (Chicago: University of Chicago Press, 1982), and he has just completed a book manuscript entitled *Paraesthetics: Foucault, Lyotard, and Derridae* (forthcoming, Methuen).

ANTHONY GIDDENS is a professor of sociology and Fellow of King's College at Cambridge University. His recent works include *The Constitution of Society* (Cambridge: Polity Press, 1984) and *The Nation State and Violence* (Cambridge: Polity Press, 1985).

STEPHEN GREENBLATT is the Class of 1932 Professor of English at the University of California, Berkeley. His books include *Renaissance Self-Fashioning: From More to Shakespeare* (Chicago: University of Chicago Press, 1980). He is founder and editor of the journal *Representations*.

WOLFGANG ISER is a professor at both the Universität Konstanz and the University of California, Irvine. His books include *The Implied Reader: Patterns of Communication in Prose Fiction from Bunyan to Beckett* (Baltimore: Johns Hopkins University Press, 1974) and *The Act of Reading: A Theory of Aesthetic Response* (Baltimore: Johns Hopkins University Press, 1978).

MURRAY KRIEGER, director of the Focused Research Program during the years that produced this volume, is University Professor of English at the University of California, with Irvine as his home campus. His books include, among others, *Theory of Criticism: A Tradition and Its System* (Baltimore: Johns Hopkins University Press, 1976) and *Poetic Presence and Illusion* (Baltimore: Johns Hopkins University Press, 1979).

DOMINICK LACAPRA is Goldwin Smith Professor of European Intellectual History at Cornell University. His books include *History & Criticism* (Ithaca, N.Y.: Cornell University Press, 1985) and *History, Politics and the Novel* (Ithaca, N.Y.: Cornell University Press, 1987).

JEAN-FRANÇOIS LYOTARD is a professor of philosophy at the University of Paris at Vincennes/Saint-Denis and a member of the Collège International de Philosophie. His books include *Discours, figure* (Paris: Klincksieck, 1978), *Economie libidinale* (Paris: Minuit, 1974) and *Le différend* (Paris: Minuit, 1983). In addition, two of his works have been translated into English: *The Postmodern Condition* (Minneapolis: University of Minnesota Press, 1984) and *Just Gaming* (Minneapolis: University of Minnesota Press, 1985).

MARK POSTER is professor of history at the University of California, Irvine. His books include *Foucault, Marxism, and History* (New York: Blackwell, 1980) and *Existential Marxism in Postwar France* (Princeton: Princeton University Press, 1976).

JOHN CARLOS ROWE is professor of English at the University of California, Irvine. His publications include *Through the Custom-House: Nineteenth-Century American Fiction and Modern Theory* (Baltimore: Johns Hopkins University Press, 1982), and *The Theoretical Dimensions of Henry James* (Madison: University of Wisconsin Press, 1984).

ROBERT WEIMANN is a professor of English literature at Zentralinstitut für Literaturgeschichte in the Academy of Sciences, Berlin, German Democratic Republic. His books include

Shakespeare and the Popular Tradition in the Theater (Baltimore: Johns Hopkins University Press, 1978) and *Structure and Society in Literary History: Studies in History and Theory of Historical Criticism* (Baltimore: Johns Hopkins University Press, 1984).

CONTENTS

xiv   **Contents**

INTRODUCTION
THE LITERARY, THE TEXTUAL, THE SOCIAL

Murray Krieger

THE essays in this volume are the fruits of a series of lectures and colloquia held at the University of California, Irvine, over a period of three academic years (1982–85) under the auspices of the Focused Research Program in Contemporary Critical Theory. The general subject to which speakers—and now writers— were to address themselves was announced by our title, *The Aims of Representation: Subject/Text/ History.* Our speakers gave papers in the following order: Jean-François Lyotard, David Carroll, and Wolfgang Iser in 1982–83; Shoshana Felman, Anthony Giddens, Mark Poster, and John Carlos Rowe in 1983–84; and Robert Weimann, Dominick LaCapra, and Stephen Greenblatt in 1984–85. The first eight of these—through Weimann's paper—were individual presentations presumably written independently of one another, four of them by visitors to our Program and four by its members. Each was followed by a lengthy colloquium. LaCapra and Greenblatt generously consented to compose papers instigated by the eight that were previously delivered and were now on the table for discussion: their comments were to be independently conceived though in some way addressed to issues generated by the eight, raising responses to them to the point of stimulating our debate. In March 1985, as an exhilarating conclusion to our three years of dialogue, the Program held a full-day colloquium devoted to the discussion of the papers of LaCapra and Greenblatt and, through them, the eight papers discussed individually at earlier moments.

Our intention was to publish all ten papers, and in the order I have described. And all of them are here, with the exception of Felman's. Unfortunately, previous publishing commitments that she had made prevent her paper ("Women and the Dream from which Psychoanalysis Proceeds: 'The Irma Dream'" from The Interpretation of Dreams) from appearing in this volume.

When the members of our program decided upon the general subject, which has come to be the title of this volume, we were less aware than we have become that the three terms in the subtitle—in the order in which they appear—represent, in brief, the focal points in the sequence of theoretical movements in recent years: the subject as controlling author of the literary work, then the work seen as produced by and absorbed within the larger textuality, and then that textuality seen as produced by and absorbed within power-driven historical forces. Subject, text, and history, in other words, can be seen as reflecting the consecutive dominance, respectively, of the criticism of consciousness, of deconstruction—whether Lacanian or Derridean—and of what we might call theories of social power, Foucaultian and/or Marxian. (Indeed, as if in echo of the subtitle and of this historical sequence, most of our essays—now including mine too—display three-part titles.) Now, at the end of this succession of essays, we can see how much our original subject reflected the direction that recent theory has been taking, so that we should expect the third emphasis to predominate. And it does. In the main these essays champion the increasing tendency to submit literary or more generally textual problems, as well as problems about the subject, to what are seen as the controlling pressures of the social-historical domain. And the debates in our final colloquium reveal a similar commitment. The extent to which literary problems could be subsumed under textual problems generally and the extent to which those textual problems could be subsumed under social-historical "realities" were what was at issue. Our principal thrust was social, although Wolfgang Iser (and I) appear to contest it from the other side. Were there still literary problems calling for special considerations, or were there only general textual problems into which so-called literary ones could be collapsed, or were there—beyond—social-historical "realities" that had not already been inscribed as a text, "realities" to which texts could be reduced rather than the other way round?

In the fall of 1982 Jean-François Lyotard sounded the opening notes—bold, challenging, and postmodern in their resistance to the comforts of harmony—and their resonance was such that we never escaped their reverberations. His paper, it turned out, framed our discourse, its terms and issues re-emerging again and again in papers and discussions right through our final colloquium. We found in it his tendency to expand language theory into social theory, or at least to encourage some slippage from linguistic forms to social forms. Though he hangs onto his discursive base, his borrowings from Austin permit him to raise language from the cognitive level to the "performative." We found also a distrust of closure as a totalizing act that masks a totalitarian act: his is a denial of the neat inclusiveness of system, a denial that opens the way to the heterogeneous "sublime" that he would have us seek. He rejects the very idea of "metanarrative" in order to indulge "little stories." At the more minute, grammatical level, he disdains the unifying "regime" of the sentence, preferring the resistance of the "regime" of the hold-out phrase. "Regime" is an effective example of a Lyotardian word whose metaphorical extensions permit him to stretch his meaning across the no-man's-land connecting the literary to the social-historical. At the same time we have in this use of terms like "regime" an example of a common figurative device and rhetorical procedure in Lyotard and among our theorists: the more the language of theory seeks to turn literary into social concerns, the more it doubles its meanings so that, in seeming to account for social-political matters, it is imposing linguistic—or even literary—categories upon those matters, leaving among them the thematic residue of the literary imagination. This is a development to which I will return at length later.

David Carroll and Mark Poster are those whose papers most obviously reflect the concerns we see in Lyotard. Carroll explicitly addresses his paper to Lyotard and to the ideas he shares with Bakhtin. He relates Lyotard's "multiplicity of small narratives," in opposition to any metanarrative, to the plurivocity of Bakhtin's notion of the carnivalesque, of dialogistic subversion. In both Bakhtin and Lyotard Carroll finds a lingering formalism which, in spite of itself, fights totalization in society with instruments forged in literary criticism. Thus the "heteroglossia" Bakhtin attributes to the several incompatible languages of carnival (like Lyotard's warring "heterogeneous regimes of phrases") is the social analogue of the "novelization" of literature, with the novel serving as the disruptive genre, enemy of all genres in that it violates them all in producing its own disorderly—indeed carnivalized—self. Is this, after all, an anti-formalism or only another, extreme thrust of formalism? Is it the collapsing of literature into social concerns or is it the ultimate—if unknowing—idolatry of literature, trimming the world to its forms, or rather in this case loosening the world into the bagginess of its monstrosity?

For Poster also the focus upon language immensely complicates and unleashes what otherwise the social theorist might be able to maintain about the social-historical forces he must theorize into submission. Posing the post-structuralist method of Foucault against the claims of Marx in addressing the contradictory forces of contemporary society, Poster sees that the totalizing assumptions of Marx must give way before linguistic deconstruction. Under the guidance of Foucault we see language as furnishing an opening for us to seek out the hidden sources of social power: Foucault permits us to "unlock the forms of domination inherent in diverse linguistic experiences." Is this so absolutely or only within a specified historical context: does the superiority of Foucault rest on inherent differences in the two analytic methods (those of Foucault and Marx), or does it hold only at our historical moment because in it the "mode of information" has replaced Marx's "mode of production" as history's controlling force? Despite suggestions of these historical differences, there is a suggestion also that the advent of the "mode of information" has laid bare the insufficiencies of Marxist analysis itself, now seen in older periods as well. But Poster sees a price for what Foucault gives us: the detotalizing power of post-structuralism, in its deconstruction of system, turns it into an anti-theoretical enterprise that leaves the theorist with his job still to do, though deprived of his instruments in advance. Alert to the lessons left him with the undermining of the Marxist theory by the Foucaultian anti-theory, the theorist must still try to put something together, to find some coherence of vision, though without neglecting the primal power of language and its resistance to the totality and continuity that any such coherence brings with it if it is to have any theoretical force at all.

John Carlos Rowe responds to the same concerns but is even more alive than the others to the dangers of formalism (indeed he calls it the "aestheticist impulse") lying within the post-structuralist method with its devotion to language and to textuality, to inscription and re-inscription, as the only cradle of being. For him the power of deconstruction must be forced beyond language and its play into becoming an agent that undermines the institutions of power by ripping from texts the disguises which those institutions surreptitiously use to manipulate readers. So deconstruction, no longer a self-indulgent fellow-player with the linguistic richness of textuality, is to serve as an instrument of ideological discovery and critique. No longer afflicted with lingering Kantianism, it is to forgo disinterested contemplation for active participation in the social-historical arena. Behind this fervent call to action is Rowe's need to allow for the extra-textual function of "real" social-historical forces and desires and deprivations even though he

apparently wants to hold onto the post-structuralist perspective that should suppress that need. He would prefer not to give
up his fealty to Jacques Derrida, though neither will he give up
on the difficult task of turning that fealty in directions where
other Derrideans (and, some would say, Derrida himself) could
not follow without abandoning the concepts of "reading" and
of "text" which gave the movement its distinctness—and, one
might add, which have for some years now been arousing the
antagonism of socially oriented theorists.

There occurred a curious incident of timing which affected our original discussion of the Rowe paper, and I believe
an introduction like mine is an appropriate occasion to mention such extraneous matters for whatever light they may cast. I
should say first that the Poster and Rowe papers, discussed
within a few weeks of each other in the spring of 1984, revealed
a striking pattern of reversals, indeed of criss-crossings. While
Poster, generally considered in his earlier work to be a Marxist
social theorist, seemed to have crossed to a post-structuralist
perspective from which to strike at Marx; Rowe, generally considered in his earlier work to be a devoted post-structuralist,
seemed to have crossed (passing Poster on the way?) toward a
Marxist perspective. Still, in this case, instead of rejecting Derrida, Rowe tried to carry Derrida with him, lamenting his fellow
American Derrideans who would rather press toward what he
thinks of as aestheticism and narcissism.

During the space between the two papers, just a couple of
weeks before Rowe's, Derrida presented as the 1984 Wellek
Library Lectures, also sponsored by our Program, the essays
that made up his memorial volume to Paul de Man. In them
Derrida clearly announces his affiliation to "deconstruction in
America" and, obviously, the Yale School. In his lengthy discussion of his relations with de Man and his work, Derrida's
allegiances seem far more "aestheticist" than those of the social
activist, if we are to accept and choose between Rowe's alternatives. (The fact that the sympathetic subject of these lectures is
Paul de Man had to be especially troublesome to Rowe in his
present position since socially oriented critics usually treat de

Man as an extreme example of aestheticist deconstruction. A most polemical example of this treatment is Frank Lentricchia's both in *After the New Criticism* and in *Criticism and Social Change*.) Derrida's lectures, then, reverberated through our discussion of Rowe's paper and perhaps made its lamentations about Yale School aestheticism the more wistful. The complicity of the timing of these occasions would appear to urge that Rowe may have even a harder time than he conceded if he is to retain both Derrida and the action-oriented interpretive strategy which he himself would champion. At this point in his career I believe we know which he would have to choose if he could not have both.

Anthony Giddens seems less troubled by these conflicts that complicate the polemical relations between the purely textual and the social-historical, relations prompted by the several mutually cancelling advantages of post-structuralism and theories of "practical consciousness," respectively. Rather he comes down, with few qualifications, on one side. His commitment to the intending self through whose "practical consciousness" day-to-day action is generated leads him to prize the ordinary-language philosophy of Wittgenstein as well as phenomenology over the post-structuralism of Derrida. His theory is dedicated to praxis, to ordinary language as it relates to "ordinary practices of day-to-day social life." Disdaining "the play of difference" that characterizes language for Derrida, Giddens must have language serving the subject "as a medium of social practice." So he sees texts as involving ordinary social activities, sees them as products of intending subjects. Rather than being taken as autonomous writing in post-structuralist fashion, texts, according to Giddens, are better described as speech acts, each one a "temporally and spacially situated conversation." He is thus poised to use texts to intervene in the arena of social-political consequences.

With Robert Weimann and Wolfgang Iser we are brought closer to the literary itself since unlike the others they return the theoretical emphasis to the differentiating character of literature, whatever its service as a text to the social-historical realm. Although Weimann is deeply concerned with the role of history, he shares with (or borrows from) Iser a concept of literature as the closing of the gap between representation and the non-representable. This also reminds us of Lyotard's definition of the *différend* as the point in language where the to-be-represented cannot be put into a phrase. For Weimann it is this fracture between the represented and the non-representable, between discourse and the non-discursive, that permits his Marxist concept of "appropriation," poised between mimesis and post-structuralism and at once celebrating and seeking to close the gap between them, to enter as the term that can both characterize the literary and give it its historical relevance. Indeed, as Weimann expands the several metaphorical realms of human labor in which that term can function in its several ways, from material to literary "appropriation," he proceeds to press formal literary values toward the reflection and criticism of society, thereby serving both literature and social history, both post-structuralism and mimesis, each separately seen as an insufficient perspective.

Though Iser accepts the notion that representation depends upon difference, for him literature consists of the representation of that from which difference has been removed; yet in this case representation is nevertheless made possible, thanks to poet and reader. Iser resolves this apparent paradox by moving literature into the "performative" mode, turning literary discourse into "staged discourse." It is the act of self-conscious "staging" that allows the self-"doubling" of the literary work, turning it into the "play" that distinguishes it from other discourse and characterizes it as literature: "It is the play element in the removal of difference that distinguishes literature as a form of staging from all conceptualizations of life as forms of explanations, but even this infinite variety does not fully explain the fascination of the aesthetic semblance which gives presence to the inaccessible." Here indeed is a privileging of literature, and it is this privileging—resting on the "performative," which produces the "staging" and hence the "doubling," the "play"—which Iser requires in his definition of literature as the presentation of the (otherwise) unpresentable. Freed from "difference," it achieves the "simultaneity of the mutually exclusive."

Iser is the only one of our critics whose interest—at least in this essay—is focused exclusively on the peculiar representational functions of the literary work, as distinguished from other discourse (other "conceptualizations of life as forms of explanation"). However, through his treatment of literature as a version of the "performative," with its relations to speech-act theory, he has clearly opened it into a social context by implicating the reader and the reader's response. His sense of the "performative," as well as his primary concern for the representation of that which, as undifferentiated, is inaccessible to being represented, keeps him still within that range of problems which Lyotard's paper put on the table for our three-year sequence of papers and discussions.

It is not surprising that these problems continued to be our focus in our final colloquium based on the papers of LaCapra and Greenblatt, since they were to comment upon the concerns expressed by the others. I will try to convey something of the spirit of that spirited occasion and my reactions to it as I comment also on the two papers that stimulated it.

Dominick LaCapra's paper pressed further the tendency he saw in our essays to empty the textual into the social-historical, and it sought to make this a representative and progressive tendency on our theoretical scene. After a discussion of Marx that shows him to stand in need of post-structuralist critique and supplementation, LaCapra's analysis of our current situation in theory takes the form of a narrative that moves, Hegelian-style, from Derrida to Foucault to Bakhtin-Lyotard. (Of course, this is Bakhtin as lately rediscovered for our Lyotardian purposes rather than the historical Bakhtin of the thirties.) I find in the narrative a certain impatience to get beyond Derrida (though the limitation of his theory to pure—or mere—textuality is strongly qualified) to Foucault's domain of social-historical power and beyond again to the continual subversion by the dialogism produced by carnivalization and the loosing of différends. But we may fear that the Foucaultian desire for coercive power will not down, not even in those committed to subvert it; instead it reappears to lead to the reification and then the institutionalization of those very anti-institutional forces unleashed by the freedom urged by the Bakhtin-Lyotard moment. How to keep in the carnivalizing act the disruptive intention that threatens the hegemonic structure without permitting one of its splintering elements to seek a newer dominance that would make it a rival structure? We have seen in recent years how such developments could vitiate Derridean or Foucaultian dispersion, despite all its inherent post-structuralist resistance, thereby revealing the pattern in which every deconstruction turns, in spite of itself, into its own construct in need of further deconstruction. Or, to put the pattern in political rather than philosophical terms, every subversive struggle against the repressive power structure becomes a struggle for its own power and thus its own right to repress.

Much of the lengthy discussion following LaCapra's presentation revolved about Bakhtin, his notions of the dialogic and of carnivalization. Some discussants echoed LaCapra's doubts about how subversive carnival really turned out to be, since it must be conceded that the established authority might encourage it in order to allow repressed steam to be released, so that—as Carroll reminds us in his paper—the authority is supported rather than threatened: to normalize the ritual of carnival is to domesticate the dangerous and reinforce the status quo. Others were as concerned as LaCapra was about the danger of seeing only the benignly disruptive elements of carnival; concerned, that is, about its potential for folk violence, a Nazi-like irrational explosiveness that can lead to "scapegoating" and its "blood-letting."

Still, the potential values of the carnivalesque were pursued. All who spoke acknowledged that the carnivalesque could have value to the extent that it let loose anti-totalizing disruptions of the dominant ideology, to the extent that it threw up splinters of alien and unforeseen possibilities. It is a way to put the deconstructive proclivities of the Derridean to social-political use—perhaps to us an echo of John Carlos Rowe's attempt to turn Derrida in the direction of social revolution. It is also a way for LaCapra to seek to undo the dominant discursive formations established by Foucault for the sequence of power structures through history. Once beyond Foucault, we can indulge the multiplicity of autonomous phrases advocated by Lyotard, of dissident voices, hold-out regimes that challenge the closure of the regime. We are not far from the wayward sequence of "conversations" advocated by Richard Rorty.

Yet another concern in our discussion centered on the action-blocking consequences of the over-indulgence in carnival. As we might have expected from his paper, Rowe saw in "endless carnival" a danger to our need for an ideology to lead us toward action. For Rowe this resistance to ideology is all too Kantian, too disinterested and contemplative: the anarchic multiplicity of voices paralyzes the clean line of action, precludes any organized social intervention. Rowe is charging this celebration of the dialogic collision of phrases with being too literary—disinterested and thus aesthetic in the Kantian sense—another version of the harmless diversions that only reinforce hegemonic power. His is a charge not unlike the charge brought long ago by social critics against the New Criticism. (Indeed, social critics like Rowe claim to find good reason to argue that theories which would promote the carnivalesque—which resist a subsequent ideology of their own—have some continuity with New-Critical doctrines of irony.) Thus Rowe complains against the university as an institution for social change, seeing that it is constituted precisely as an unending carnival for the young who, like Mann's Hans Castorp, are pleased to experiment and experience while, seeing them so occupied, the dominant institutions can relax their anxiety and extend their dominance. The von Humboldt ideal of liberal education, like Schiller's ideal of "aesthetic education," with its idolatry of Kantian disinterestedness, builds a structure dedicated to a projection of literary irony onto our contemplation of all intellectual and social-political alternatives. In effect, Rowe charges, the academic community has appropriated the notion of carnivalization and turned it into yet another of its self-paralyzing formalisms.

What Rowe helps make important to our discussion is the analogy to which I have earlier referred between the function of disruption in society and the function of discontinuity, of gap, of aporia, in the text. This is the analogy we saw Bakhtin create between carnival as de-totalizing force in society and the novel as anti-genre in literature. The movement in recent theory, as in Lyotard and as applauded by LaCapra, which collapses the literary into the social on these grounds, is rejected by Rowe as being only literary and inconsequential after all. Rowe's attack on the irresponsibility of the de-totalizing spirit, like the claims I have attributed to Anthony Giddens, is made on behalf of the necessary role of ideology as a ground for action. (I will continue to use *ideology* even though it may be only a fancy word for the rationalization of institutional pressures.) His attack rests on the assumption that ideology will intrude its control upon our critical texts in any case (including the de-totalizing cases), so that the underminings by Derrida or even Bakhtin and Lyotard may as well face up to the ideology being served by *their* moves and should consequently become unironically ideological themselves in the service of change. Thus Rowe would resolve the conflict between ideology and the de-totalizing spirit (such as we have seen in Bakhtin and Lyotard) on ideology's side: he finally has recourse to a metanarrative (one that would delegitimate any discourse authorized by a universal critical method directed against the heavy, closed hand of institutional power), even when the "little stories" would undermine that metanarrative at every step. We have seen that Poster and Carroll have similar concerns, but they remain more persistently alive to the anti-totalizing force in post-structuralism that threatens the theoretical impulse itself and would pull down theory and doctrine alike.

But how are the anti-totalizers among us to reconcile themselves to what seems to be inevitable: to the drift of their anti-ideological discourse into ideology, its own ideology, an institution of the anti-institutional questing for the power that goes with discourse? How to accommodate within a de-totalizing discourse its gradual transformation of a persistent series of moves into a movement? This troubling problem to which I have already alluded, only implicit in LaCapra's paper, was taken up by many of its discussants afterwards. If the drive to delegitimate the ruling totalized discourse is so continuously pursued that it begins to legitimate itself, then of course we are faced with the formation of a new totality, however self-contra-dictory it may be to form it. The deconstruction, thus con-verted, then stands in need—by its own arguments—of being itself deconstructed in turn. Once the carnivalizing impulse turns into carnival as a way of life to be justified—just as the anti-generic novel turns into a literary genre with its own defin-ing and controlling characteristics—a reification has occurred in the guise of a naturalized fiction. And all discourse, from closed ideological systems to freely playing *différends*, seems eventually to face this affliction. No one has witnessed the continuous rise and fall of rival movements and the competi-tion among them without sensing the imperialistic motives that undermine the commitment to de-totalize the theoretical im-pulse.

If the dialogical habit, in self-defiance, closes in upon itself, it requires either a surrender to ideology or a later rescu-ing by another secessionist discourse. But what if there was a discourse devoted exclusively and self-consciously to the play-ful pursuit of dialogue, without direct and explicit concern for existential and social "realities"? What if it alone could pursue its resistance to closure because it had no "interest" that would fix its undermining motion? What if its "stagings" took place only on an actual stage and the "performatives" of its persons were literal performances, so that they were not persons with actual destinies but characters with dramatic denouements? These questions propose that the very dilemma of the dialogic in discourse suggests a way of re-privileging (indeed reestab-lishing the existence of) the literary as a means of serving the plight of the rest of discourse. At least it has suggested some-thing of the sort to Iser in his paper and to me in the wide areas of agreement which I share with it.

Iser distinguishes between those discursive fictions

which stand in need of being unmasked and those which enact a continual doubling that unmasks itself in the very act of making its illusion. The dialogical tendencies in discourse or society may succumb to the temptation of formalizing themselves until they are ripe for the deconstructive activities of the next dialogical opposition: extended carnivalization leads to the fetishizing of carnival as an institution and requires further carnivalizing activity to unsettle it and then disestablish it. But literature, seen by Iser's eyes through the performatives that stage its doubling, is a projection to all its texts of the "novelization" of genres proposed by Bakhtin. The endless doubling of the literary text commits it to nothing except its own resistance to any closure within a totalization. It can thus become the model of a dialogic that does not resolve: it is the model of a disruption that does not, as it extends itself, seek to repair itself. Its continuous self-undoing spins it into a *mise en abyme* (in the phrase made familiar by American Derrideans), unlike the undoings of "nonliterary" texts, which finally find solid ground on which to institutionalize themselves in an unconscious but unavoidable act of bad faith, all too quickly pointed out by their rivals.

From this perspective literature as self-consciously fictional discourse is a permanently self-unravelling non-institution, even though we must be quick to concede that it has become necessary to institutionalize the very discipline that surrounds it via canons, "periods," university departments, journals, professional associations, etc. (Further, it is typical of the institutional habit of the American literary academic, under continuing pedagogical pressures to teach the texts of a canon, to domesticate apparent revolutionary methods and alien texts into familiar classroom patterns.) Nevertheless, what presumably has been institutionalized is a body of texts, literary texts, each with a resistance to totalization that seeks only to extend itself indefinitely, each in flight from the coercive force of discursive closure. As for "nonliterary" texts, those discursive fictions that claim to be pointing toward an outside reality, so that they do not acknowledge their fictionality, these may well stand in need of a deconstruction that exposes the fiction for what it is. And any tendency to institutionalize the fiction may be resisted by means of a carnivalizing disruption that the self-conscious fictionalizing of literature supplies for itself. I suggest again that we may see in this move a reflection of Bakhtin's use of novelization as the literary analogue to the carnivalization of culture. The view I have outlined privileges literature as a model discourse that epitomizes, as, in its endless gyrations, it protects, the carnivalizing *différends* that other discourse may indulge but then must abandon if they are to institutionalize themselves. Of course, my argument here sacralizes the literary, though its power is seen as a de-sacralizing power.

A social critic like Rowe would be quick to complain that it is just this proposed function of literature as model for a carnivalizing discourse-without-end that points up the bankruptcy of this program for discourse. Discourse is being valued as it is anti-ideological, with the literary (or the self-consciously fictional) as the extreme version in its resistance to the compromise with institutions which the quest for power induces in the others. The literary can continue to whirl round its de-totalizing objective and hold that motion instead of moving on toward an ideological sanction for corrective action in a world beyond its language and its fiction. As a model, it is to warn its nonliterary imitators away from the arena of the rivals who vie for power through the coercion of discursive closure. For the critic interested in the consequences for social action, this argument reveals the mere literariness of the anti-ideological discursive ideal. Hence it is a roundabout way of resubscribing to a formalism, a reassertion of Kantian disinterestedness which worships art as its ultimate realization and, from the perspective of that formalism would—consciously or unconsciously—aestheticize all discourse and the interpretative categories used to analyze it. The history of recent theory supports this charge, although there may well be disagreement about whether or not a theorist finds these ubiquitous formalisms invidious.

Bakhtin's use of the novel as an instrument to open us to the dispersion of ideological forces is actually a representative notion similar to what the formalist tradition of Anglo-American literary criticism has repeatedly given us this century. It was I. A. Richards who, from his writings in the early 1920s, urged that poets use irony as their means of making their work an alternative to action by "bringing in . . . the opposite, the complementary impulses," thereby neutralizing the dominant impulse to act on a single side. Presumably this irony, clearly derived from the earlier irony of the German Romantics, is "constantly a characteristic of poetry" "of the highest order." Here too we have the paradoxical notion of a constant inconstancy. Cleanth Brooks and other New Critics extended this notion, with its anti-ideological implications, to a more explicitly formalistic doctrine.

Indeed John Crowe Ransom expands upon the special freedom of the poem to resist the authoritarian character he sees in nonpoetic discourse, this latter a totalizing character he associates sometimes with Platonism, sometimes with Hegelianism. Ransom's anti-organic attack on closure in the late 1930s and early 1940s sounds almost like a foreshadowing of what we have been associating with post-structuralists. And the political implications of his position are seen in his choice of metaphor, as he himself concedes: the poem has "a huge wealth of local detail, which sometimes fitted the plan functionally or served it [as is exclusively the case in nonpoetic discourse], and sometimes only subsisted comfortably under it [though with 'no structural value,' as in the poetic increment to discourse]. . . . But it was the political way of thinking which gave me the first analogy which seemed valid. The poem was like a democratic state, in action, and observed both macroscopically and microscopically." It is "democratic" because of the freedom of its elements to be independent, indeed "irrelevant," as they resist any overarching unity. It is hardly likely that Ransom knew Bakhtin, but he felt the carnivalizing impulse and shared its antagonism to the blanket of holism. Though he remained a narrowly *literary* critic, he is clearly aware of the political analogue of his commitments to a poem's "local texture" as it holds out against the overriding "logical structure" that tyrannizes over the prosaic alternative. It must be conceded that Ransom considers himself a dedicated Kantian looking for a kind of discourse that will restore to experience "the world's body," which the action-ridden discourse of prose must exclude because of its single-minded objective. It is this "body" which Ransom has found in the disinterested realm of poetic discourse.

To make a politics out of Ransom's poetics and then to seek to order other kinds of discourse by what he grants to poems is of course to aestheticize discourse and to render it "escapist" in just the way our contemporary advocates of social relevance warn us about when they deal with the Bakhtin-Lyotard line of resistance, social-political and literary. We can look across the yawning theoretical abyss between the New Critics and that model deconstructionist Paul de Man and see a similar Romantic irony leading to a similar focus upon those errant moments in discourse that would undermine its supposedly dominant claim. I have more than once observed also that the self-deconstructive activity of texts dwelled upon by de Man resembles the "unmetaphoring" activity of poems described by Rosalie Colie, who acknowledges her post-New Critical lineage—or resembles my own anti-Hegelian arguments on behalf of poems whose apparent closures disclose their illusionary and hence self-denying character. More importantly, all these varieties of methods that search out the de-totalizing propensities of texts resemble that emphasis we have seen in Bakhtin and Lyotard, even though these latter have an explicit social-political concern beyond the more narrowly literary realm of the others.

In these comparisons spread over these decades we see the extent to which anti-totalitarian social theory, represented throughout our discussion by the names Bakhtin and Lyotard, can be seen to be derived from notions generally used in literary interpretation. (I am calling "literary" what today it is more fashionable to term "rhetorical" in a flight from the privilege implied by "literary." But I believe my claims would be unaffected by substituting the one term for the other.) In effect a mode of specifically literary interpretation expands into a mode of generically textual interpretation and then into a mode of social interpretation. But, it can be argued, it remains a literary mode throughout; it is only that this interpretation now ranges far beyond the literary and even beyond the textual realm in search of the objects it makes available to itself, even if it treats them as if they were literary. And the question follows which asks whether literary texts have been deconstructed into an equality with all written texts or whether all texts are being constructed, if not into literary texts, then at least into texts worthy of being submitted to the categories of interpretation imposed by the literary habit. What is suggested is that the recent tendency to flee literature's self-enclosure is accompanied by that literary habit and induced by it to strike back from its exile and to see all the world as literature.

So we may well ask whether we have surrendered the literary to the social or permitted an insidious universal conquest by the literary. The rivalry in recent theory between the literary and the social seemed to move against the privileges reserved for the literary and to treat the literary as exhaustively reflected in the social and thus to abandon the literary for the social. But by applying literary categories to the social, we may well have transformed the social into a literary text: the loss of literary privilege disguises the imperialistic triumph of a monolithic literary method. Further, the imposition of this method, even on alien materials, domesticates them and cannot help but leave them with the thematic residue of literary considerations, so that they take on the subtlety and the ironies that complicate them and carry them further from ideology, bringing them to rest in their *différends*. And the literary text itself, as I have already suggested, remains the model of discourse theoretically secure from the lapses into ideological temptation to which the more mixed character of the others exposes them.

Stephen Greenblatt's paper and the position he took during our discussions seemed to carry forward this attempt to impose the methods of literary criticism on nonliterary materials. The very phrase, "cultural poetics," as the description of the project with which his work is associated, reveals its mission. He seeks to formulate a compound discipline which can treat the "circulatory" interrelations between the literary text and surrounding social-historical texts of every kind in order to provide a literary domestication of apparently alien brother-texts from other supposedly (but hardly) remote areas. Although Greenblatt's primary concern for the subversive play of aesthetic forms may keep him close to the Iser end of our spectrum of theorists, he is anxious to show these forms equally at work in nonliterary texts. [The paper that Greenblatt delivered at our colloquium paid a more extended attention to canonical literary texts (and their relation to contemporary nonliterary texts) than does the version of that text which appears in this volume.] The interflowing of forms he traces among contemporary texts is to persuade us of the common discursive figures and narrative structures that inform a culture at a given moment in its history. The socially oriented theorists in our colloquium suggested that Greenblatt's metaphor of "circulation" (like his self-consciously economic metaphor of "exchange"—or, worse, "negotiation") between the literary and the rest of culture was less balanced than he may have intended because of the primacy of literary figuration which seemed to control his readings of the nonliterary source texts. (In his presentation at the colloquium Greenblatt also dealt with the relation of *The Tempest* to William Strachey's account of the Bermudas experience.) But Greenblatt remains unwilling to forgo the distinction between the aesthetic and the social, rejecting the warning of Fredric Jameson who would conglomerate them in spite of capitalism's attempt (according to Jameson) to keep them separate in order to cultivate "privatization." On the other hand, Greenblatt must hold back from licensing the multiple discontinuities among discursive regimes proposed by Lyotard (and, according to him, repressed by capitalism) because Greenblatt requires the cultural continuum within which the circulatory pattern can sustain itself. Still, despite his near-Marxist affiliations, Greenblatt, here at the close of our three-year sequence of papers, was privileging a method that can be (and was) seen as representative of the tendency to literary imperialism that I have been tracing, not altogether unsympathetically.

Let me recall that early in his paper David Carroll singles out this tendency as he remarks the inevitable return of formalism to assume control of the several anti-formalistic impulses we have had these past two decades. He speaks of the frustration that accompanies the reaction "to the fact that formalism in some form or other just won't go away no matter how often and how forcefully history and politics are evoked to chase it away or at least put it in its place (in the place they assign it). Another version of formalism always seems ready to rise out of the ash can of history to take the place of previously discarded versions." Thus, he argues, every "return to history," once it is forced to face up to the challenge of the post-structuralist perspective, ends in self-defeat by being turned into yet another formalism, just around yet one more bend that puts us in a place we think we have been. It is not surprising that those who would now again force us to move from textual form to social-historical "realities" should seek to reduce the post-structuralist's continuing critique of ideology to a formalist escapism. It is by now hardly new to charge the Yale deconstructionists, for example, with being a new (and more reckless) variant of the old New Criticism. And in our discussion we saw a similar complaint by John Carlos Rowe in his desire to warn us off too sympathetic a response to the anti-ideological fragmentation of Bakhtin and Lyotard.

But, as we saw in Rowe's paper, this desire to reopen the way to ideology carries its own difficulties in the face of the post-structuralist critique. Anthony Giddens' defense of "practical consciousness" reveals these difficulties even more clearly. The confrontation between Marx and Foucault staged by Mark Poster effectively displays the flimsiness of ideology when so confronted. On the other hand, Poster also surveys the cost to theory (perhaps in the end only a euphemism for ideology) of the anti-theoretical thrust of post-structuralist dispersion. This balanced concern recalls us also to Robert Weimann's attempt to mediate between theory and an errant history, between the representation and the unrepresentable, by appropriating Marx's "appropriation" for post-structuralist uses. And this collision between the inaccessible and the discourse that gives us access to it brings us once more to the "performative" realm of Wolfgang Iser.

Thus the spectrum created by our own authors returns upon itself, from the literary to the social and back again. Yet in their joint effort we find the anxiety to seek a balance: each time the unleashing of the anti-ideological seems headed for the *mise en abyme*, with the threat of turning that negation into its own institution, theory resurrects itself in its own ideological quest for a ground. But once that ideological fixity beckons— and threatens—it offers itself for deconstruction, as the subversive urge of a neo-formalism, fostered by too much literature, moves our skepticism still.

Or at least it moves *my* skepticism still. And that my bias has given the direction these remarks have taken is evident enough—a bias still influenced by my defensive posture with respect to the literary, let me confess. So for me the recognition of the conflict between theory as dominated by ideology and the post-structuralist splintering of all totalities leads back toward literary texts and toward the methods we have developed to interpret them as duplicitous. Literature, losing its definition and reduced to an egalitarian status with all texts, is returned to the greater privilege of providing the model for a mode of interpretation to which all texts are now made eligible. But since the anti-totalizing tendencies in nonliterary texts, now perceived through turning literary analysis upon them, move toward reification and self-legitimation into a new totality, we have to assess anew how institutionalization and its resulting institutions relate to discourse.

So I see literary discourse and its exemplary resistance to ideology as a "sublime" archetype of what a discourse in flight from institutional power can perform. (Mine is little more than the answer Shakespeare gives in his paradoxical Sonnet 65 which, looking at empires, sees that "sad mortality o'ersways their power," against which is his poem: "How with this rage shall beauty hold a plea, / Whose action is no stronger than a flower?" The balance of the sonnet seeks to justify his daring to rhyme "flower" with "power." It closes by urging the miracle of "flower power," hoping to attribute "might" to the "bright"-ness cast by the poem's lines: "unless this miracle have might, / That in black ink my love may still shine bright." This is, of course, a self-mystifying statement in its anti-worldliness. But those possessed of—or by—the literary habit cannot quite give it up.) This attitude represents, of course, only one side, my side (at least sometimes). And still there, arrayed against it, is our urge for theory, for ideology, our urge to use texts to manipulate a profoundly unjust society at a critical moment in its history.

Almost all our authors seem astraddle the fissure between post-structuralism, which may turn out to be no more than another, more embattled and self-aware formalism with its literary models, and new social theorizing, which may turn out to be no more than another ideology with its mimetic and totalizing consequences. This is where theory now hovers, in a moment in its way as tentative, and as promising if as unresolved, as was that moment in the late 1960s, poised between structuralism and post-structuralism, which was marked by the Macksey and Donato volume (The Languages of Criticism and the Sciences of Man: The Structuralist Controversy, 1970). It is a presumptuous hope, but one shared by members of our group, that the present volume may serve the present moment in a similar way.

1

JUDICIOUSNESS IN DISPUTE, OR KANT AFTER MARX

Jean-François Lyotard
(Translated by Cecile Lindsay)

War itself, if it is carried on with order and with a sacred respect for
the rights of citizens, has something sublime in it . . .
—*Critique of Judgment*, J. H. Bernard, tr.
2d ed. (London: Macmillan, 1914), Sec. 28, p. 217

AT seventy-four, Kant complained to Hufeland of having suffered for two years from an "epidemic head cold accompanied
by a *heaviness of the head (Kopfbedrückung)*."[1] This morbid
state accompanies thought, rendering it painful "inasmuch as
thought is the maintenance (*Festhalten*) of a concept (the unified consciousness of related representations)." Kant explains
that the mind has the power, by force of sheer human will, to
master illnesses taking the form of spasms, cramps, coughing,
sneezing, insomnia, and hypochondriac paralysis. But in the
case of this inflammation of the head, he confesses, one has the
sensation of a "spasmodic state of the organ of thought (the
brain)—a sort of oppression." This state apparently does not
weaken either thought or reflection themselves (*das Denken
und Nachdenken*), nor does it affect memory (*Gedächtnis*) in
respect to what was previously thought (*das ehedem Gedacht-*

en). But "in the explanation (be it written or oral) where it is necessary [here, by a *lapsus* that proves the malady he describes, Kant omitted the *it is necessary*] to secure against distraction a solid collection of representations in their temporal sequence, it [this headache] produces an involuntary spasmodic state in the brain, a certain inability to maintain a unified consciousness of these representations during their succession." "This is what happens to me," he adds, "I always begin a discussion (*Rede*) by preparing the listener or reader for what I am going to say. I direct attention first to the object I am aiming at, and then to the object from which I take my point of departure. Without this dual direction there would be no coherence in the discussion. But when I come to linking the second object with the first, I suddenly (*auf einmal*) have to ask my listener, or myself: Where was I? Where was I going? This lapse is due less to a mental flaw or even to a flawed memory than to a defect in one's presence of mind (*Geistesgegenwart*) in making connections. This involuntary distraction is a most trying defect, and one that should be avoided in writing, especially philosophical writing, since it is not always easy to look back at one's own point of departure in philosophy."

Jean-Luc Nancy analyzes this "fainting spell" of discourse from the perspective (as Kant would say) that is his own: The perspective of the impossibility, or at least the undecidability, of a properly philosophical presentation (*a Darstellung*); the impossibility of a presentation of thought. His argument, transcribed in Kantian terms, is that any philosophical treatise worthy of its name must seek to furnish a "direct presentation" of the entire system of thought. Since, however, this entire system is hypothetically a whole, and since the whole is the object of an Idea which cannot be directly presented, then the philosophical treatise can only *indicate* the speculative object that is the system. The treatise can furnish one or more *signs* of the system, but cannot provide through schemas or examples any intuitions about it. It follows that, considered as a perceptible (that is, artistic or literary) work, philosophical discourse (*Rede*), whether spoken or written, is always found

lacking in respect to the connections that assure the maintenance of the system. It is thus itself afflicted with a spasmodic
ailment. The feeling inspired in connection with this torturous
distraction must consequently be a sublime one. This sign (or
should we say symptom?) that is the discursive cramp provokes
in the reader or listener three sensations: First, the pleasure
deriving from reason's infinite capacity to formulate an Idea
(namely that of the systematic whole of thought); second, the
pain born of the inability of the faculty of presentation to
furnish an intuition of this Idea in philosophical discourse; and
finally, the benefit arising from this disorder among the faculties. This latter benefit (which is not a secondary gain, but
rather the ontological stakes of criticism) lies in the fact that the
convulsion in which "before" and "after" lose their co-presence in the discourse is also a signal that discourages the transcendental illusion by which the Idea of the presentation of the
system itself in its entirety would claim to be realized in some
written or oral discourse.

This is the reason why the condition that constitutes an
illness or even a torture for the empirical patient named Kant (a
patient who suffers only because he is susceptible to this transcendental illusion, especially as the author or presenter of
philosophical discourse) also constitutes a "transcendental
health."[2] This illness comprises even that ontological health
which *is* criticism. I would thus like to begin by saluting in this
agitation—which is the emblem of a busy life and of the synco-
pated rhythm of health—the shadow cast over experience by
the critical condition, or what anthropologists would call its
judicious complexion. To judge is to open an abyss between
parts by analyzing their *différend*;[3] this act is marked by the
camera obscura of that complex feeling Burke called "delight."

Always, in the Kantian text on man, be it the *Anthropology,* the *Quarrel between the Faculties,* the historico-political
works, or the critique of teleological judgment, health—whether that of the body, of the mind, of institutions, or of "the
organization" in general—is presented as a *Wechsel.* That is, as
an alternation, an exchange between two poles, a thrust inhib-

ited by an obstacle, a movement to and fro, a race from one point to another and then back again, a visceral *vibrato*, an excitation of the life force. In section 25 of the *Anthropology*, causes capable of increasing or diminishing sensory impressions are ranked in a hierarchy ranging from contrast to novelty to the *Wechsel* and beyond, on a scale of increasing intensity. Section 79, which deals with the emotions, announces at the outset that through certain emotions, such as laughter and tears, "nature mechanically promotes health." At the end of the paragraph, Kant spares, in the name of mirth, even the court jester, the *Hofnarr* whose task it is to spice with laughter the meal of the elite; his situation, Kant writes, "is, whichever way one takes it, either above or beneath all criticism."[4]

If we remember the "quality of the satisfaction in our judgments upon the Sublime" that Kant analyzes in section 27 of the *Critique of Judgment*, we recognize the same extreme agitation that gives this judgment an ontological advantage over the sense of the beautiful. Here, the agitation is attributable to the transcendental subject rather than to the empirical individual. Kant writes: "The mind feels itself moved (*bewegt*) in the representation of the Sublime in nature," while in aesthetic judgments about the beautiful, it is in a state of restful contemplation. This sublime motion "may be compared to a vibration (*Erschütterung*); that is, to a quickly alternating attraction towards and repulsion from the same object."[5] We know that in this movement the imagination is repelled by reason as if by an abyss where it would perish, while at the same time it is attracted to it. That the mind, eluding all forms of exemplification, is reserved for Ideas is evinced in the insufficiency and impotence of the faculty of presentation. From the very beginning of the "Analytic of the Sublime" in section 23 of the same *Critique*, the same transcendental agitation characterizes that indirect pleasure, that delight which is the sublime, and which is born, Kant writes, from "a momentary checking (*Hemmung*) of the vital powers and a consequent stronger outflow of them."[6]

Agitation does not serve here simply as a predicate distinguishing one pleasure from another within the realm of human experience. It is, rather, a transcendental feeling, a distraction or a dispersion in the strict sense of the word *Zerstreuung*. As a paradoxical feeling, like pleasure in pain or even pleasure through pain, this agitation is one of the conditions of possibility for the human experience of the sublime. The "subject" that is thus affected is not an individual human in experience, but rather the subjective entity, itself unpresentable, to which Kant persists in attributing the power of Ideas and presentations as if these were faculties of that entity. It is evident that this "subject" is still far too heavily patterned on human experience, and that there remains much that is analogically "humanist" or anthropomorphic in what is, after all, scarcely even a series, but more precisely a dispersion, a *Zerstreuung*, of conditions of possibility for sensation, for positive knowledge, speculation, ethics, the beautiful, the sublime. We shall see that it is precisely this persistence of what Kant called, in 1770, his "phenomenology" in his subsequent critical strategy that motivates our own *différend* with his thought. But we must grant that with Kant, an emphasis is placed on the sublime with an energy unprecedented in the already long tradition of meditation on the sublime that had begun, at the latest, with Boileau's translation, in 1674, of the treatise of the pseudo-Longinus. The accent is placed on the dispersion of the subjective entity and on the paradox which results. What Kant calls the "freeplay" of the faculties, in respect to reflective judgments in general, is in the case of the beautiful immediately harmonious. In the case of the sublime, it is harmonious through meditation. Kant writes in section 27 of the *Critique of Judgment* that the play between imagination and reason in the sublime is "harmonious through their very contrast (*Kontrast*)," and that if there exists a subjective purposiveness, it is paradoxically produced "*durch ihren Widerstreit*": through this conflict.[7] The appeal to judgment results from a conflict between faculties. Two phrases from heterogeneous regimes, here, imagination and reason, do not succeed in agreeing about an object that gives rise to a feeling of the sublime. Their conflict is signaled by a sign, an eloquent silence, and by a feeling that is always an agitation, that is, an impossible phrase.

These analogies between the transcendental and the anthropological are admittedly debatable in themselves, and yet are properly critical in the Kantian sense, as are signs, symbols, and monograms. It is by means of these analogies that we are led to suspect that critical activity itself—the activity that is at work in reflective judgment and that should constitute the object of a Critique of critical reason, and which is in fact surreptitiously woven into the three (or four) written Critiques—we are led to suspect that this activity falls less under the sign of a jury or judge acting according to a body of laws or jurisprudential provisions than under the sign of the agitation of an uncertain and shaken watchman who is always on guard as to cases and rules—a sentinel.

The analogy with the tribunal occurs frequently in the Kantian text. It decrees a happy ending for the fiction of the war of doctrines that is sketched in the first Preface of the first Critique, but goes no further. The indifference (Gleichgültigkeit) toward questions of metaphysics resulting from the episodes of this war is not entirely negative; it also attests to a "profound way of thinking," a "strength of judgment, an Urteilskraft" which purportedly anticipates the institution of a tribunal: "This court of appeal is no other than the Critique of Pure Reason."[8] The battlefield, the arena (Kampfplatz) where metaphysical combat takes place, thus becomes a courtroom. And the verdict will be rendered "according to (nach) the eternal and immutable laws" of reason. The triumphant tone of this text from 1781 makes the act of judging appear to be no more than the subsumption of a given case under a predetermined concept. The fiction of war does not explain why criticism did not come into play at the very beginning, in order to spare thought the useless torment of dogmatic quarrels; it doesn't even raise the question.[9] We can only surmise that the welcome birth of critical philosophy must have taken place at the cost of these misfortunes. From a polemical point of view the discipline of pure reason suggests what may be the purpose of these wars, or of this single war lasting two thousand years. By an excellent disposition of nature, these wars promote the development of investigational reason as well as critical reason. Such a purpose ought to suffice in forbidding the exercise of any censure in speculative controversies. It is in this sense that Kant writes: "There really is no antithetic of pure reason."[10] Once again, criticism puts an end to war, replacing it by "the peace of a legal status, in which disputes [our *différend*, our *Streitigkeit*] are not to be carried on except in the proper form of a *lawsuit*."

We should note, however, one small indication of an unexpected critical reward. Even if the champions of various doctrines are allowed to fight at will, reason can only benefit from the struggle in its progress toward criticism. However painful the battle for the combatants, we who are firmly ensconced in the critical position (if we can call it a position) can observe the struggle in peace (*geruhig*) and even make of it an entertaining pastime.[11] If he is a judge at all, the Kantian judge takes a strange, ironic, Lucretian pleasure in the chicanery.

Thrown into polemics with Schlosser fifteen years later, Kant abandons his materialist or stoic irony to adopt a "critical" sense of humor. The figure of the judgmental instance becomes in Kant's writing less judicious than ever. The subject of the portrait is the critical philosopher who, as a man, partakes in the realm of experience. The figure is once again anthropological; it belongs to the "physiological knowledge of man" which, according to *Anthropology from a Pragmatic Point of View*, "aims at the investigation of what nature makes of man."[12] Since, with criticism, nature makes something of the thinking man, there must thus be a physiology or a physics of a philosophy that judges. Here is what physiological anthropology discovers in the philosophical mind: A penchant (*Hang*) or even an impulse (*Drang*) to reason or ratiocinate (*vernüfteln*), to argue, and, in the excess of the *Affekt*, to quarrel (*zanken*). The combative complexion of reason is probably "a wise and beneficial disposition of nature," since, by unsettling the validity of the arguments of both empiricists and idealists, this combat arouses the critical spirit, leading it to institute critical philosophy. The familiar schema is thus repeated; with the tribunal, one hopes, peace will replace war. This anticipation is much encouraged by the title of a small work published in 1796, *Proclamation of Imminent Peace in Philosophy.*

And the first section of this work does in fact establish the serene perspective of this permanent peace. But even before the second section can acknowledge that with the Schlossers the aforementioned perspective was disturbed, the promised peace itself offered something unexpected.

Critical philosophy, Kant writes, "is a permanently armed state (*ein immer bewaffneter Zustand*) aimed at those who wrongly take phenomena to be things in themselves." (I would add: equally aimed at those idealists who treat things in themselves as phenomena). This armed state "always accompanies the activity of reason." If "the perspective of perpetual peace among philosophers" does indeed arise in respect to the Idea of freedom, it is not because philosophers manage to arrive at a consensus on this Idea, but rather because this Idea can be neither refuted nor proved, while at the same time there exist the most pressing of practical reasons for admitting the principle of freedom. That is why this peace presents in addition (*Überdem*) yet another privilege (*noch ein vorzug*): that of "always keeping in a state of alertness or agitation those of the subject's forces that aggressions [like Schlosser's] seem to put in danger." At the same time this restless peace is a means of "promoting, thanks to philosophy, nature's plan to continually revive the subject and defend it against the sleep of death."[13] In nature's plan, philosophy is thus "a means of reviving (*Belebungsmittel*) humanity in light of its ultimate goal." If, therefore, someone like Schlosser launches an attack on philosophy, he unintentionally contributes to the reinforcement of the "combative disposition or constitution (*die streitbare Verfassung*) which is not war, which in fact can and should prevent war," but which is not on the other hand the peace of a graveyard.

From an anthropological point of view, the benefit deriving from philosophy is immediately physical: health, *status salubritatis*. But as human health is simply the incessant movement between illness and cure, the salutary effect of philosophy is not that of a regime which would protect a stable health against illness; it also requires a treatment which will reestablish health. Kant recalls that Cicero tells of the Stoic Posidonius who cured himself, before Pompey's eyes, of a violent attack of gout by means of a lively dispute (*durch lebhafte Bestreitung*) with the Epicurean school. A good dialectical argument on liberty, one which purports to refute the adversary (although the *Critique of Practical Reason* accords neither combatant the victory) at least results in the body's health. Kant confesses to Hufeland in the third *Quarrel Between the Faculties* that with age he has begun to suffer from cramps that prevent him from sleeping, and that are generally considered to be symptoms of gout. He writes: "One feels at that moment a sort of spasm in the brain—something like a cramp." To overcome his insomnia, Kant fell into the habit of fixing his thoughts on some object: "For example," he writes, "on Cicero's name, which calls up many associations" (*Nebenvorstellungen*). The course of these associations suffices to turn his mind from the disorders afflicting it, permitting him to sleep. Firmness in this sort of resolution (aided by a proper regimen) should see one through episodes of gout as well as convulsions, epileptic attacks, and even podagra.[14]

Kant leads us to think that we are dealing here with the Stoic therapeutics leading to apatheia. If apathy comes into play here, however, it would necessarily be Sadic—that is, an agitated apathy. Kant writes: "The act of philosophizing, even though one is not a philosopher, is a way to fend off a number of undesirable feelings. At the same time it is an agitation (*Agitation*) of the mind that introduces into whatever occupies it an interest that is independent of external contingencies. Although it is merely a game, this interest is nevertheless powerful and profound; it prevents the vital forces from stagnating."[15] If one is not intelligent enough for philosophy, even as unskilled work, then any other "pointless amusement" would render the same therapeutic service.[16] For example, one might make sure that none of the clocks in one's house chimed at the same moment. This practice definitely prolonged the life of one old man (presumably from Konigsberg), while it made money for the clockmaker. In this way, the lover of parachronisms who creates "cramps" in chronology thereby revives his forces and prolongs his own life. The lover of abysses, for his part, either listens for or provokes convulsions among the mental faculties, which serves to keep him alert. Looking for passages (*Übergange*) where there are none, he lives long and well, accomplishing the ends that nature pursues by means of the philosophical condition.

In this way, the exercise of judgment can be considered stimulating. The root of the word *gescheut* (judicious) is *scheiden*: to separate. The judicious spirit described by the *Anthropology* (Section 46) no longer conjures up the image of a venerable magistrate armed with a code to be used in settling contested issues. We see, rather, a sort of insomniac night watchman, a vigilant sentinel who defends himself against the torpor of doctrines by the practice of criticism. Doctrines weave a spell that prefigures death; the spasm is a salutary illness because it shakes us out of the doctrinal torpor. And if insomnia in turn becomes an illness, then sleep becomes the critical antidote, permitting the agitation to transfer to another domain while the vital forces are at rest. This domain is that of the imagination: dreaming is in animals as in man that agitation which nature maintains even in rest in order to prevent that very rest from spilling over into death.[17] The critical sentinel is alternately an insomniac and a dreamer in the same way that he lives in the city and in the country, writes stories and poems, works and rests, travels and stays home; and in the same way that he likes to gamble because he feels both fear and hope, he goes to the theater because he finds both apprehension and joy there, he smokes because tobacco is harmful but at the same time arouses new thoughts and sensations; and in much the same way, he works because although work is painful, it is less so than idleness, and vice versa, he rests even though it is painful because it is less painful than working.[18]

This agitation is without end, except that one does die after all. But we die in spite of the agitation, not because of it. It promotes long life, which is the only objective symptom of good health, since health is like the voice of God: "One can certainly *feel* well, basing his judgment on a sensation of well-being, but one can never *know* that he is well."[19] Health is the object of an Idea, not of a concept of the understanding. At least old age allows us to say that we *have been* healthy. Not only does judging make for long life, old age is reciprocally necessary for good judgment. Judgment is that "understanding which comes only with the passage of time."[20] Judgment cannot be learned, but only exercised; its development is called *Reife*, maturity, because it is a fruit that nature cultivates in the mind. Judgment is a macrobiotic prescription. How should we judge? Often and intensely. Since it makes for a long life, we should judge a great deal. For the more we judge, the better we judge.

What maintains the health of the critical watchman? The war of doctrines is salutary in that it comprises a game, an exercise serving to sustain a state of agitation. But war in itself is bad; the only benefit deriving from war lies in its mechanics: confrontation, contestation, alternation, *Wechsel*. This becomes all the more evident when wars are replaced by commercial transactions. Money is good not because it enriches, for then we would have to presuppose "that riches mean happiness," but because it allows for dispersion (*Zerstreuung*). Take, for example, the dispersion of the "Palestinians who live among us," as Kant writes in a note to section 46 of the *Anthropology*. Their world-wide diaspora, which is also termed *Zerstreuung*, is not a curse but a blessing. The manuscript of this note originally read: "Therefore the greatest disaster of the state turned into the greatest luck of its citizens. . . . Provided that riches means happiness."[21]

The diaspora is a convulsion. It can be salutary, provided one doesn't slumber under the effect of the remedy it offers (for example, money). The watchman's power of discernment is not brought to bear upon the content of the doctrines presenting their respective pretensions. This power of discernment is logical; it is brought to bear upon the relationship of the rule (or of meaning) to the individual case. It asks the question: what are the claims made by the doctrine—truth? goodness? beauty? the common interest? Analysis delimits the stakes, and the stakes situate a regime of phrases or sentences. What is at stake in an imperative phrase is not whether it is true, but whether it is obeyed. In a work of art, what is at stake is not the work's ethical value, but its ability to elicit pleasure. Analysis elaborates the subtle conditions of the respective stakes: the conditions involved in the obligation to obey an order, and the conditions governing the pleasure that a work of art must produce. These conditions are not found in experience in the general sense. Ethical and aesthetic experience are not experience in a strict Kantian sense, but are the effects, in experience, of that which is not empirical. The diversity of these experiences is only possible because there exist diverse regimes of phrases calling for validation, and thus necessarily cases which are themselves diverse in their modes of presentation. This is what Wittgenstein calls "grammatical remarks" when he notes, for example, in section 717 of the Zettel: "You cannot hear God speaking to others; you can only hear Him if He speaks to you. This is a grammatical remark." Is it a lapsus or a deliberate paradox that this remark is in the second person?

The critic thus moves between rules and cases, not between doctrines. There lies the real war, the right war, the true différend, the Streit and the Widerstreit. And the différend between the academic faculties of 1798 is a différend between mental faculties, that is, between regimes of heterogeneous phrases. The case must be found for the rule, or the rule for the case, and that is not something that can be learned. It is something that is only exercised; it is what we call judgment. If it cannot be learned, neither can it be taught. For it is, as Kant explains in section 42 of the Anthropology, the "faculty of distinguishing whether something is under the rule or not." Teaching, on the other hand, consists of communicating rules:

"Therefore, if there were any doctrines concerning judgment, then there would have to be general rules by which we may distinguish whether or not something agrees with the rule. Such a process would ask questions *ad infinitum.*"[22] This argument had already been presented in the introduction to the "Analytic of Principles."[23]

How can we know if a given case comes under a given rule if the subsumption of the case under the rule has not previously been determined, as it is in the schema? We don't *know* it, but we are able to discover it. In section 44 of the *Anthropology*, Kant writes that judgment is "the faculty of discovering (*ausfinden*) the particular for the universal (the rule)." What about finding the rule for the particular case? This, he writes, is the work of the *ingenium*, of the *Witz*, which "succeeds in thinking (*ausdenken*) the general for the particular." These two movements within the realm of critical agitation are due solely to talent. The most important aspect of this talent is, in both cases, acuteness, or *acumen*: judgment "concentrates on detecting the differences within the manifold as to partial identities," while the *Witz* "concentrates on marking the identity within the manifold as to partial differences." Each culminates in "noticing either the smallest similarity or dissimilarity." If we pursue the minute difference, we have a sense of exactitude (*Genauigkeit*), but if we pursue infinitesimal resemblances, we enjoy the *Reichtum des guten Kopfs*, the fertility of a good mind, which produces the blossoms of intelligence. With its blossoms Nature is at play, while it tends to business with its fruit. We usually judge the talent for games to be inferior to the talent for business; the inventor of rules is only the artist of criticism; its real head of state is the inventor of cases.

This distribution of roles is somewhat at odds with the rigid, militaristic hierarchy established in section 42 of the *Anthropology* in respect to the three faculties of knowledge. Understanding is right (*richtig*); reason is well-founded (*gründlich*); judgment is exercised (*geübt*). The first, understanding, is sufficient for the domestic or civil servant whose task it is to follow orders. A general, on the other hand, needs reason in order to devise (*ausdenken*) the rule for potential cases. It is the subordinate officer who needs judgment, for he is given general rules that he must apply to particular cases. This hierarchy of talents reappears in section 43; it had previously been mentioned in 1784 in a text entitled "What Is Enlightenment?"[24]

This stratification of tactical intelligence is clear-cut in appearance only. Is the devising of a rule for a case ultimately an act of reason or of *ingenium*, otherwise known as *Witz*? And if we consider judgment as a game without rules, isn't it, too, in search of the rule? Or must we limit judgment to the search for cases? The judgment of the critical watchman, at least, doesn't settle for simply discerning cases that fit a given rule; it isn't satisfied with providing examples or exemplary representations for various preestablished regimes of phrases. The critical watchman's judgment also seeks to discover, for a given case, a rule that it doesn't know. For example, what rule could govern cases as apparently disparate as the emotion produced by tragedy, or political pathos, or intellectual heroism, or the feeling of guilt? If these are cases, then they are also phrases, albeit complex ones, which obey certain rules of formation that are in themselves complex. Or, inversely, what about a rule for which there are no cases? The question posed by criticism presupposes a possible relationship between these extremes. All in all, at least one case—however singular it may be—does exist for at least one rule. It is this presupposition—that is, that we must not neglect singularities or existences—that provides the motor force for the "Critique of Teleological Judgment."

But there are all sorts of *différends*, and they are not all equally lighthearted. What diverts the observer of the first "Conflicts of the Antithetic" in the *Critique of Pure Reason*? It is the futility of the dogmatic arguments offered on all sides. This futility results from an illusion which causes one regime of presentation to be taken for another. Does the world have a beginning? Is there an absolutely unconditioned totality? The thesis and antithesis are consistent in relation to negation; they are not intrinsically contradictory. However, cases for either one cannot be directly presented: no palpable fact, no here and now can be found to prove the disputed phrase. The illusion derives from a certain confusion as to the nature of the present-able. Phrases from the dialectic of reason do not have as their object (or, as we would say, as their referent) something that could also be the object of a designation, of a phrase that says "here it is."

The conflict (*Streit*) of reason with itself in its dialectical usage cannot be resolved (*nicht abzuurteilenden*) before the tribunal of reason. We would be arguing about nothing (*um nichts*) if we indeed meant by "something" the possible object of a designation.[25] This isn't, at bottom, a true *différend* according to the rules of knowledge established in the Analytic, rules that are invoked by both sides. It is not a true *différend* because it can be dispelled—that is, thrown outside the realm of knowledge. It is dispelled by analysis. Both the defender of the thesis and the defender of the antithesis concerning the infinity of the world can produce a given, a "this." Subsequently, thanks to what Kant calls the regressive synthesis of the conditioneds (*les conditionnés*), they can produce another "this" which will precede the first, and so on. Each one thus undertakes to retrace the series of conditioneds themselves, with one seeing this series as endless and the other disagreeing. The rule they obey in so doing is the one which dictates that the synthesis of a given fact must always take as its point of departure the conditions of that fact. The term "rule" is taken here in the strict Kantian sense, as a regulative rather than a constitutive principle.

The position (*Anstellung*) of this synthesis is not in the series, but rather in the admonition "and so on," which dictates the repeated application of a given operation to its own results.[26] The explanation of empirical facts is no more than the application to referents furnished by designation, i.e., "given a," of the operation Kant called empirical synthesis. This operation proceeds by implication: "if a, then b"; and so on: "given

b; and if b, then c." The explanation is thus infinite (or indefinite—we won't pursue the distinction here) by reason of the
"and so on" included in its formulation. As to whether the
world itself is infinite or not, we cannot know (savoir) this in
the sense that we perceive it or are aware of it (connaître). For
the world is a totality of givens, and thus the object of an Idea.
But this object cannot itself be designated. Even if it were
capable of designation, it would necessarily fall under the rule
of explanation governing all objects of designation. Thus the
différend that Kant calls mathematical is not at all settled, but
simply dismissed as the product of an illusion or mistake common to both parties.

When it comes to causality through condition and
through freedom, it's a different matter entirely. Kant thema-
tizes this difference between différends in the following way:
the quarrel (Streithandel) can be dismissed (abgewiesen) in
respect to the world because its object, which is the cosmologi-
cal series of phenomena, derives from a synthesis that is homogeneous with itself, and because both sides make the same
mistake as to the position this synthesis should be given. But
with causality through freedom, a heterogeneous position (Anstellung) is introduced into the series of conditions. This position is doubly heterogeneous if the above analysis is pursued:
first, any cause (or condition) classified as free causality cannot
be demonstrated. Second, Kant's empirical synthesis, or the
admonition to apply the operation to its own result, is excluded. The free act is not demonstrable; its reasoning is not
repeatable. Not only is the totality of the series of conditioneds
not presentable here and now, but there exists in this series a
conditioned for which is postulated a condition that is not
presentable here and now.

At this point, if the critical watchman is sensitive to
differences between différends (which are nevertheless
grouped together under the single rubric of the Antithetic), he
will stop smiling and enjoying himself as he did with the false
Streit between idealism and empiricism over the issue of the
world. In that case, the watchman was able to discern the

identical in what appeared to be different or even opposite: that is, the same illusion which situates in the referent what actually belongs to a set of rules (designation, implication, repeated application). In the *différend* concerning freedom, the watchman discerns the differences in things that appear to be similar. The two sides don't speak in the same idiom, although they are talking about the same thing. And since they don't speak in the same idiom, both sides can be right.[27] Which means that the same "this" can be shown by one side to be implied by a "that" which is also implied and can also be designated. At the same time, the same "this" can be designated or at least invoked by the other side as the result of a "that" which can neither be designated nor implied, in its turn, in a regressive synthesis.

If the tribunal were competent to judge questions of knowledge, it would have to declare a mistrial. For even the tribunal would have to decide in favor of the defender of determinism who, since he speaks the language of the tribunal, makes himself perfectly understood. The court in question decrees that arguments must be implications with no free play, that demonstrable proofs must be produced, and that the procedure for administering the proofs must be capable of reiteration as often as necessary. This tribunal can *know* (*connaître*) nothing of the cause that the defender of freedom advocates. As Kant writes, "the judge himself supplies perhaps the deficiency (*Mangel*) of legal grounds (*Rechtsgründe*).[28]

In the same passage we learn, however, that the judge will "supplement (*ergänzt*)" this deficiency, will fill in where the law defaults, so that the *différend* "may be adjusted (*vergleichen*) to the satisfaction (*Genugtuung*) of both parties."

What might be the constitution of this supplement, this complement? Does it consist in the establishment of another tribunal, one that would be competent to pass judgment on freedom's suit? This seems indeed to be the case, since a new Critique was established to examine the suit. This institution requires a complement to right that would be based on the regime of cognition, since a rule must be devised (*ausdenken*) under which the case for free action can be presented. Yet the only relationship that could possibly exist between this rule of presentation and the rule governing the presentation of "this" that allows for the validation of knowledge is an *analogical* relationship. The analogy consists in the necessity, in both, of a *type* borrowed from cognition: that of the universal legality inscribed in the categorical imperative.[29] In fact, the only presentation capable of validating the ethical phrase according to its own stake—lawful prescription—would not be some "this" that could be designated, but rather a feeling—that is, a sign whose designation must remain problematic. This means that without the possibility of direct presentation, the question "Is it true that freedom exists?" can find no answer in the regime of cognitive phrases. It also means that in the regime of ethical phrases, it is not truth itself that is at stake, but the obligatory nature of truth. From the first to the second Critique, the heterogeneity is such that it comes to bear upon the very stakes of the phrases involved. It would seem that here the dispute is not over nothing, but rather over two entirely different things.

But this way of "filling in" the law, of supplementing right's deficiencies in the area of freedom does not, finally, result in completeness. Far from filling out the jurisdiction of knowledge, the institution of a second Critique dealing with right creates an abyss between the two sides or regimes of phrases and, at the same time, between the two jurisdictions. This separation or insulation which continues to proliferate in the third and "fourth" Critiques, in what I have called elsewhere an archipelago of regimes of phrases, is in fact the opposite of a completion. But this completion is nevertheless called for; and despite appearances, it is not only or essentially called for by the Idea of a system. It is called for by the nature of the real—and not illusory—*différend* opposing the cognitive phrase to the moral phrase. This *différend* is real not only because the two sides speak in different idioms, but because they make their claims in respect to the same case.

The separation between regimes of phrases is not in itself new. We can assume provisionally that it corresponds, *grosso modo*, to the divisions made since Aristotle among the various disciplines within philosophy. From a doctrinal point of view, this division would propose the reunification of the disciplines into a systematic whole as the task of the philosopher, or at least of the modern philosopher. But here a litigation occurs, stemming from a *différend* between two of the said disciplines in respect to the same case. This *différend* assumes first of all some sort of claim—call it rivalry or jealousy—whose stakes are the case which each side claims. This claim then assumes that a given case, at least before criticism sets it straight, is capable of belonging to two or more different regimes. Even after it has established separate jurisdictions, criticism is still impelled to demand, as Kant does in the second introduction to the third Critique (although we might concede that he does so to satisfy the system's demands), that despite the abysses separating heterogeneous regimes, whatever is presented as a referent for the various phrases deriving from the respective regimes must at least be compatible with all admitted phrases. There must exist between the phrases, a *Zusammenstimmung*, a concordance of voices. The passage (*Übergang*) from one to the other must be possible "*ohne Abbruch zu tun*," with injury to none.[30] This is clearly, if not distinctly, expressed when Kant writes that "the concept of freedom is meant to actualize in the world of sense the purpose proposed by its laws."[31]

Any critique of the Critique must in its turn take note of this demand for compatibility. It can go in two completely divergent directions. And it is in our suspicion as to this divergence that we most feel our own divergence, our *différend*, with Kant. For the required compatibility—that is, the liability of a single referent before several different critical tribunals—can dictate one of two things: either that the extreme equivocacy which criticism discovers in the referent need not destroy the referent's identity as a fact (or a real human act when we are dealing with the Third Antinomy); or that the dissociation of the entire field of all objects into domains or territories separated by abysses can be restored to a unity that is at least teleological, through a movement subordinated to an ultimate end. In the first hypothesis the unity of the referent is called for

by the very possibility of a confusion of regimes (by the possibility of error), and thus by the possibility of discerning between regimes through criticism. In the second hypothesis the
unity of the field, which can only be postulated as an ultimate
end, is called for by the *Idea* of systematicity. This unity does
not necessarily compel that a single, Leibnitzian world be formulated for all the phrases; with Kant, in fact, it remains simply
a field. But this unity does require that the phrases' heterogeneity, while conserved, must at least be ordered toward a
single end comprising the object of an *Idea*.

The deficiency supplemented by the judge of the Third
Antinomy, which is the dynamic antinomy par excellence, is
not the missing identity of the referent. For it is supposed that a
given fact can give rise to controversy as to its causality, which
is considered to be conditioned for one side, and free for the
other. The judge remedies the absence of a universal tribunal, of
a final judgment before which the regimes of knowledge and of
freedom can be, if not reconciled (for they will never be reconciled), then at least put into perspective, ordered, and finalized
according to their difference. This supplementation is so evidently on the order of a reconciliation between phrases themselves, and not between their referents, that it must be attributed to nature rather than to the world in the Kantian
sense.[32] Nature is the object of the Idea of objective purposiveness, and this is in turn called for by reflective judgment in its
attempts to account for the singular existences that the lawful-
ness of a "mechanically" determined world does not explain.
But inversely, if the activity of precise discernment (*Genauigkeit*)—or, in other words, the attention paid to *différends* that is
at work in criticism—could assume this function of supplementation through the objective purposiveness of a certain
nature, then that activity or attention would itself be a means
used by nature to achieve its own final purpose.[33] This purpose
must be accomplished by man because he is the only being in
the world that is not entirely conditioned.

Therefore if the critical watchman believes it is possible,
in the absence of legal provision, to pronounce a sentence on

the *différend* concerning freedom, it is because the Idea of a natural purpose authorizes critical philosophy to do so. But then, what authorizes critical philosophy to find in this Idea of natural purpose the authorization to judge without law? Since what is in question is an Idea—that of nature and thus of purpose—the critic can designate no "this" to validate that authorization. But he can present an "as if this"—that is, a sign. As always, the sign is a sensation, a feeling. Does the feeling that signals (and only signals) the possibility of judgment even in the absence of law constitute a sensation of good health? In other words, is it the sensation of passing quickly from life to death and from death to life: the delightful vertigo of leaping above (*au-dessus*) the abyss rather than over (*par-dessus*) it? And would we have to call this sensation the sign of judgment, as when Kant elsewhere calls enthusiasm for the French Revolution a "sign of history"?[34] But the sensation of health thus described is only anthropological; it has to do with what nature seeks in the empirical individual who judges. We must further acknowledge that the critic can use this sensation as proof (*Beweisen*) of the existence, outside of law, of a right to judge. But he can only admit to the existence of this right according to the Idea of a nature pursuing its ends even in the process of supplementation.

According to this development, then, the example permitted by the schema authorizes knowledge by providing the concept (or descriptive scientific statement) with the direct presentation of a perceptible given—that is, by providing a case for the rule. If this is the case, then the question that follows is: whether all other regimes of phrases (whether dialectical, ethical, aesthetic, or political) are validated only by means of indirectly perceptible givens, which in Kant's work have several names that I have grouped here under the term "sign." But the value of signs for the critical watchman, apart from the fact that they liberate the play of judgment for their subject (finding the case for the rule and the rule for the case), lies in the frank presupposition of a sort of intention or purposiveness on the part of whatever uses signs. A sort of subject has to be assumed, which Kant does under the name of "nature." But it is an "as if" subject which signals, at least for the philosopher, and by means of the sensation he experiences—cramps, fainting spells, that is to say, *health*—that a quasi-phrase is taking place under the auspices of a given sign; and that the meaning cannot be validated by procedures applicable to knowledge. Is it possible to make judgments on signs without presupposing, even problematically, such an intention? That is, without prejudging?

This presumption or presupposition, even in the qualified form Kant lends it, is at once too consistent, and not consistent enough. It is not consistent enough if we want to *know* how to judge. For then we would have to establish this quasi-subject who makes signs as though it were a subject. The critical philosopher would have to become speculative, but speculative in the sense intended by absolute idealism: not only must the subjectivity of his thought become substance, but the objectivity of the object must be transformed into a subject. But then signs would cease to be signs. Signs would no longer be needed. Nor for that matter would feelings. There are concepts, and there are realities; the former exist for themselves (*pour soi*), while the latter only approximate themselves (*auprès de soi*). This is, at least, the principle of speculative thought. In fact, as Adorno writes, reality now serves only as a reservoir of examples for concepts.[35]

On the other hand, however, the Idea of a nature that sends signs to the critical watchman weighs a little too heavily; it is too rough an instrument when it comes to analyzing and elaborating *différends*. Today we would say that this Idea masks by closing too quickly the wound suffered by the referent when the unity of language totters under the blows administered by the Critique. If we do away with this overly consoling Idea, we are left with the naked convulsions of the *différends*. Without hoping that this Idea might bring about health (the sign of judgment), or that it would mark some progress for the better (the sign of history), we at least wonder how it is possible. We have already said that *différends* could only take place if a given case could belong to at least two systems of hetero-geneous phrases (which Kant called the synthesis of the hetero-geneous).

Those of us for whom the *différend* strikes a blow at the referent must necessarily reverse the question. Given: two phrases that criticism establishes as belonging to hetero-geneous regimes. How can we know that in spite of their hetero-geneity, these phrases, as is supposed in all quarrels, are talking about the same referent? Take the descriptive statement "That door is closed" and the order "Close that door." In the universe presented by each sentence, it is not only the meaning that undergoes an obvious modification in passing from one regime to the other, but also the sender and the addressee. The entity that receives an order is not expected to act upon it in the same way as the entity to whom a description is addressed. As for the entity (whatever it may be) who declares the door open, it is not situated by this declaration in the same way as the entity who orders it closed. Different things are expected of each party. This expectation is in no way a psychological state, but rather an anticipation of the enunciations or acts (if we provisionally allow this term) that normally follow description or prescrip-tion. This "normality" corresponds to what I have called the regimes of phrases, in the same way that the meaning presented by (or deriving from) the form of the phrase corresponds to those phrases. It is thus provisionally accepted that there is only one meaning, a "pure" or "proper" meaning. Normally, for example—that is, purely or properly—an interrogative sen-tence (including, in the case of an oral sentence, the curve of intonation) presents the meaning of a question, or a questioned meaning. The sender and receiver are consequently situated as two poles, between which a meaning presented as suspended *there* should be presented as established *here*. Whether or not the intended connection is actually made, or even whether it is made more often than not is another question, and one that cannot be treated here.

Let us return to the referent. How can two heterogeneous phrases be made in respect to the same referent? Doesn't the referent meet with the same fate as the other instances in the universe of phrases—such as the sender, the receiver, or the meaning—when the regime of phrases changes? How can it be determined that the door referred to in the statement "This door is open" is the same door presented by the sentence "Close that door"? Doesn't a descriptive sentence call up its referent differently than a prescriptive sentence? Isn't being the object of a piece of information entirely different from being the object of some future transformation? An order, as René Thom has noted, is not a piece of information.[36] If the referent is an instance in the universe presented by a phrase (and what else could it be?); if the instances of these universes of phrases are simply poles across which various expectations play themselves out in the manner described; and if these expectations are finally different according to the differences in regimes of phrases, then we would be able to conclude that the instance called the referent is not the same in both declarative and prescriptive sentences.

The question is even more pointed if the entity involved in phrases from heterogeneous regimes is not involved, in both regimes, in the same type of instance. It is here that we rediscover heterogeneity in the Kantian use of the word. The door in the preceding example served as a referent in both sentences. But how can we know that we are talking about the same entity when we say: "Albert is going to leave Marie"; and to whom we say: "Albert, think before you act"; or about whom we say: "What courage Albert has!" and who himself says: "I think it would be best if I left Marie"? These shifts in instance, added to the heterogeneity of the phrases, seem to complete the dissolution of the identity of that entity who answers to the name of Albert.

Certainly in questioning the identity of this entity through the various instances and regimes, we too take it to be the referent of our inquiry; the examples cited here are cited in order to argue the said inquiry. In respect to philosophical inquiry, the situation of that referent often causes the investigator to admit with no further debate the reality of the entity in question, and to conclude that the various enunciations cited are only variations on the meaning allowed by the substance or substratum called Albert, which is from that moment held to be real. This is an error. The investigator's phrase is the "nth" (here, the fifth) in a series along the lines of "What then is the reality of Albert?" This sentence, which belongs to the interrogative regime, has in itself no privilege enabling it to endow the entity named Albert with a real identity. This is a frequent error in philosophical discourse: its nature as phrases about phrases causes it to disregard referential value, as Frege would have said; or, as we might say, the stakes inherent in each of these phrases. Herein lies the error of the Hegelian speculative discourse in particular; it places all phrases, regardless of the regime to which they belong, within the regime of cognitives, thus making pronounced sentences into autonomous quotations. Instead of the order "Close the door," the Hegelian tribunal (or, as it is called, the tribunal of the world) can only know the interrogative-descriptive sentence "Was the door really ordered closed?" The synthesis of the heterogeneous has no difficulty in being effected on this level of metalanguage.[37]

Once we have rejected this speculative refuge, the question remains: does the entity bearing the name of Albert really exist? As the referent of a description, this entity derives from what can be called, in the Kantian sense, a judgment based on experience. As the receiver of a prescriptive phrase, it falls within the province of practical reason. As the occasion for evaluation, it belongs to the sphere of ethics or aesthetics. As we have seen, Kant poses the problem of the incompatibility of these different phrases in the dramatic terms of a leap above abysses. Here, however, the problem must be presented in its most urgent form: are the ethical Albert and the "conditioned" Albert the same entity? What we term the "referent" is for Kant called the "object." For Kant, objects are always objects of litigation; they are always put into play in legal proceedings. But they are always put into play for their meaning, which will determine the regime of phrases to which they belong. Are they also put into play for their reality?

We know that for Kant, the reality of the object comes under the safeguard of direct *Darstellung*. This presentation (and I use the word in its Kantian sense) complies with the regime of perception. The forms of the latter are rules which transform enigmatic sensory matter into given facts situated in time and space. We would say today that Kant's direct presentation, once it is divested of its phenomenological trappings,[38] corresponds to a designatory or ostensive phrase, one on the order of: "Here is the case." For, as Kant knows, a referent is only designated as real in order to prove an assertion. The ostensive phrase is an indispensible moment in a line of reasoning: it appeals to reality for the validation of an argument. The ostensive sentence declares: "There is, here and now, this thing that confirms the validity of what I am saying." It implies the use of deictics or their equivalent. Deictics designate reality; they designate the referent of the ostensive sentence as being endowed with an "extra-linguistic" existence. But deictics also connect the whole universe presented by the sentence where they are used to a "present" spatio-temporal "origin," something like I-here-now.

This origin does not itself constitute any sort of permanence. Presented or co-presented (that is, presupposed) along with the universe of the sentence in which deictics are evident, it appears and disappears with that universe, that is, with that sentence. That which was before the here-and-now is, here and now, the *here and now of a moment ago*. The same goes for the "I." How then can an ostensive sentence serve as proof in arguing an assertion? In order for the citing of a case to carry the weight of a proof, it must be accompanied by some means of repeating the presentation of that case. But repeating the same deictic is not sufficient for citing the same case a second time. The validation of a cognitive phrase requires, at least, that a given referent be locatable in an unchanging place and time. The validation can only do this by means of referentials that are independent of the phrases' occurrences, and which thus are not deictics. The *here*, the *now*, and the *I* must be replaced or at least completed by designators of place, person, and time that will be independent of the sentence that present them.

The problem posed is thus that of finding a designator that will always indicate the same referent independently of the time, place, or person of the designation. It doesn't seem plausible that this problem could find a solution in the domain of transcendental or phenomenological philosophy, at least insofar as it comprises a philosophy of the subject. I do not intend to reopen here the discussion of the general aporia of the *Ich denke* in its relationship with time, nor do I want to deal with the enigma of schematism. The elaboration of these two questions has become a philosophical staple. As it is more precisely a question of *Darstellung* and of the possible constancy, through what Kant called the *Zeitreihe*, or temporal series, of the designated referent, I will only note here that the difficulty is treated in the first "Analogy of Experience." This is the one that is entitled, in the second edition of the *Critique*, the "Principle of Permanence of Substance" (and no longer, as in the first edition, simply the "Principle of Permanence"). The revised version is also found in the "Refutation of Idealism," which was similarly added in 1787. The argument of the Analogy is the following: any change in time presupposes that time is a permanent, changeless form. Now, Kant writes that "time, as a form of internal intuition, cannot be perceived in itself." Permanence must thus be located in external objects, as substance. Kant's "Refutation," as modified by a note in the second preface, directs this argument at Descartes' problematic idealism: there is no empirical determination of self-consciousness that does not presuppose a permanent substance. And this permanent substance "must therefore be something external, and different from all my representations." [39] It follows that the determination of my existence in time proves the existence of objects in space.

We can certainly designate the permanence of the referent in various ostensive phrases as "substance," since, as Kant himself notes, "the proposition that substance is permanent is tautological."[40] But what is not tautological is the fact that substance or subsistence is a thing. In saying thing, Kant certainly can't mean the thing in itself, but only something which isn't caught up in a temporal series of "representations." (We are now back to the heart of the problem of preservation and convulsion in presentation: hysteria and "heaviness of the head" are, after all, a sort of "cramp" in time, and in this sense perhaps constitute an ontological endeavor.)

The problem is thus: given that "I," "here," and "now" are designators that depend on the ostensive phrases supporting them, how can we find independent designators without falling back on the concept of a permanent substance which can itself receive no validation by designation?

Nor is this the only problem raised by the synthesis of the heterogeneous—that is, by the constitution of the différend. The problem as we have just delimited it consists only in the synthesis of referents of demonstrative phrases, and particularly in their identity throughout their succession. This synthesis essentially corresponds to what Kant called experience. But the heterogeneity of regime existing among phrases that we assume to present a single entity—whether or not that entity occupies the position of a referent—seems necessarily to constitute a new attack on the unity of experience. Take, for example, the event: Albert opens the door and leaves. How can it remain an event if we are able to attach to it all the various phrases from heterogeneous regimes that I cited earlier: "He's going to leave Marie"; "Think before you act"; "What courage!"; "I think I should leave Marie." Or others, such as Marie's "You'll regret it," and of course our own: "Albert opens the door and leaves"?

It is precisely on the question of this specific diversity that judgment must be exercised. Judgment must recognize and bring to light the abyss that exists between these sentences: their incommensurability. The problem of the identity of the referent of ostensive phrases (in this case named Albert) is, in this respect, only a preparation for the problem of judgment. Of course, this latter problem would not be raised at all if the entity named Albert were not the same in the various universes presented by the sentences cited. But showing that it is the same entity—that is, solving the problem of the identity of the referent named Albert—does not solve the problem of the synthesis of the heterogeneous. In fact, it only makes it more acute. The entity named Albert must be the same not only in order to make knowledge possible, but also in order to make possible the coexistence of those worlds that Kant calls fields, territories, and domains[41]—those worlds which of course present the same object, but which also make that object the stakes of heterogeneous (or incommensurable) expectations in universes of phrases, none of which can be transformed into any other. *Ohne Abbruch zu tun.*

One striking feature of philosophical discourse in most of the forms it borrows (for it borrows from other genres, literary and otherwise) is that it avoids, on principle, any use of proper names in its arguments. The names of authorities and adversaries that nevertheless remain persist only as the names of arguments. I will not examine here the reasons offered to justify this exclusion. More often than not, none are offered. It seems to go without saying that in philosophical discourse we are not operating on the level of names. On the other hand the discourses of history, of the great classical or romantic poetic genres, of geography, of biology, anthropology, paleontology, or physics would simply be impossible without proper names, however different their usage may be in the various discourses. Even the "hard" sciences must use them. For example, if electrical science recognizes a "Joule's Law," it does so not only to honor the physicist who discovered the variables governing the intensity of electrical current, but also because this name designates an experimental procedure that can be repeated by an "I" at any time and in any place. For the permanent conditions of the procedure's execution are strictly determined, and have up to now always permitted the observation of identical results. But what does "strictly determined" mean? It means that once the names of measurements (of duration, extent, weight, volume, or intensity) have been fixed and acknowledged, the variables constituting the experimental schema can be introduced in named quantities by means of these measurements. Thus the repetition that assures the validity of Joule's Law can be only executed thanks to the stability of the names of measurements (of systems of units in physics) which must be considered as a network of proper names.[42]

No evidence of any order can be admitted as proof unless it is accompanied by names that permit it to be reiterated. It does not suffice to say: "I was there." We have to be able to say who, when, and where; that is, we have to give the names that make it possible to locate the *here* of "there" in a world of place names; to locate the *now* of "then" in a world of dates; to locate the *I* of "he or she" in a world of personal names. In addition, for each of these worlds, we must give the name of measurements (of duration and extent at least) that situate the names in respect to each other in a repeatable fashion, so that a journey in this network can be retraced from the "here-now-I" of the phrase pronounced.

If it is true that all referents are litigations, and that judging is finding the case for the rule (and probably also the rule for the case), then judgment cannot be passed if the case, the object of litigation, is not attested to. And the case can be attested to only by its positioning in a world of names, which permits the evidence to be repeated as often as desired. Any tribunal requires names in order to establish the reality of a referent. The reconstruction of a crime serves as a model for any assertion of or about the reality of a referent.

This is why the detective story whose hero is a criminal trying to erase any clues provided by names (dates, places, people, measurements) constitutes, as Kracauer suggests, an archetypal form of the ontological question in the modern or postmodern age.[43] In the classical age, tragedy was the form taken by that question. What distinguishes modernity is that the destruction of identities and the assassination of experience through the effacement of proper names is a willed effect. The psychoanalytic investigation should also be examined in this light. Freud's passion for the cryptic inscription, for the *rätsel-haften Inschriften* that he deciphered at night in the *Fliegende Blätter* had much more to do with the style, or more precisely the genre, of the *Traumdeutung* than his rereading of *Oedipus Rex* or *Hamlet*. Causing proper names to be forgotten (an amnesia which is also one of the first signs of old age) is the perfect crime because it prevents the reconstruction of the crime. This is the criminality of the unconscious: a solitary confinement in which one finally forgets oneself; where the self, grown nameless, can no longer even take itself to be another in the momentary salvation of a pseudonym like that taken by Nietzsche, Hölderlin, or Wilde, but can only drift into anonymity. And if measurements are also proper names, then Assassination must be considered the art most admired by the unconscious. It was Thomas de Quincy who watched over Kant's last *lapsus*, in the *Kantswake*.[44]

I would be tempted to think that in blinding the proper name and its function in the establishment of reality, philosophical discourse can only be one of two things: either it is dogmatic because it must assume a permanent thing or some absolute witness (which is a non-sense, or *unsinnig* in Wittgenstein's sense); or it is autistic because it is incapable of taking the step which leads from the deictic of the ostensible phrase to the reality of the referent. The latter incapacity is evident in Kant's impossible schematization, which can only furnish the possibility of experience, and not experience itself; it is also evident in the impossible constitution of the other in the course of the *Fifth Cartesian Meditation*, from which there can only be derived a *him* or a *you* dependent on the constitutive direction of the *I*.

Like executions or death sentences, there are ways of summarily putting an end to reality's trial. But the trial is nevertheless without end, affording neither summation nor sleep. And while it is true that this trial makes an appeal to proper names, it doesn't necessarily follow that their application puts an end to the *différends* in question. In fact, the opposite happens. For names are, as Kripke characterizes them,[45] constant quasi-deictics; in this sense they are what Kant would call *analoga*. But they are *analoga* of deictics, not semantic equivalents of given facts. Proper names are empty, but they are, in a certain sense, empty twice. They are first either empty of meaning or too full of meaning, which is in effect the same thing; and they are also empty of reality.

A name is no proof of the reality of the referent that bears it. As Louis Marin has noted, we show our inheritance from Pascal's nominativism when we say "That's Caesar" both when we meet the man bearing that name, and when we see his profile on a coin.[46] A fictional universe is a world of names in which, more often than not, all the referents named can be located or situated in respect to each other. Sometimes it takes no more than a name to achieve the effect of reality—for example, the longitude and latitude of the island of Utopia in Thomas More's story. Or the names Waterloo and Napoleon in *The Charterhouse of Parma*. This proves at the very least that the same name can provide one indicator in the world of names comprised by Stendhal's fiction and another in the world of names verified by historical science—and this without wronging either world. This entanglement provides a good example of a *différend*: is Napoleon the emperor of France, or is he the Ideal of political reason for Fabrice and Julien? We consider that a referent for a given name is real when we can attach to a nominative phrase such as "It is Rome" the corresponding ostensive phrase: "And here it is." While we certainly cannot simply settle for designation, neither can we do without it.

But we should recall that elsewhere the nominative phrase "It is Rome," whether it be an acknowledgment or a baptism, is always appealed to in a search for the proof of a meaning—that is, in a legal argument. This meaning doesn't necessarily have to be introduced by a sentence taken from the realm of descriptive phrases. We would naturally respond with the designation "*This* door" when asked "What door are you talking about?" But this question could just as well be linked to phrases from regimes as heterogeneous as that of description: "The door is open" or exclamation: "What a door! It's always open!'' or narrative-interrogative: "Did he open the door?" or simply narrative: "It was at that moment that he opened the door." What is certain is that the answer—the designation "*This* door"—does not provide sufficient proof of the reality of the referent of these sentences. Between the said designation and the sentence or sentences cited above there must be interposed a nominative phrase on the order of: "You know, the Eastern door of Albert's house at Villeurbanne."

The case is clear in the now proverbial examples of Aesop or Plutarch: *Hic Rhodus, hic salta. Salta* presents meaning within the regime of prescription. *Rhodus* gives the name, while *hic* serves as the articulation, marking the designation. And since it is an order—the order to jump—that must be validated, *hic* also signals a state of urgency. The question of the reality of the referent is thus never resolved by a single phrase falling under a regime specifically charged with this duty; it is always resolved by the play, or free play, of three phrases: one carrying the meaning, one carrying the name, and the third carrying what Kant calls the presentation. This tripartite complex is not without complications. Once again, however, the question of the reality of the referent is no more than a stage in the problem that concerns us here: the problem of the *différend*. Therefore, I will not dwell on the first question. As for the second, I will note only that, unlike a concept (or an essence) or a deictic, the proper name undergoes no changes in its value as a designator when placed in any instance in the universe of phrases, or when placed in the most heterogeneous of regimes. We have seen that this is the case for Albert. For example, in a descriptive phrase, Albert is situated, as a predicate, in the instance of meaning: "She has stopped loving Albert." In an interrogative, he is situated in the instance of the referent: "Was Albert here?" Or Albert can occupy the position of the addressee in an imperative: "At this moment, I opened the door" (taken from Albert's diary or memoirs). It is precisely because its value as a designation remains constant that the proper name lends itself so aptly to *différends*.

The plasticity of the proper name is evidently limited by

its inclusion in one or more worlds of names, as well as by the place constitutively assigned to it among other names according to spatial, temporal, and anthroponymic distances which themselves have names: kilometers, decades, generations, degrees of kinship. And this place is in constant agitation. Within these limits, nevertheless, a nondeterminable swarm of meanings can descend upon a name without changing its capacity for designation. From among this swarm, of course, certain of the attributed meanings will be singled out by means of the name's relationship with the other names given, and also by means of designators. Even then, however, the swarm of possible meanings still remains enormous at any given moment; nor will it ever be ended. No one could have known in 1932 that Karol Wojtila would one day become Pope, just as no one could have known, around 340 B.C., that one of the meanings attached to the referent named Aristotle would be that a French philosopher at the end of the twentieth century would show how the ontology contained in Aristotelian metaphysics is not a science, but rather a dialectic. In other words, names are very capable of accommodating future contingencies, as well as ambiguity, polysemy, and even contradiction. This accommodation is possible because names are neither definable essences nor designators of essences (although Leibnitz believed the opposite to be true, just as Kripke still does to some extent). Names only designate landmarks which indicate procedures for reiteration, but which, in so doing, also allow the institution or attempted institution of new networks in which the given names will be included.

The nominative phrase thus presents a double advantage: first, that of corresponding to a necessary moment in the procedures for establishing the reality of the referent; second, that of making possible an infinite number of *différends* concerning the referent. Kantian *Darstellung*—designation—is insufficient for the first task, that of establishing reality. And it seems to constitute an obstacle to the second task, that of promoting *différends*. Kant is condemned, by a transcendental aesthetic that is also phenomenological, to make a distinction between direct presentation and analogical presentation. This distinction causes him to accord an excessive privilege, which is otherwise inexplicable, as is his schematization, to the cognitive phrase. At the same time, this distinction sets in orbit outside the sphere of the perceptible all those "objects" that are not objects of knowledge. In this way, the question of the *différend* is not posed with its full cutting force, but can be blunted in the Idea of a reconciliatory end.

The question of the *différend* has to do with language rather than anthropology. In spite of all appearances, what is at stake in *différends* is not the satisfaction of "human" interests or passions. To allow this claim would be to presuppose some sort of nature which, be it human or not, would have to obey a purpose. And this idea is much too rough, too pathetic, or too heroic to account for *différends*. It would be just as futile to replace the *anthropos* by a *logos* if it were only in order to attribute anew to the logos some "nature"—whether expressive, communicational, or "poetic"—which would assure its ultimate unity. It does not even suffice to say, as Wittgenstein does, that: "Language (*die Sprache*) is a labyrinth of paths (*ein Labyrinth von Wegen*)," because this still supposes that someone walks there, even if it is only to get lost. What Wittgenstein subsequently adds comes closer to the *différend*: "You approach from one side, and you know your way about; you approach the same place from another side and no longer know your way about."[47] Wittgenstein uses the same verb (*sich auskennen*) that serves in section 123 of the *Philosophical Investigations* to present the problem of philosophy: "A philosophical problem has the form," he writes, of the expression, "I don't know my way about." Kant said: "Where was I? Where was I going?" This spasm in the labyrinth of legal arguments attest to the fact that language is not "something unique"[48] in the sense that it is composed of phrases from heterogeneous regimes, phrases which should forbid any recognition of "the same place," the same referent.

But neither can it be said that no one knows that "here" is the same place as "there." The possibility of identifying a referent does exist—certainly not by direct presentation, but by the procedures that we briefly indicated, and which are fixed paths marked in the labyrinth: pieces of paper. This identification is required by the validation of cognitive phrases; it still takes place, at least as a demand. Why? In order to put an end to *différends* both theoretical and practical. But it is precisely in the attempt to bring an end to *différends*, to transform war into a litigation and pronounce a verdict that will settle the dispute, that a *différend* can manifest itself. It manifests itself by a feeling. Even damages for which reparations have been made can evidently arouse a feeling of irreparable wrong. The purposiveness thus undoes itself, and peace remains an armed state.

I will term a "wrong" any damage accompanied by the loss of the means to prove the said damage. We can recognize in this "wrong" what Marx said in 1843: "a class with radical chains, a class in civil society that is not of civil society, a class that is the dissolution of all classes, a sphere of society having a universal character because of its universal suffering and claiming no particular right because no particular wrong but unqualified wrong (*ein Unrecht schlechthin*) has been perpetrated upon it."[49] To explain why I had to introduce this word here would take too long—would be interminable. At any rate, this word is diverted here from the perspective that was Marx's at that time: a perspective that was still Feuerbachian—that is, humanist, Lutheran, and perhaps still dialectical. But it is perhaps the most decisive way of marking the break with Hegel's philosophy of right—a break that has not yet been either reversed or *aufgehoben*, which is why "Marxism has not finished."[50] Indirectly, it marks the break with a thought that proposes mediation or reconciliation: with the Kantian Idea of the *Zusammenstimmung*. Whatever suffers a wrong is a victim. It is in the nature of a victim to be incapable of proving that a wrong has been suffered. For the judge says to the victim: one of two things is possible; either you are the victim of a wrong, or you are not. If you are not, you are either mistaken or you are lying when you testify that you are a victim. If you are a victim, and since you can testify to this wrong, as I am informed is the case here, then this wrong ceases to be a wrong. It becomes a damage; and you are mistaken or lying when you testify that it is a wrong.

Faurisson complained that he had been lied to about the existence of gas chambers. To verify that a place is a gas chamber, he would only accept, he declared, "a former prisoner capable of proving to me that he actually saw a gas chamber with his own eyes."[51] According to Faurisson, then, there can be no direct witness to a gas chamber other than its victim; and there can be no victim except a dead victim, for then this gas chamber would not be what Faurisson's opponent claims it to be. Thus, no place can be identified as a gas chamber, because there can be no eye witness.

This argument is called the dilemma, and was known by the sophists, notably Protagoras. It provides the mechanism for the Epicurean maxim: if death is there (at Auschwitz), you are not there; if you are there, death is not there. In both cases, it is impossible for you to prove that death is there.

This double bind also provides the mechanism for the lawyers' arguments in the great political trials of Berlin or Moscow: if you are a communist, you are in agreement with the Politburo; if you are not in agreement with the Politburo, you are not a communist. In either case, there is no way of proving that a disagreement exists within communism. But the double bind also provides the key to positivism in its generality: only that which can be validated under the regime of cognitives is real. If for some reason you are deprived of the means to prove the damage you have suffered, then your judge cannot "reconstruct" the damage; that is, he cannot accomplish a reiteration of the case through the accepted procedures. Your case is thus dismissed. Extended to all statements, this criteria is called performativity. It compels any plaintiff to prove any damage he alleges according to the rules of cognition—that is, according to technological science. If the regime of phrases to which the plaintiff belongs is different from that of cognitive phrases, and thus necessarily different from that of the only tribunals he can appeal to, then he is certain to lose his suit. This is the case, for example, with a philosophy whose regime of phrases, if indeed there is one, cannot by hypothesis be limited to the cognitive regime. In *The Quarrel Between the Faculties*, Kant marks his position as that of the impossible witness of *différends*, as the judicious position. In so doing, he fully assumes the inferiority which necessarily results in respect to disciplines armed with a code.

What forbids any "return" on our part to Kant is capital, or the power of indifference. Marx is himself a name around which many *différends* have arisen, and which still provides material for litigation and vengeance. But something in Marxism has not finished being critical, has not stopped demanding that we be judicious. With Marxism, the *différend* has been transmitted by a reception that is at once sharp and blurred. It is sharp because Marxism has welcomed a rejected feeling, that of class hatred, and has sought to invent the idiom for which that passion was at a loss. But the reception becomes blurred when Marx insists on furnishing proofs of a wrong for which no one can point out a case, and, moreover, when the wrong is treated as the only one whose reparation, through revolution, could put an end to most *différends*—or, in its Stalinist version, to all of them.

Contracts and agreements between socioeconomic partners do not preclude (indeed, they presume) the fact that the wage earner or his representative must have spoken—and will continue to speak—of his work as if it were the temporary transfer of merchandise, or the "service" which he owns. Marx terms this situation "abstraction" (but the term is deceptive: what "concrete" does it imply? what more real reality does it oppose to the provable reality of earning wages?); this "abstraction" is nevertheless required by the idiom in which the litigation is decided: "bourgeois" social and economic law, the language of capital. Unless he makes use of this language, the worker cannot exist in the domain governed by it; he would be a slave, for example. By using this language, he can become a plaintiff. But, precisely because he does use it, he cannot stop being a victim. Does he indeed possess the means of establishing that he suffers some damage, not because his salary or the conditions of his salaried work are unjust, but from the very fact of wage-earning itself? No. How can he—or anyone—*know* (savoir) that the wage earner is something other than the owner of an ability which he rents out to his employer according to the conditions of social legislation? How could the arbitrating magistrate understand that the worker's "being," his Idea, is a force that creates surplus value, and that his real name is the proletariat (according to Marx)? The arbitrator does not need to know what the worker is, or what his Idea is; he needs to know what he owns and what he is exchanging. For the judge, it would seem impossible for the worker to have nothing, since his employer is in the process of buying something from him. Moreover, as Kant would add, the referent "labor force" is perhaps the object of a concept, but since no intuition can be subsumed within it, this concept is a concept of reason—an Idea. No direct perception is possible for a case that could validate this concept or the phrase that signifies it; the worker's counsel will never be able to furnish proof of it.

The arrangement worked out between the different sides by the arbitrators—even if we assume no denial of justice on their part—cannot accede to the petitions of the other phrases, which we can call Marxist, but which also relate to the same name, that of the wage earner. This phrase belongs to a regime which is not that of the phrases by which judgment is rendered. A wrong and a victim therefore exist by the mere fact that the wage earner's suit is tried in a language whose regime excludes the very Idea that a labor force capable of creating value could be associated with the name "wage earner."

How can we know that the wage earner's name is also that of a proletarian, in the Marxist sense? We don't know any proletarians, but we can form the concept of one. We cannot point to an example of a proletarian. The proletariat is the object of an Idea, and this Idea is elaborated reflexively, taking signs as a point of departure. And signs, as Kant shows in respect to the French Revolution,[52] are feelings. But in order to signal that a noncognitive regime of phrases is attached to names given in the various worlds of names, a feeling must be inexplicable, like free action. Class hatred—at least as it is usually understood—is explainable. What escapes the administration of cognitive proof, and can serve as the sign of a phrase from another regime, is the feeling of solidarity manifested by spectators who are not themselves involved with the actors in the class struggle. In the same text from 1843, Marx seems to support this view when he writes: "No class of civil society can play this role [of emancipation] unless it arouses in itself and in the masses a moment of enthusiasm, a moment in which it associates, fuses, and identifies itself with society in general, and is felt and recognized to be society's general representative."[53] Without this solidarity, Kant would continue, there is no sign that the proletariat is the object of an Idea. The empirical establishment of even an international association of workers takes the place of this feeling of solidarity. Kant would say that such an association obeys, like all organisms, the principle of a technical purposiveness.

That is at least how the critical watchman would judge the case after a full century of Marxism. But this watchman would also add: other objects of Ideas are possible, and they must be constructed reflexively, taking as a point of departure signs that derive from other names. For example: what is the object of an Idea whose sign arose out of the 1968 movements to elicit the solidarity and enthusiasm of many people who had no stake in the events, and who were at a considerable remove from them? This object has not been elaborated reflexively. The movement has merely been explained; it has been placed, for judgment, under the regime of proof. The wrong to which it was perhaps trying to testify has not found its idiom.

What has been lost, at least for the critical philosopher, with this century of Marxism (and Hegelianism), is the speculative principle of the Result. There is no contradiction between two phrases attached to the same name but deriving from heterogeneous regimes; they can both be "true." The "truth" may not even be at stake in these phrases. Their synthesis—the result—cannot be the object of a concept; the very principle is absurd. Moreover, when the advocate of synthesis claims to produce proofs of it, absurdity makes way for terror.

What has perished here, along with Marxism, as the victim of the transcendental illusion, is a principle symmetrical to that of the Result: the principle of the origin. This principle only recognizes as fundamental the *différend* in which work is at stake. The watchman wonders: the Algerians are not the proletariat; but were they not victims of a wrong merely by the fact that they were unable to express, either in the framework of French constitutional law or international law, the damage they suffered by being French? Or the Quebecois, who are not the proletariat, by being Canadian? Or women, who are not the proletariat, by being at best placed under the same judicial regime as men?

A certain form of Marxism objects to this Idea of a multiplication of *différends*: none is fundamental, it would say; capital accommodates them all, transforming them one by one into litigations that are judged according to the criteria of performativity. The means used to make this judgment is a universal measure applicable to all entities, regardless of the regime of statements from which they derive: money. This is evident in the new technology of language, which has as its corresponding unit of measure the bit of information. The response to this objection is the argument that the totality of phrases, like the whole in general, is an Idea. This is why capital can only be the "virtual" totality of phrases. Capital's madness, or even its sanity, its transcendental illusion, is perhaps that the enigma of will, which is (since Descartes) the infinite, seeks to transform itself into experience. Thus there results a confusion of regimes of phrases. The task of the critical watchman is clear: illusion must always be dissipated. Yet that task is also obscure: that very dissipation may be an illusion.

Hidden within the litigations and the verdicts is a wrong that can be threatening (but even this isn't sure, for the Antithetic tells us that there are false *différends* that are merely amusing). Through these litigations and verdicts, phrases—and thus meanings—are attached to names. As a result, other heterogeneous phrases that were attached to the same names can be dismissed. Proper names are indeed, if not passages, then at least points of contact between heterogeneous regimes. Taken to the extreme, this threat of a wrong promises to strike from history and from the map entire worlds of names: extermination of the Communards, extermination of counter-revolutionaries, extermination of the Armenians. The final solution. The purposiveness that the twentieth century has witnessed has not consisted, as Kant had hoped, of securing fragile passages above abysses. Rather, it has consisted of filling up those abysses at the cost of the destruction of whole worlds of names. A Polish adage says that when the people and the government disagree, the government changes peoples. Capital is that which wants a single language and a single network, and it never stops trying to present them. The means capital employs to diminish the *différends* is what Marx called the *Gleichgültigkeit*, or the indifference, of money. This "equivalent value" conceals surplus value in the same way that equality hides *différends*.

Vengeance hovers around names. Vengeance does not precede legal cases; it follows them. It can invoke no right, for right is always "right" according to a tribunal that is unique and that demands proofs, names, and measurements. What cries out for vengeance are the forbidden phrases of defense, phrases that have suffered a wrong because they can only make an appeal to feelings. A *différend* takes the form of a civil war, of what the Greeks called a stasis:[54] the form of a spasm. The authority of the idiom in which cases are established and regulated is contested. A different idiom and a different tribunal are demanded, which the other party contests and rejects. Language is at war with itself, and the critical watchman posts guard over this war. The name "Palestine" belongs to several worlds of names. Within each of these worlds, several regimes of phrases quarrel over the name "Palestine." Here we have an analogon of language: not simply the complexity of a large city, but the complexity of a large city at war. In 1956, at Budapest, the names of the streets were changed to mislead the Soviet tanks; the government doesn't change peoples, the people change names: this is the clandestine. And this is why philosophy must remain in arms. The armed state that is philosophical peace procures health neither for humanity nor for philosophers: it is the health of language.

In the *différend*, something cries out in respect to a name. Something demands to be put into phrases, and suffers from the wrong of this impossibility. This affect comprises the silence, the feeling, that is an exclamation; but, because it has to, it also makes an appeal, through its ellipses, to possible phrases. Humans who believe that they use language as an instrument of communication and decision learn, through the feeling of pain that accompanies the silence of interdiction, that they are conscripted into language. The "delight" that they also feel at this conscription does not derive from any hope of thereby increasing their power, but only from the hope of permitting other phrases, perhaps heterogeneous.

Notes

1. *The Quarrel Between the Faculties*, Kant, *Werke* (Frankfurt: Insel-Verlag, Wilhelm Weischedel), 6:389–90. All references are to this edition. Where possible, I have used a standard English translation of the Kantian texts cited. These references follow the author's references to the German edition—tr.

2. The expression is borrowed from Jean-Luc Nancy, *Le Discours de la syncope* (Paris: Flammarion, 1976), p. 74.

3. I have chosen to leave *différend* in the French throughout the text. The term denotes at once a difference of opinion, a quarrel, a dispute, or a state of discord. The term *différend* connotes both the subtlety of a difference and the antagonism of a dispute (translator's note).

4. 6:599. *Anthropology from a Pragmatic Point of View*, Victor Lyle Dowdell, tr. (Carbondale: Southern Illinois University Press, 1978), p. 172.

5. 5:345. *Critique of Judgment*, J. H. Bernard, tr. (London: Macmillan, 1914), p. 120.

6. 5:329. Bernard, p. 102.

7. 5:346. Bernard, p. 121.

8. 2:13. *Critique of Pure Reason*, F. Max Müller, tr. (Garden City, N.Y.: Anchor Books, 1966), p. xxiv.

9. Obviously, the theme of the war between doctrines has long been a rhetorical staple of preambles in general, and of prefaces to philosophical works in particular. Hume makes use of it in the introduction to *A Treatise of Human Nature*. But he doesn't intend to put an end to the war with a verdict; he simply wants to win it with a decisive blow: "instead of taking now and then a castle or village on the frontier, to march up directly to the capital or center of these sciences [the human sciences], to human nature itself; which being once master of, we may everywhere else hope for an easy victory" (London: Dent, 1911), p. 5. This Blitzkrieg strategy did not exactly achieve the anticipated success. This was for the most part due to Kant's parry. But the strategy was destined to have another success, at once less "clear" and more fearful: the installation, in the course of two centuries (including, as it has been shown, to some extent with Kant himself), of the human sciences in the place of metaphysics, as well as the installation of positivism at the heart of methodology, whatever may have been Hume's own thoughts on the subject.

10. 2:640. Müller, pp. 481, 486.

11. 2:636. Müller, p. 484.

12. Preface, 6:399. Dowdell, p. 3.

13. 3:409.

14. 6:381–303.

15. 6:377.

16. *Opus postumum*, Liasse 11, fo. 5, p. 3.

17. 6:381–383.

18. Dowdell, pp. 132–133.

19. 6:374.

20. Dowdell, p. 93.

21. Dowdell, p. 102.

22. 6:519. Dowdell, p. 102.

23. 2:184. Müller, pp. 118–119.

24. 6:55–57.

25. 2:467. Müller, p. 350.

26. The problem is posed in this way by Wittgenstein in the *Tractatus*, sections 5.251 to 5.254, but only in respect to the logical-mathematical series.

27. 2:488, 491. Müller, pp. 366, 371.

28. 2:486–487. Müller, p. 365.

29. 4:157, 186–191. *Critique of Practical Reason*, Thomas Kingsmill Abbott, tr. (London: Longman, Green, 1909), pp. 133, 159–163.

30. This expression recurs frequently in Kant's text. It signifies the minimum requirement for compatibility among the regimes. Its French translation (*sans en léser aucun*) was suggested by Jean-Pierre Dubost.

31. Vol. 2, Introduction, in fine. Bernard, p. 13.

32. 2:408. Müller, p. 302.

33. 2 (KUK), section 84. Bernard, pp. 359–361.

34. 6:357.

35. *Dialectique Négative*, Groupe Collège de philosophie, tr. (Paris: Payot, 1978), avant-propos.

36. *Modèles mathématiques de la morphogenèse* (Paris: Editions 1018, 1974), p. 186.

37. See J-F Lyotard, "Essai d'analyse du dispositif spéculatif," *Degrés*, no. 26–27.

38. In a letter to Lambert dated September 2, 1770, Kant terms "phaenomenologia generalis" the entirely negative science in which the value and limits of these principles of perception would be determined. The fourth part of Lambert's *Nouvel Organon* is called "Phenomenology."

39. 2:254–257. Müller, p. xiv.

40. 2:222. Müller, p. 150.

41. Introduction, 2:245. Bernard, p. 11.

42. Saul Kripke, *La Logique des noms propres*, Jacob and Recanati, trs. (Paris: Payot, 1982), pp. 42–44.

43. Siegfried Kracauer, *Le Roman policier*, Rochlitz, tr. (Paris: Payot, 1981), pp. 38 sq.

44. *Les Derniers Jours d'Emmanuel Kant*, Pierre Legris and Marcel Schwobt, trs. (Paris: Gallimard, 1973).

45. Kripke, *La Logique*, pp. 36 sq.

46. Marin, *Le Portrait du roi* (Paris: Editions de Minuit, 1981).

47. Wittgenstein, *Philosophical Investigations*, 3d ed., G. E. M. Anscombe, tr. (New York: Macmillan, 1958), section 203, p. 82e.

48. *Ibid.*, section 110, p. 47e.

49. "Contribution to the Critique of Hegel's 'Philosophy of Right,' " in *Critique of Hegel's Philosophy of Right*, Annette Jolin and Joseph O'Malley, trs. (Cambridge: Cambridge University Press, 1971), p. 141.

50. See J-F. Lyotard, "Pierre Souyri, le marxisme qui n'a pas fini," *Esprit* (1982), vol. 13, no. 2.

51. *Le Monde*, January 16, 1979, and Serge Thion, *Vérité historique ou vérité politique?* (Paris: Librairie La Vieille Taupe, 1980).

52. Section 5, 6: pp. 356 sq.

53. Marx, "Contribution," p. 140.

54. Nicole Loraux, *L'Invention d'Athènes* (La Haye: Mouton, 1981), pp. 200–204 and Index: Stasis; id°, L'Oubli dans la cité, *Le Temps de la réflexion* (1980), 1:222 sq.

2

NARRATIVE, HETEROGENEITY, AND THE QUESTION OF THE POLITICAL: BAKHTIN AND LYOTARD

David Carroll

Returning to History and Politics

Simplifying to the extreme, the "postmodern" is characterized by an incredulity concerning metanarratives.
—Jean-François Lyotard, *The Postmodern Condition*

WITH an ever increasing urgency we hear the cry today from
various quarters that we must stop treating literature as an
entity unto itself and must instead begin again to investigate its
historical and political implications, its links with society. The
problem is of course how to establish such links and what forms
of history, what concept of society and politics, one is proposing to connect literature to or ground it in. Too often the cry is
made simply out of frustration and in reaction to the various
types of formalism that still seem to dominate the intellectual
marketplace, to the fact that formalism in some form or other
just won't go away no matter how often and how forcefully

history and politics are evoked to chase it away or at least put it in its place (in the place *they* assign it). Another version of formalism always seems ready to rise out of the ash can of history to take the place of previously discarded versions. This may in large part be due to the fact that the critique of formalism has too often taken the form of a naive, precritical historicism, one whose shortcomings certain types of formalism (for example, a certain Russian formalism and early, critical structuralism) have quite effectively exposed and challenged. Such critiques, rather than being post-formalist (or post-structuralist, if this term has any sense), are really preformalist (prestructuralist). Perhaps the problem even is not really how to become postformalist at all, as if one could ever really leave the problem of form behind, but rather how to establish a critical perspective on form and history that does not depend on either formalist or historicist, post-formalist or metahistorical assumptions.

Any "return to history," any rethinking of the sociopolitical realm, if it is to be critical, that is, more than a return to the safe, secure ground of traditional history and politics, must do more than such pseudo-returns have done in the past. Rather than posing as an alternative to the various formalisms vying for dominance today, a truly critical return to history and politics must question itself in the same terms it uses to question the various formalisms it opposes itself to. That is, it must question itself as a particular form, series or narrative, as it situates and undermines the notion of form as a closed, integral, autonomous, and self-reflexive entity. It must confront its own philosophical and ideological limitations as it challenges the idealist, metahistorical pretensions of all theories or philosophies of form.

Rather than establishing *a ground*, a critical return to history and politics will inevitably be forced to confront not an abyss, total absence or pure groundlessness, as a certain textual formalism would have it, but the conflictual interpenetration of various series, contexts, and grounds constituting any ground or process of grounding. A critical return to history and politics in this sense is an unending process that can never reach its destination, that never quite returns, not because there is no ground at all but because there is no one, ultimate, totally determining ground, no ground of all grounds—neither in history, society, nor politics. A theory of history or the political that posits itself as such a ground in fact ends up denying or putting an end to historicity rather than affirming it, resolving the question of the political rather than pursuing it critically. It produces in this way the conditions and urgent necessity for a return to (or through) formalism, aesthetics, or textualism in order once again to begin to question the certainties of the historical-political realm.

The safest way to resolve the problems involved in any critical rethinking of history and politics is to fall back on either a historico-political or formalist metatheory that, when confronted with the limitations and contradictions of all other theories, situates them within itself, makes them elements of or steps on the way to its own formalist system or historical-narrative schema. No matter how critical such metatheories are of the theories they situate, and regardless of whether they are rooted in a system of tropes that accounts for all dialectics (and other forms of narrative and history) or in a dialectical theory of narrative that accounts for all tropes, they demand that one believe in them, adhere to them, accept their priority and efficacity. In other words, they demand that all critical questions, even or especially the ones they themselves ask of all other positions and theories, not be directed at them; their metatheoretical status depends on it.

But do we still have—and should we even be encouraged to have if we don't—the faith, the confidence, the conviction, the naiveté or the "piety," as Jean-François Lyotard would say, to commit ourselves to such a belief in either a formalist or dialectical metatheory and to ignore the shortcomings and repressive effects of any and all metatheories? It would seem that for many today such "faith" is no longer possible and is moreover an impediment to critical analysis.[1] If all theories are really dissimulated narratives and thus have no real claim to universality or omnitemporality, as Lyotard, for example, claims in *Instructions païennes* (p. 28), then the decline in belief in metanarratives of all sorts that Lyotard asserts is typical of our age should not be seen as a sign of our own modern (or postmodern) "decadence," but rather as a positive sign, an indication of radical critical possibilities. For Lyotard, this "condition" of disbelief has made it possible and necessary to rethink the whole question of the social and political, not in order to derive them once again from another theory of history or society, but in order to confront the most fundamental and urgent historico-political issue, one that cannot be "theorized," that is, resolved, by any theory or system: the issue of justice. For Lyotard, a justice of the "postmodern condition" can no longer be conceived in terms of universal laws that resolve diversity, difference, or contradiction; rather it demands that the alterity of the other be respected and that the conflictual diversity of the social space itself, which can then no longer be determined in terms of *a* history, *a* theory, or *a* narrative, be maintained. In this sense, the impossibility of believing in metanarratives is the beginning of "postmodern" critical thought, for the end of the reign of the "grand récits," whose function was to unify, synthesize, totalize, and legitimate, makes it necessary to develop different strategies for dealing with the heterogeneity of the millions of "petits récits" now freed from the place and sense assigned to them within the various metanarratives.

Lyotard's postmodern disbelief in metanarrative is rooted in a confidence in the potential critical force of small narratives, at least insomuch as their conflictual multiplicity and heterogeneity resist totalization—and he sees, moreover, narrative heterogeneity to be indicative of the complexity and diversity of the social fabric itself. Fredric Jameson in his "Foreword" to the recently published English translation of *The Postmodern Condition* takes issue with Lyotard's critique of all metanarrative and considers it in this instance to be paradoxical and even contradictory insomuch as "the vitality of small narrative units at work everywhere *locally* in the present social system are accompanied by something like a more global or totalizing 'crisis' in the narrative function in general."[2] But in spite of what Jameson claims, there is really nothing paradoxical or contradictory about this situation, even though there is something conflictual about it. For if metanarratives for Lyotard repress the critical, disruptive potential of small, local narratives, then their decline and the "totalizing crisis" accompanying it can only be seen as presenting radical critical possibilities, not only for small narratives but for the narrative function in general. In fact, narrative diversity for Lyotard has always had a detotalizing, that is, critical, function; the belief in metanarrative, the opposite function.

Jameson undoubtedly presents the situation as contradictory (at least, like most contradictions, it is a "seeming contradiction") because contradictions can in principle always be resolved in dialectical terms—and this is what Jameson will propose to do:

> This seeming contradiction can be resolved, I believe, by taking a further step that Lyotard seems unwilling to do in the present text, namely to posit, not the disappearance of the great master-narratives, but their passage underground as it were, their continuing but now *unconscious* effectivity as a way of "thinking about" and acting in our current situation. (p. xii)

With this resolution of the "seeming contradiction" between metanarrative and the multiplicity of small narratives, a resolution made in terms of metanarrative in a new form or rather on a different level, Jameson attempts to rescue the master-narrative function in general and the Marxist metanarrative in particular from Lyotard's critique. In fact, Jameson's entire "Foreword" attempts to show that the "crisis in narration" can be resolved (it is in this way a false crisis) if we situate it within a master-narrative that shows it to be just a passing phase, no matter how recurrent. For Jameson, the postmodern is a superficial moment in a narrative of all narratives, and it is only as we are able to ignore the disbelief around us that we are able to act in and think effectively about our current situation.

But Lyotard's "unwillingness" in *The Postmodern Condition* and elsewhere to posit either a conscious or unconscious critical effectivity for any form of metanarrative is exactly what separates him from Jameson and constitutes on a more general level his *différend* with Marxism, even in its critical form.[3] It seems to me that the "open Marxism" championed by Jameson and used against Lyotard here, no matter how forceful and critical it might be in particular contexts, is limited by its defense of metanarrative, for would it still be Marxist in any significant way if it did not defend the dialectical metanarrative? The chief difference between Lyotard and Jameson can perhaps be stated most economically in the following way. For Jameson, "the great master-narratives here are those that suggest that something beyond capitalism is possible, something radically different; and they also 'legitimate' the praxis whereby political militants seek to bring that radically different future social order into being" (p. xix). For Lyotard, on the contrary, "something beyond capitalism," "something radically different," and, more importantly, "*something just*" is possible only in opposition to master-narratives, which always bring the different back to the same, only with the multiplication of small narratives that both the capitalist and Marxist metanarratives attempt to limit, control, and repress. As Lyotard demands, "One must maximize as much as possible the multiplication of small narratives,"[4] as part of "a politics that would respect both the desire for justice and the desire for the unknown" (*The Postmodern Condition*, p. 67). For Lyotard, then, a belief in metanarrative is an impediment to action, a constraint on justice, and a repression of the desire for the unknown. No wonder he is unwilling to believe in "the political unconscious" and the underground existence of metanarratives as effective supports for action and critical thought.

Lyotard has argued that the loss of credibility of the Marxist metanarrative, for example, is largely due to the unjust effects it produces everywhere it is executed completely,[5] the most obvious of these effects being the way it deprives even the "heroes" of the Marxist narrative, the workers, the right to

narration: "The grand narrative could only acquire the pre-
dominance it had on the condition that its own addressees, the
workers, who were also its heroes, were denied narration"
(p. 23). Being denied narration is not just a metaphor for injustice for Lyotard, it is already injustice itself. The totalitarian
state is one in which all narrative functions are fixed and
assigned in advance and where no deviations from the master-
narrative are possible:

> As a citizen of one of these regimes, you are taken at the
> same time for the co-author of its narrative, for the priv-
> ileged listener, and for the perfect executor of the episodes
> that are assigned you. Your place is thus fixed in the three
> instances of the master-narrative and in all the details of
> your life. Your imagination as a narrator, listener or actor is
> completely blocked. . . . A mistake in execution, an error of
> listening, a lapsus of narration, and you are locked up. . . .
> You are forbidden narration. Such is devastation. (pp. 31–
> 32)

The question of political justice is here cast in terms of narrative, or rather, what one could call the right to narrative is for
Lyotard a fundamental political right. For how can the political
nature of narrative, even of the most insignificant of little narratives of daily life, be denied when the totalitarian state defends
its master-narrative with all the means at its disposal? When
those who circulate their own little narratives or those of others
in spite of political oppression and at great risk are considered
enemies of the state ("nonbelievers")?

Hundreds, thousands of little dissident narratives of all
sorts are produced in spite of all attempts to repress them, and
they circulate inside and eventually, or even initially, outside
the boundaries of the totalitarian state. The importance of these
little narratives is not only that they challenge the dominant
metanarrative and the state apparatus that would prohibit or
discredit them, but that they also indicate the possibility of
another kind of society, of another form of social relations in
fact already functioning "laterally" within the totalitarian

state: "a shadow of civil society made of distended circuits and improvised circulations" (p. 33). And Lyotard attributes to small narratives this critical, oppositional function in relation to the capitalist metanarrative as much as in relation to the speculative, Marxist metanarrative:

> If the networks of uncertain and ephemeral narratives can eat away at the grand, instituted narrative apparatus, it is in multiplying the somewhat lateral skirmishes as pro-abortionists, prisoners, draftees, prostitutes, students, and peasants all did in your country during the last decade. One invents small stories, even segments of stories; one listens to them, transmits them, and acts them out at the right moment. (pp. 34–35)

For Lyotard, only with such small stories is the honor of narrative, honor itself, preserved (p. 33), and this is because more is always at stake in story-telling than the story told. For in the right to narration—to narrate, listen (read), and act in ways not determined in advance by any metanarrative—the political is in question, a nondetermined, critical sense of the social, indicated.

Lyotard, then, focuses on narrative to raise the question of the political, and he does this at least in part because of the critical advantages he sees in certain strategies derived from narrative pragmatics. He opposes pragmatics to metaphysics, dialectics, and the entire theoretical, speculative, dogmatic genre in the following terms: "Pragmatics is a word that designates the set of very complicated relations that exist between the person who narrates and what he is narrating, between the person who narrates and the one who listens to him, between the latter and the story told by the former" (p. 16). The critical advantage of narrative pragmatics for Lyotard is that in order to talk about narrative it does not implicitly or explicitly assume a metanarratological position, one that gives the rules according to which narrative should be judged, one that proposes laws which determine the truth of narrative, the nature of the real to which it is supposed to conform, and the ideal form narrative must be modeled after. On the contrary, a critical pragmatics admits that one can only analyze, respond to, and counter narratives with other narratives, or as Lyotard puts it: "My narrative like all narratives has for its referent other narratives. It's always: I say that one says. . . . The *diégèse* of my narrative, but also of yours, is never made of brute events or facts, but these are always carried by other narratives that ours take as referents" (pp. 18–19). The point is then that one is always already situated within narrative, within various and conflicting philosophical, political, historical, biographical narratives and that one *acts* by countering and responding to these narratives and by occupying different places within different narratives: that is, as narrator, listener-reader, or actor. The possibility of *responding* is thus crucial to all narrative; it is an opening in narrative to other narratives, an opening that is fundamental to the very structure or form of narrative.

A metanarrative, on the contrary, demands that all alternative narrative possibilities be repressed or subsumed into it; it is terroristic or totalitarian in the sense that it assigns every narrator, listener, and actor *a* place and makes each responsible for the place assigned to him. It programs all responses in advance and blocks all nonprogrammed responses. From this perspective, a theory and practice of discourse can be considered to be critical, therefore, only if they resist, subvert, and undermine such blockages, if they reinsert openings that have been closed off through brute political force, philosophical coercion, or rhetorical persuasion. Any narrative that predetermines all responses or prohibits any counter-narratives puts an end to narrative itself by suppressing all possible alternative actions and responses, by making itself its own end and the end of all other narratives.

Read in this way, Lyotard's focus on narrative as a way of recasting the question of the political or the social could be linked to the work of another critical "narrativist" who also used a certain notion of narrative to undermine the authoritarian characteristics of what he called monologic discourse (what Lyotard would consider a form of metanarrative). I am of course referring to M. M. Bakhtin. Bakhtin's approach to narrative, like Lyotard's could be considered a pragmatics and defended on grounds similar to those proposed by Lyotard. For Bakhtin too, narrative is privileged not only because it is closer to reality or history than other forms of discourse (a truism since reality and history have traditionally been modeled after *a* form of narrative, made to conform to a metanarrative), but also because it establishes a complicated set of social, political, philosophical, and formal relations among narrator, actor, and reader (listener) that are dynamic rather than fixed. In principle, the reader or listener of one story always has the possibility of becoming, and is even demanded to become, the narrator of another, the narrator of one becoming the reader of another, the actor of one, the narrator of another, etc. This possibility, this opening to the other, to alternative narratives and thus to a rearrangement of relations and positions, is at the heart of all narrative in Bakhtin's as well as Lyotard's approach.

For Bakhtin, in the novel, no voice, no language, no narrative ever goes unanswered; none is presented as having the first or last word. Of all the literary genres, if it really is a genre at all, Bakhtin privileges the novel in that it provides him with "objective evidence" of the fundamental plurivocity and alterity of all narrative, and ultimately, of all discourse. The novel displays openly its origins in heterogeneity and multi-languagedness; it is structured (or destructured) in terms of *dialogue*—the dynamics of narrative and counter-narrative— while all other genres in one way or another disguise or repress this "original situation." It is in this sense that the novel is for Bakhtin not just one genre among the others but the *original genre*, not really a metagenre but a parody or primary mixture of genres, languages, narratives, forms, voices, and social dialects:

> The novel can be defined as a diversity of social speech types (sometimes even diversity of languages) and a diversity of individual voices, artistically organized. The internal stratification of any single national language into social dialects, characteristic group behavior, professional jargons, generic languages, languages of generations and age

groups . . .—this internal stratification present in every
language at any given moment of its historical existence is
the indispensible prerequisite for the novel as a genre.[6]

The novel is thus one of, if not the best, example of the dialogic,
for it exploits as part of its form and content the primary dialogic nature of discourse and thus society; alterity is a fundamental component of its very structure.

One senses in Lyotard's work the same kind of emphasis
on the openness, the "plasticity," the inherent heterogeneity
not just of the novel but of all narrative. For Lyotard too, narrative distinguishes itself from other genres by admitting all
genres into itself:

> Narrative has a privilege in the way it assembles diversity.
> It is a genre that seems to be able to admit all others.
> (Everything, says Marx, has a (hi)story.) There is an affinity
> between the people and narrative. The popular form of
> "language" is the small deritualized story. . . . Prose is the
> people of little stories (historiettes).[7]

Deritualized narrative is "popular," it could in fact be considered synonymous with "the people," because it is nonexclusive and assembles rather than resolves or represses diversity.
In this way Lyotard opposes the little narrative to the speculative didactic genre, and in the Aristotelian terms he adopts for
his own purposes, narrative is a form of dialéktikè (not the
Hegelian or Marxist dialectic), an art of discussion: "Aristotle
opposed the art of discussion, the dialectic where opinions
confront each other, that is, where little everyday narratives
enter into competition with each other, to learned didacticism"
(Instructions païennes, p. 41). The confrontation of opinions,
of little narratives governed by no unique law, purpose, or end,
defines the political for Lyotard, and narrative has a relative
privilege in this area because it seems to be more overtly embedded in these conflicts than any other genre and in this sense
more directly "political" than other forms of discourse. And
this is argued not so much because of its content as because of
its "form," its capacity to assemble and not reduce or suppress

diversity and heterogeneity. Neither the "prose of the people" nor the "people of prose" is one.

For Lyotard and Bakhtin, then, the heterogeneity characteristic of narrative, a heterogeneity that is primary and unsynthesizable, a plurality that no single genre, metadiscourse, or master-game encompasses, is in itself an indication of the heterogeneous quality of the social space itself, defined by Bakhtin as the heteroglossia of various languages and dialects and by Lyotard as "a multiplicity of confrontations of interlocutors placed in different pragmatics" (Au juste, p. 142). The problem each then has to confront is how to link the heterogeneity they find characteristic of narrative to a notion of "sociability" or community that is open but not simply pluralistic, how to develop a narratological-political strategy that neither suppresses this heterogeneity in the name of a historico-political ideal nor makes it an end in itself at the expense of the social community. The social space may not be one, but it is not made up only of random, unconnected entities either. Social relations that are rooted in and that respect diversity are the goal of both.

The novel can, then, neither be determined by an assumed preexisting social reality nor preformed by formalist or generic categories. In the novel, according to Bakhtin, a battle takes place in discourse and among discourses to become "the language of truth" or reality, a battle for what Foucault calls power-knowledge, or what in Lyotard's terms is characteristic of différends. All realisms and all theorisms attempt to end these battles and disputes by assigning to one form of discourse the privilege of effectively capturing or being adequate to the real, of presenting the truth. Bakhtin, in arguing against such realisms and theorisms, claims that the "realist imperative," which was "often hailed as constitutive for the novel as a genre (in contrast to other epic genres) and usually formulated as: 'the novel must be a full and comprehensive reflection of its era,'" should be formulated differently: "the novel must represent all the social and ideological voices of its era, that is all the era's languages that have any claim to be significant; the novel must be a microcosm of heteroglossia."[8] The conflicting plurality of voices that Bakhtin insists the novel must present is not accumulative and synthetic, however, but auto-critical in nature: "This *auto-criticism of discourse* is one of the primary distinguishing features of the novel as a genre. Discourse is criticized in its relationship to reality: its attempt to faithfully reflect reality, to manage reality and to transpose it (the utopian pretenses of discourse), even to replace reality as a surrogate for it (the dream and the fantasy that replace life)" (p. 412). Internally stratified within themselves and refracting the intentions of the speaking subject as well as the referent, the languages of the novel are representational only in that they demonstrate why *representation as such* is impossible, why novelistic representation is always an open, unresolvable conflict of representations. No representation, no narrative, and no theory can encompass and resolve such a fundamental conflict without denying its own dialogic foundations and becoming authoritarian and dogmatic.

The novel is not only critical of the relationship assumed to exist between language and reality in representational theories of literature, but also of all formal, generic categories which assign to each genre a specificity, form, and truth. As Bakhtin vividly puts it: "The novel gets on poorly with other genres. There can be no talk of a harmony deriving from mutual limitations and complementariness. The novel parodies other genres (precisely in their role as genres); it exposes the conventionality of their forms and their language; it squeezes out some genres and incorporates others into its own peculiar structure, reformulating and re-accentuating them" (p. 5). Bakhtin even goes so far as to call for the "novelization" of all genres, but this is not to establish the novel as a metagenre, an unquestioned canon from which to judge all others. It is rather to demand in a manner quite similar to Lyotard's that the historical and formal specificity of generic distinctions be taken seriously but at the same time that links to other languages and genres be established: "The novelization of literature does not imply attaching to already completed genres a generic canon that is alien to them, not theirs. The novel, after all, has no canon of its own. It is, by its very nature, not canonic. It is plasticity itself. It is a genre that is ever questioning, ever examining itself and subjecting its established forms to review" (p. 39). Like the realisms to which they are usually opposed, all traditional theories of genre are limited by metanarrative assumptions: they posit or assume that the conflict among genres and theories of genre can be resolved, that genres exist, in other words, prior to and outside the conflict of languages constituting them. The "novelization" of all genres would serve on the contrary to wear away the abstract, ahistorical, formalist distinctions used to define genres and undermine the metageneric, metanarrative systems or theories in which these distinctions are rooted; it would establish links among diverse elements without destroying their relative generic specificity.

But even though all the major genres are considered by Bakhtin to be *established genres* and therefore closed off to history—to their own past and to any future development—and thus opposed to the critical and open-ended, historical perspective of the novel, poetry is made to take the brunt of the opposition with the novel: "In genres that are poetic in the narrow sense, the natural dialogization of the word is not put to artistic use, the word is sufficient unto itself and does not presume alien utterances beyond its own boundaries. Poetic style is by convention suspended from any mutual interaction with alien discourse, any allusion to alien discourse" (p. 285). "The language of the poetic genre is a unitary and singular Ptolemaic word outside of which nothing else exists and nothing else is needed. The concept of many worlds of language, all equal in their ability to conceptualize and to be expressive is organically denied to poetic style" (p. 286). Poetry is everything the novel is not; it is dominated by a concept of formal integrity and rhetorical, linguistic uniqueness, as well as an ideology of identity and single-voicedness. It is thus formally and ideologically suspect.

Bakhtin's anti-poetic stance, stated in this way, is undoubtedly too polemical and simplistic; his concept of poetry, too monolithic and "abstract," to use his own terms. His critique of poetry is more effective, however, when it is directed not at the practice of poetry in general but at what I would call the poetic ideology that has dominated the history of literature from its origins. This ruling literary ideology, which consists in the idealization of literary or poetic language, is not confined, as Bakhtin sometimes seems to argue, to poetry as a genre but cuts across genre lines—it also informs the conceptualization and writing of prose and certainly the theories and critical strategies used to interpret and delineate the form of works of all genres. This ideology is at work whenever any genre or discursive practice or theory posits closed borders around itself or its object of study, whenever it puts an end to the dialogic differences and *différends* constituting it and becomes, as Bakhtin argues, "authoritarian, dogmatic and conservative, sealing itself off from the influence of extraliterary social dialects" (p. 287). It is the ideal of a singular, poetic language unlike any other that is the ultimate object of Bakhtin's attack:

> Therefore such ideals as a special "poetic language," a "language of the gods," a "priestly language of poetry" and so forth could flourish on poetic soil. . . . The idea of a special unitary and singular language of poetry is a typical utopian philosopheme of poetic discourse. . . . The ideal of a "poetic language" is yet another expression of that same Ptolemaic conception of the linguistic and stylistic world. (pp. 287–288)

The attack against poetry is then an attack against the "poeticization" or "sacralization" of language wherever and whenever it occurs.

In the history of philosophy and literature, various languages and critical strategies have been sanctified by different theories of literature, and what all these theories and languages have in common is their determination by a poetic, textual, or sociohistorical ideology, that is, their privileging of one language, one form of discursive practice, one historical, political, or narrative strategy, over all others, their reduction or diversity and heterogeneity to sameness. Each refuses, as Bakhtin puts it, "to look beyond its own boundaries"; each puts up defenses so that these boundaries cannot be crossed except in the terms it lays down. "Poetry behaves as if it lived in the heartland of its own language territory, and does not approach too closely the borders of this language, where it would inevitably be brought into dialogic contact with heteroglossia; poetry chooses not to look beyond the boundaries of its own language. If, during an epoch of language crises, the language of poetry *does* change, poetry immediately canonizes the new language as one that is unitary and singular, as if no other language existed" (p. 299). The poetic in this sense and the monologic or metaphysical are one and the same thing for Bakhtin; each is a violent denial or suppression of its own conflictual history and of other-languagedness. Any dialectical synthesis of difference, opposition, contradiction, any positing of a Narrative of all narratives, would, then, also be considered by Bakhtin to constitute a "poetic," formalist position, no matter how forcefully and how often history or politics were evoked to defend it. The novel for Bakhtin is dialogic (and not "poetic") only insomuch as it is not dialectical (it is not antidialectical either), only insomuch as it keeps open and unresolved the conflicts or disputes of voices and languages constituting it, only as it resists the temptation to reduce the alterity of the other to the identity of the same.

Carnival, Justice, and the *Idea* of Community

> The partition (*partage*) of the *hermeneia* is infinite. It is the partition of dialogue in the widest sense of the word, which is not only literary but also ethical, social, political. The question of dialogue is . . . that of "understanding the discourse of the other." . . . The community remains to be thought according to the partition of the *logos*.
> —Jean-Luc Nancy, *Le Partage des voix*

History is made up of wisps of narratives, stories that one tells, that one hears, that one acts out; the people does not exist as a subject but as a mass of millions of insignificant and serious little stories that sometimes let themselves be collected together to constitute big stories and sometimes disperse into digressive elements. Generally though, these are the stories that come together at least approximately to form what is called the culture of civil society.

—Jean-François Lyotard, *Instructions païennes*

Given their insistence on narrative heterogeneity and their critiques of monologism and metanarrative, no approach to narrative could be considered critical by Bakhtin and Lyotard if it attempted to situate itself outside or above the conflict of languages and opinions (narratives) it hopes to account for. On the contrary, it must attempt to be as dialogic, as heterogeneous as the "objects" it treats. Lyotard, for example, has used different strategies in his recent work to deal with heterogeneity: he has moved from the narrativist strategies discussed above to strategies associated with a Wittgensteinien notion of language games, to, most recently in *Le Différend*, strategies associated with what he calls a philosophy of phrases. In spite of the differences of emphasis and procedure as he moves from one strategy to the next, the one constant in his different texts is his insistence on a fundamental socio-discursive heterogeneity that resists unification, dialectization: that is, theorization. This means that any theory dealing with the multiplicity of little narratives would itself have to be considered localized, strategic. It would have to confront its own limited status as just one narrative among many; any language game attempting to account for all the other language games would be limited by the fact that it was only one game among many and that its rules were not those of the other games; any genre of discourse would be restricted by the fact that it could not account for those phrases falling outside its territory. In the "postmodern condition," when no form of discourse or narrative—scientific, philosophical, political, historical, literary—can claim to legitimate all others, all legitimation must thus be considered relative, even that of science: "Science plays its own game; it is incapable of legitimating the other language games. . . . But above all, it is incapable of legitimating itself, as speculation assumed it could" (*The Postmodern Condition*, p. 40). Critical discourse, thus, cannot claim to do what science is incapable of doing; it is rather constantly faced with the problem of its own legitimation and that of the discourses it interacts with.

Perhaps the most serious consequence of this relativization of all discourse and the "crisis" of legitimation associated with it is the destruction of traditional notions of society and the social subject: "The social subject itself seems to dissolve in this dissemination of language games. The social bond is linguistic, but is not woven with a single thread" (p. 40). The same could be said of the effects of dialogization on the subject, for the Bakhtinian dialogized subject, penetrated from the start by alterity, by the voices and languages of others, is hardly a stable, unique, unified origin from which or in terms of which to construct a unified concept of society. Neither Bakhtin nor Lyotard, however, sees this dissemination or dissipation of the social subject in negative terms, for it is not something to be mourned, not a loss to be regretted and whose recovery is nostalgically desired. Each on the contrary will attempt to think this dissipation affirmatively as a positive principle in view of an alternative notion of the social space. Bakhtin is for the most part untouched by nostalgia for an original subject (I shall discuss further on where there is evidence of nostalgia in his work); and Lyotard is even more direct, claiming that such nostalgia and mourning are things of the past and can no longer be taken seriously: "Turn-of-the-century Vienna was weaned on this pessimism. . . . We can say today that the mourning process has been completed. There is no need to start all over again. . . . Most people have lost the nostalgia for the lost narrative. It in no way follows that they are reduced to barbarity. What saves them from it is their knowledge that legitimation can only spring from their own linguistic practice and communicational interaction" (p. 41). What has been lost then is the desire for an original subject and a justification for society coming from religion, philosophy, history, science, or some other form of metadiscourse; what has not been lost is the desire for community, for sociability—for if this were to be lost too, the postmodern would indeed be the condition of barbarism.

It could be argued that neither the dialogism of Bakhtin nor the pragmatics of Lyotard is governed by a definite *concept* of society, a knowledge of what society is or a foreknowledge of what it could and should be. Each attempts to indicate, however, an "Idea" of sociability that is not conceived in terms of a unique end;[9] each strives to keep the question of the social *as a question*. In the case of Bakhtin, perhaps the best way to present the sociopolitical "Idea" indicated by his critical strategy is to analyze the term most commentators have emphasized in their discussion of Bakhtin—at least until recently when the dialogic has replaced it in importance—the term in his work that seems to have the most radical political-historical implications: *the carnivalesque*. The figures and rhetorical-political strategies associated with the carnival—the fool and the clown, laughter and parody—could be argued to be the very foundation and the most subversive elements of his critique of tradition, bureaucracy, religion, philosophy, and ideology. In a certain sense, laughter could be considered the most crucial element of the carnivalesque, for it is more fundamental and subversive than dialogue, or perhaps more accurately, it is the most radical form of dialogue. It is laughter that resists and even undermines the power of all political-religious-philosophical systems and institutions and thus makes dialogue possible, even within monolithic, authoritarian, totalitarian structures whose function it is to exclude or repress it. Laughter indicates that dialogic interaction is still possible even in the most repressive of situations; it is an indication of sociability, of community, of a nondetermined relation to others, even at those moments when community is most threatened.

The advantages of laughter are many: of all literary-philosophical strategies, Bakhtin claims that laughter alone serves no master theory of philosophy, no institution or ideology. Throughout history, laughter has remained marginal, popular, and unofficial: "Of all aspects of the ancient complex, only laughter never underwent sublimation of any sort—neither religious, mystical nor philosophical. It never took on an official character, and even in literature the comic genres were the most free, the least regimented. After the decline of the ancient world, Europe did not know a single cult, a single ritual, a single state or civil ceremony, a single official genre or style serving either the church or the state . . . where laughter was sanctioned (in tone, style or language)—even in its most watered-down forms of humor or irony" (p. 236). Laughter is critical and disruptive, undialectical and dispersive. It cannot be raised to a higher level in any system of any sort. It is antisystematic and thereby subversively critical of the hierarchical levels and separations all systems institute. It emphasizes contradiction and multi-sidedness rather than synthesis and unity: "Parodic-travestying literature introduces the permanent corrective of laughter, of a critique of the one-sided seriousness of the lofty direct word, the corrective of reality that is always richer, more fundamental and most importantly *too contradictory and heteroglot* to be fit into a high and straightforward genre" (p. 55). Laughter is thus the affirmation of unresolved and unresolvable contradictions; it is the opening to difference, heterogeneity, and alterity.[10]

Laughter is the most evident characteristic of the carnival, which is for Bakhtin, as is well-known, the privileged social-historical chronotope (space/time) insomuch as it is a reversal or rearrangement of the structure of society and the kinds of relations determined by it. The carnival reveals that all relations are arbitrary, that alternative structures permitting other kinds of relations are always possible. Historically, the carnival is the special time of year when religious dogmatism and the social hierarchy are suspended, when the language and actions of the people are free from all constraints and become forms of aesthetic and social "free-play." Situated between art and life, in both at the same time and separating each from the other, the carnival is the privileged chronotope of passage between the two, the space and time of their dialogue. As Bakhtin argues in his "Introduction" to *Rabelais and his World*:

> The basis of laughter which gives form to carnival rituals
> frees them completely from all religious and ecclesiastic
> dogmatism, from all mysticism and piety. . . . But the basic
> carnival nucleus of this culture is by no means a purely
> artistic form nor a spectacle and does not, generally speak-
> ing, belong to the sphere of art. It belongs to the borderline
> between art and life. In reality, it is life itself, but shaped
> according to a certain pattern of play.[11]

The carnival offers a critical perspective on society, a momentary, "aesthetic" break with the structures, laws, and dog-
matically imposed "truths" which determine the place of "the
people" under normal conditions.

The carnival does more than offer an interlude from the
restrictions of daily life and the social hierarchy, for it represents or "refracts" in its masked figures and by means of the
flexible relations existing among them a less restrictive sense of
the social, an alternate idea of community. The "free-play"
made possible by the suspension of social, political, and philosophical constraints functions in Bakhtin's work as a universal
aesthetic and social ideal, a sign of a truly human, free society:
"Carnival is not a spectacle seen by the people; they live in it,
and everyone participates because its very idea embraces all the
people. While carnival lasts, there is no other life outside it.
During carnival time, life is subject only to its laws, that is, the
laws of its own freedom. It has a universal spirit; it is a special
condition of the entire world, of the world's revival and renewal, in which all take part. Such is the essence of carnival,
vividly felt by all its participants" (*Rabelais*, p. 7). The Idea of
society suggested here is very seductive: total participation by
all members of society in all aspects of social existence, continual renewal of the world and of self with the only laws being
those of freedom itself, where revival, renewal, change prevail.
The carnival indicates an Idea, then, of what the "truly human"
is; it is the space/time where humanity momentarily but completely realizes its human potential by being freed from all
restrictions and laws except those of freedom itself. "As op-

posed to the official feast, one might say that carnival celebrated temporary liberation from the prevailing truth and from the established order; it marked the suspension of all hierarchical rank, privileges, norms and prohibitions. . . . People were, so to speak, reborn for new, purely human relations. These truly human relations were not only a fruit of imagination in abstract thought; they were experienced. The utopian ideal and the realistic merged in this carnival experience, unique of its kind" (*Rabelais*, p. 10). The carnival is the fluctuating form of freedom itself, the acting out or performance of nonrestraint, flexibility, multiplicity, otherness. The carnival could thus in this sense be considered to be a form of the Kantian aesthetic, made social, lived or "played" as a counter-reality.

The carnivalesque could, however, be challenged not only for being a naive, utopic, aesthetic ideal, an idealistic model for social relations that is unrealizable outside of momentary, exceptional, *predetermined* conditions—that is, when the authorities allow it—but also for acquiescing to the power of the authorities and accepting the sociopolitical status quo and the few moments of freedom it parcels out. Any society, the argument might go, no matter how repressive, could, at least in principle, always afford, with no threat to itself, to allow the momentary freedom and social reversals of the carnival (and of the carnivalesque in literature) precisely because they *are momentary,* "normalcy" having been established before the carnival and the return to it therefore guaranteed after it. This kind of critique is a serious one, but it could be answered by arguing that Bakhtin does not really present the carnival as an end in itself; it is not, as a momentary interlude, a sufficient alternative to the repressive, hierarchical, bureaucratized social structure. It is not so much a social reality as an indication of the possibility of alternative forms of social relations that are unrealizable except in play, as fictions. Rather than indicate that momentary reversals and precisely defined and limited interludes of freedom are sufficient and all that can be hoped for, the carnival is an affirmation that "normalcy," order, orthodoxy, hierarchy, and determined, monolithic social relations are themselves to be considered momentary, and arbitrary, even if they are serious reductions of social and political possibilities, powerful defenses against alterity and change. The carnival is the repeated affirmation of the possibility of alternative relations in the midst of order and control; it is the model for a society that is not slavishly determined by any one structure or conceived in terms of any one model or theory.[12]

A more serious challenge to Bakhtin's notion of the carnival might be raised by focusing on the contradictions within his presentation and defense of this privileged chronotope. Perhaps the chief contradiction has to do with the way he claims language is used during carnival. The "special type of communication impossible in everyday life," but possible during carnival, demands a language that has been liberated from the constraints of language itself: "This led to the creation of special forms of marketplace speech and gestures, frank and free, *permitting no distance between those who came in contact with each other* and liberating from norms of etiquette and decency imposed at other times" (*Rabelais*, p. 10, my emphasis). All reversals of social hierarchies, all ambivalence in speech and action, all masks and costumes, all laughter, parody, and irony—all those things that are seen by Bakhtin in a positive critical light as subversive complications of language and action, products of mediacy, indirectness, and distance and thus affirmations of the alterity of the other—seem to be rooted in the ideal pre- or post-linguistic immediacy of aesthetic free play, in the immediacy of oneness. A certain form of art, then, a form that is "experienced" at its fullest in the carnival, is the most profound, original, and universal form of language and of life itself.

Bakhtin, as if to prove that the immediacy the carnival makes possible was once an integral part of the social fabric and thus could be again, as if he felt he needed the testimony of history to defend such an idea, posits a time before the "lies and hypocrisy" of both feudal and modern society have taken over. It is the time/space *of the folk*, the source for Rabelais' chronotope and for the novel in general, a "pre-class, agricultural stage in the development of human society." "This time is collective, that is, it is differentiated and measured only by the events of *collective* life; everything that exists in this time exists solely for the collective. . . . This is the time of *productive growth*. It is a time of growth, blossoming, fruit-bearing, ripening, fruitful increase, issue. . . . Perishing and death are perceived as a *sowing*, after which follows increase and harvest, multiplying that which had been sown. . . . This time is *profoundly spatial and concrete*. It is not separated from the earth or from nature. . . . Human life and nature are perceived in the same categories. . . . Such a time is unified in an unmediated way" (*The Dialogic Imagination*, pp. 206–208). This idealized version of natural existence is totally positive; all negativity, even death, is immediately overcome and made productive. Nothing is lost, nothing perishes, all alterity seems to have been eliminated. The unity of collective existence is present everywhere, and all differences are derived from its "original" identity. The radical implications of the dialogic are thus subsumed in a myth of the natural integrity of the original community and an original subject, the people. It is the closest Bakhtin comes to piety and being victim to the desire for a lost origin and social-aesthetic plenitude.

The people realize their natural essence fully during the carnival (and in the public marketplace); here is where they manifest their true identity and where they act *in their own name* and organize themselves *in their own terms* and not in terms dictated by the political and religious institutions ruling them everywhere else. "The carnivalesque crowd in the marketplace or in the streets is not merely a crowd. It is the people as a whole, but organized *in their own way*, the way of the people. It is outside of and contrary to all existing forms of the coercive socioeconomic and political organization, which is suspended for the time of the festivity" (*Rabelais*, p. 255). The problem with this presentation of "the people" is how to define what is proper to the people, what constitutes "their own way," without predetermining their identity and the form of society appropriate to that identity, and in the process establishing the norms for equally coercive and restrictive socioeconomic and political organizations, now conceived in the name of "the people." To follow the most radical implications of Bakhtin's critical strategy and his presentation of the carnival, one would have to say in fact that the people have no one way; their way is a multiplicity of ways that sometimes conflict, sometimes work in harmony. The people then are not one but originally heterogeneous, for as soon as the people are constituted as a subject, the carnival is over.

The people are aided in "becoming themselves," that is, remaining heterogeneous, by the rogue, the clown, and the fool, the privileged figures of the carnival who also have a special role to play in the history of the novel. Their special status comes from their particular historical place and function: they go back through all of history to the very origins of time, "into the depths of folklore that pre-exists class structures" (*The Dialogic Imagination*, p. 159). Their function is to disrupt, undercut, and complicate the status quo, to lay bare the contradictions and falsities of the ruling philosophical, religious, and formal conventions. They symbolize the struggle against convention and truth which is the motor force of history for Bakhtin. Their existence is purely metaphorical, however, because this struggle can only be performed indirectly, marginally, when social time and institutions are momentarily suspended. These figures are indirection itself: "the very being of these figures does not have a direct, but rather a metaphorical significance. Their very appearance, everything they do and say, cannot be understood in a direct and unmediated way but must be grasped metaphorically. Sometimes their significance can be reversed—but one cannot take them literally, because they are not what they seem. . . . Their existence is a reflection of some other's mode of being—and even then, not a direct reflection. They are life's maskers; their being coincides with the role, and outside this role they simply do not exist" (*The Dialogic Imagination*, p. 159). These metaphorical figures, these "pure tropes" whose being is to be impure, other from themselves, seem to indicate that properness, identity, and naturalness are all effects of indirectness and non-identity; for the only way back to the immediacy, naturalness, and identity of the people is paradoxically through these figures that are indirect, mediated, and other from themselves and from all identifiable others. The question is whether it is possible to return from such radical alterity to sameness, whether the people, presented in this way, ever constitute a subject.

If it is true in general, as Bakhtin argues it is for feudalism, that "internal man—pure 'natural subjectivity'—could be laid bare only with the help of the clown and the fool, since adequate, direct . . . means for expressing his life was not available" (*The Dialogic Imagination*, p. 164), then one can only wonder with and against him how "internal" and "natural" this man and this subjectivity really are. If the only way to achieve naturalness and to present directly "internal subjectivity" is through the unnatural, indirect ways of fools, clowns, and novelists, the unmediated, natural ends themselves end up inevitably being contaminated in the process, the purity and naturalness of man and his subjectivity, complicated and differentiated, that is, masked, as they are externalized and presented in the public light. The contradictory complexity of Bakhtin's dialogism is perhaps most evident at such moments: when parodic, double-voiced language is used to complicate all single-voiced utterances in order to lead back to the immediacy of a language which would be the true voice of natural man, but which at the same time can only be ventriloquated through "unnatural," masked figures and never enunciated and heard in itself. When the masks of the buffoon are used to unmask the hypocrisy of those who claim to be without masks (other kinds of buffoons) and to point to the presence of "the people" who have no need of masks but who appear as themselves only as masked and other from themselves. When laughter and parody are used to undermine the ideological seriousness of the authoritarian and hegemonic discourses of the Church, the State, and all political and intellectual bureaucracies and institutions in order to return to the immediacy and proximity of the object in itself, which, however, is presented and appears in itself only in the Babelic conflict of languages and representations surrounding and refracting it. There is really no way out, no before and no after, no way to put an end to the critical process constituted by the carnivalesque, no way to finalize the dialogic. The myth of the people, of an original human subject, dissipates as it is presented; it is presentable only in its dissipation.

In my mind, then, Bakhtin's approach to narrative and to the sociopolitical does not in the last instance constitute a metatheory; it posits no fully constituted, original subject-narrator or subject-hero that can stand on its own and speak in its own voice. Rather it remains opposed to all forms of metanarrative, even, or rather, especially those that would make "the people," defined as a collective identity, an unmasked, unified presence, the universal subject and privileged narrator and actor in and of history. The fundamental heterogeneity Bakhtin's critical strategy testifies to undermines even the ends it projects for itself, and in this way heterogeneity is affirmed and retained in terms of those ends. Bakhtin's "people" are the people of the carnival and the marketplace, not a subject to be realized in the course of history but the dissemination of self in the multiple possibilities of the masks, voices, dialects, and jargons of the social space freed from the control of authority and class structure. This "freedom" never makes possible just one thing but always a multiplicity of contradictory things; it is the sign that something else is always possible.

The carnivalesque, which could be considered the ultimate form of the dialogic, the space-time where the dialogic heterogeneity of the social fabric is given its maximum play, does not then in the strictest sense constitute a socio-historical reality or even a very precise model for society from which it would be possible to derive the means for reforming society, for making it more carnivalesque. The carnivalesque is rather an unreal, fictive, theatrical element within history and society (within discourse) that serves to give critical perspectives on social reality, on "things as they are." It dramatizes the initial conditions necessary for any critical questioning of society by *performing* the heterogeneity that no theory of society or literature, no aesthetics or political or social "science," can ignore or repress without taking on the dogmatic, authoritarian characteristics the carnivalesque parodies and turns upside down.

The carnivalesque seems to demand something other than another theory of society or a new form of political science or history; it demands rather an approach to the social that does not determine in advance the essence of the social or its ultimate destination. Perhaps the best way to raise the question of the social in Bakhtinian terms would not be as a theorist, scientist, or historian, but as a "clown," a "joker," a novelist perhaps, as someone open to the voices and discourses of others and responding to and speaking (with) them. In this sense, the critical thinker is as much a fabricator of fictions as a philosopher or theorist, a fabricator or applier of systems. To *know* the social space from the outset, from outside or above, to be able to define it, delineate it, and thus theoretically to master it is in Bakhtinian terms a contradiction; for the "essence" of the social for Bakhtin is precisely what is more dynamic, unpredictable, playful, and cunning than any system of knowledge, that is, than any authority. The question of the social in its critical form could be said, then, to be just beyond or to the side of what all authorities and authoritarian discourse tells us, the complexity of the social fabric indicated (indirectly) and performed more forcefully in the fictions and theatricality of the carnival than in the sterile and repressive politics of instituted parties and social institutions, than in the dogmatism of philosophical-political systems. After reading Bakhtin, one is led to ask the question that Lyotard asks near the beginning of *Au juste*: "What is the real difference between a theory and a fiction? After all, doesn't one have the right to present theoretical utterances under the form of fictions, in the form of fictions? Not *under* the form, but *in* the form" (p. 15). Without *a* (*meta*)*theory* in place to distinguish between theory and fiction, the question of the difference between them has no simple answer, and one obviously *has the right* to present theory in the

form of fiction. It may be one of the strategies needed to safeguard socio-discursive heterogeneity and the freedom of social
relations.

Heterogeneity in itself (as if it could ever really be in
itself), however, is obviously not enough, not an adequate answer to the question of the social, even if it is an indispensable
starting point, Lyotard and Bakhtin would agree, from which to
raise the question, a check on all tendencies to universalize and
systematize. There is still the question of justice to be considered, the question central to all of Lyotard's recent work. In
Instructions païennes, the question of justice is phrased at one
moment in terms of an obligation having to do with narration:
"One is not right to be coherent and unchanging, that is, equal
to oneself, but one is right to want to be equal to the potency of
narrating what one thinks one hears today in what others do
and say" (p. 29). Narrative in Lyotard's sense brings obligations
of a special sort with it, but this is not true of one type of
narrative, the one that privileges the narrator at the expense of
the other poles of narration and treats the act of narration as an
autonomous activity (p. 56). It is true, however, of what Lyotard
calls a "pagan" approach to narrative—the previous type is
exemplified in capitalist narrative—whose "gods" are an indication that no narrator is ever first or autonomous, that no
narrative is ever only "his": "We are always under the force of
some narrative or other; something has always already been
told to us and we have always already been told. We are weak,
and there are gods because we are not first" (p. 47). It is in this
fact of not being first, of having a fundamental responsibility to
what is not oneself, that the Lyotardian notion of justice is
rooted, that his "ethics" and politics, ungoverned by any law or
ethical system, begin to take form.

The example used by Lyotard in both *Au juste* and *The
Postmodern Condition* to illustrate this notion of narrative-
ethical obligation is that of the narratives of the Cashinahua
Indians of the upper Amazon, as they are related by Marcel
D'Ans in his *Dit des vrais hommes*.[13] The example is surpris-
ing, for in many ways the sacred and profane narratives of this

collection are what Bakhtin would call epic literature, that is, a literature rooted in tradition that is nationalistic (tribal), religious, and authoritarian, a literature that is univocal and imposes its discourse on its listeners, that demands narrators who respect its authority and never try to counter it—in other words, it is a literature made up of the "words of the fathers." One has to wonder why Lyotard doesn't find these narratives "pious," how he is able to use them, at least initially, as positive examples of a critical narrative pragmatics and, more importantly, of ethical obligation. It will be important to understand exactly what in these narratives is extracted from the dogmatism and piety characteristic of them as a whole, what in them Lyotard is able to make serve a critical function.

The most important aspect of the pragmatics of these narratives for Lyotard is that the originality and autonomy of each narrator is explicitly undermined: "Every narrator presents himself as having been a listener: not as autonomous, but on the contrary as heteronomous. The law of his narrative, if I can speak of law in this case, is a law that he received. . . . When he gives his own name, he designates himself as someone who was narrated by the social body" (*Au juste*, p. 64). Lyotard makes much of this situation because he feels that a critical ethics or politics must *begin* here, with the destruction of all notions of autonomy and with the admission (acceptance) that relations to alterity are primary. He claims that this lack of autonomy is precisely what has been repressed in Western philosophy and narrative: "This is a trait that is absolutely essential to paganism and that has been destroyed the most in Western thought" (*Au juste*, p. 65). The situation of the narrator in the Cashinahua narratives (and in what Lyotard calls "paganism"), then, is never primary or dominant; he is always obliged in some way to what is other, not just temporally and socially other, but ontologically other as well.

The lack of autonomy of the Cashinahua narrator is not an indication that he must accept the "words of the fathers," the long narrative tradition that precedes him, as they are, without response, that he must repeat by rote what was said to him and what has always been said. Each narrator responds differently to what has been narrated to him and "invents" or transforms as much as repeats:

> The pertinent trait is not fidelity; it is not because one has conserved the narrative that one is a good narrator, at least as concerns profane narratives. It is on the contrary because one has "added something," because one invents, because one introduces different episodes that form a motif with the narrative chain which remains stable. . . . The narratives repeat themselves but are never identical. This whole problem is avoided by someone like Lévi-Strauss and in general by a structuralist approach; it is the problem of variants. (*Au juste*, pp. 66–67)

Even though obliged, or rather in Lyotard's terms, because obliged to narrate, the narrator is not assigned a response but obliged only *to respond*; narration is not prohibited to him but demanded from him. Tradition may not be countered or undermined in these narratives, but it is in a sense "invented" each time anew.

The nature of the obligation imposed on each narrator is thus crucial, and Lyotard works very hard to free the Cashinahua narratives from the piety and traditionalism usually associated with such narratives. By emphasizing the priority of the position of the listener (addressee) rather than the narrator in terms of the question of obligation, he is following Emmanuel Lévinas in his attempt to free ethics from the ethical, religious, metaphysical systems that have traditionally determined it. As slight as it might be, it is the link between the Cashinahua narratives and a certain radical Jewish ethical tradition exemplified by Lévinas that Lyotard wants to stress:

> In other words, someone speaks to me and obliges me. And that is exactly what Lévinas was thinking of. Obliges me to do what? Here to retell, but not necessarily to my narrator. He doesn't oblige me to give it back to him, that's not what it is all about, but I am obliged like a transmitter that cannot retain its charge, that will have to transmit it. . . . That's the

question of prescription in the sense where there is a kind of imperative that necessitates that at the moment one speaks to me and that I have been spoken . . . I have to speak. And in this sense, the will is never free and freedom never first. . . . That afterwards there is will, I agree, but this will takes form only on the foundation of an obligation that is first, that is much more ancient and archaic than will, and that is not a matter for legislation, that has not been decreed, that is literally anonymous. (*Au juste*, pp. 69–70)

Lyotard thus attempts to locate obligation outside of dogma, outside of any philosophical, moral, or political system, in order not to define it in advance and yet at the same time to make obligation primary, even prior to freedom and will. The free, desiring subject is first of all an obliged subject (not an autonomous subject) and is obliged to act, respond, here retell, but not under the specific authority of any power. If the "speculative game of the West is a game . . . without listeners," then "the game of the just" is one in which "one speaks as a listener . . . and not at all as an author. It is a game without an author" (*Au juste*, p. 137). To speak as a listener is to be open to the other, to be responding to an obligation in terms of others that has not been and cannot be decreed.

In *Le Différend* and in interviews given after its publication, Lyotard complicates his references to the Cashinahua narratives and begins to make more explicit and question critically his own and modernity's relation to traditional narratives of the Cashinahua type and to the mythic universe they exemplify. In insisting on the critical aspects for modernity of the priority given in these narratives to the listener or receiver of narrative (and narrative prescription), Lyotard obviously underplayed the consequences of the circularity of their pragmatics and the very confined or reduced relation to alterity therefore permitted by them. For if the authority to narrate comes from having listened and already been narrated oneself (named), the name of the narrator is authorized by the stories relating to the genesis of names. The narrator may have no priority, then, but the narrative and social universe is closed, rooted in a mythical past the present is derived from, one that authorizes the Cashinahua to call themselves "les vrais hommes." There is in this sense a predetermined, original Cashinahua "we," and this is why, says Lyotard, traditional peoples make war on the borders of their territory to protect this "we" and its tradition.[14]

If Lyotard was perhaps a bit too easily taken in by the critical dimensions of the pragmatics of such narratives and too anxious to connect the Cashinahua narratives to a Lévinasian ethics to analyze their limitations when he first presented them, in his more recent work he analyzes the consequences when a traditional, mythic narrative pragmatics are taken on as a model for modernity to follow. His example is Nazi Germany, which he considers to have practiced what could be called a "politics of myth," claiming its legitimacy and superiority from a mythic national tradition and distant origin. As Lyotard puts it in a recent interview: "We respect the Amazon peoples to the extent they are not modern, but when modern men make themselves into Amazons, it is monstrous."[15] The problem is that of the origin in terms of which the Cashinahua or any mythic narrative legitimates itself, and in order to distinguish the modern and postmodern from the traditional, Lyotard insists that obligation cannot be thought in terms of any origin whatsoever. In this sense, the determination of obligation in terms of an origin, any origin, is the source of the monstrosity of the modern imitating the traditional; and a certain relation to an end or ends is characteristic of the justice Lyotard proposes to combat the monstrous.[16] It is of course Kant who will supplement the Cashinahua in Lyotard's work (as well as the central role given to narrative) and who will make it impossible to confuse origin and end, traditional and modern, servitude and "just" obligation.

This is not the place to pursue an analysis of the important role served by Kant (the Kant of the Third and "Fourth" Critiques) in Lyotard's recent work because it would take me too far away from the problem of narrative that interests me here, but suffice it to say that even in those works where there is an emphasis on narrative, the references to Kant serve two major functions. The first is to indicate that because there is a fundamental incommensurability among the various faculties no genre, no language game, no family of phrases, no narrative can account for all others.[17] And second, because of this incommensurability, there can be no determination of obligation or ethical conduct (of the sociopolitical), no universal ethical rule or historico-political law. As in the Cashinahua analyses, obligation is still primary, but now it is because it is oriented toward an unknown future, an indeterminable end, rather than a mythic past. The moral faculty for Kant is incommensurable with the cognitive faculty, and "this use finally *leaves* the conduct to be followed . . . undetermined. Super-sensible nature *does not* determine what I have to do. It regulates me without telling me *what* is to be done" (*Au juste*, p. 163). To be just in Kantian-Lyotardian terms is a question of responding to obligation while keeping the finality of justice, the regulating "Idea" of justice and therefore of a truly human society, undetermined, that is, always to be formed, never presentable as such as an object of knowledge.

But just as he parts company with the Cashinahua and moves beyond a strictly narrativist emphasis with Kant, Lyotard parts company with Kant over the question of ends, for what separates him from Kant is his skepticism concerning the Kantian notion of totality: "It is not a question for us of thinking what is just and what is unjust on the horizon of a social totality, but, on the contrary, on the horizon of a multiplicity or diversity. . . . I believe that . . . in order to distinguish [between just and unjust 'opinions'] it is necessary to have an Idea, but different from what Kant thought, this Idea is not for us today an Idea of totality" (*Au juste*, p. 167). As Lyotard is Cashinahuan out of respect for their difference from "moderns" and in terms of the obligation to narrate as a listener, but horrified by the totalitarian nature of any modern recuperation of the notion of a society based on a concept (myth) of "true men," he is Kantian in terms of an undetermined notion of obligation but postmodern as concerns totality. His Idea of sociability inserts heterogeneity even into the Idea of the human itself: there are not and cannot be "true men" but only a diversity of men and women pursuing various ends in the name of the truly human, in the pursuit of community in diversity.[18]

The Idea of community, then, is not a *concept* and not determined by any empirical or mythic model; strictly speaking, it is unpresentable as such.[19] Here is where it seems to me Lyotard's work and Bakhtin's both lead: not to *a place* but to critical strategies that indicate indirectly an Idea (or "fiction") of heterogeneous humanity as the foundation of the social, an Idea that must be pursued in the name of justice, in the name of an obligation to others and alterity in general. For each, the prescription "Be just" could be said to mean something like the following: Resist and undermine authoritarian metanarratives and let the dialogic interaction of languages, discourses, little narratives, and phrases produce their multiple effects in the pursuit of a human community still to be formed and *imaginable*, not knowable, in terms of a multiplicity of ends.[20]

It would be misleading, then, to imply that the work of either Bakhtin or Lyotard is limited to narrativist strategies and a dominant concern with narrative pragmatics, that their questioning and recasting of the political begins and ends with narrative. For Bakhtin, more fundamental than narrative is the interaction of voices, languages, and dialects given free play in the carnival and the carnivalized novel, but not only there. Narrative is thus rooted in a socio-discursive dialogism that is not necessarily narrative in form. For Lyotard, an emphasis on narrative was clearly a stage in a developing critical strategy, and his interest in narrative was from the start an interest in the fluidity of its pragmatics and nonexclusive, "popular" characteristics: the way it is open to other genres, language games, and families of phrases and includes them within itself without reducing their specificity or diminishing their incommensurability.

After reading both Bakhtin and Lyotard, it could be concluded that narratology, whatever its form, could be considered critical only to the extent that it indicates its own limits and those of the narrative genre itself, that it provides an entry into or indicates openings onto the non-narrative. A definition of sorts of critical discourse in general might even be derived from the narrativist strategies of Bakhtin and Lyotard: a discourse would be considered *critical* only if it inscribes within itself the obligation to go beyond it, only if it opens onto what it is not. A politics in the same vein would be considered critical (and just) only if the end it pursues is not *an end* but a multiplicity of ends, only if the "(re)turn to the political" it delineates can never be completed but most be perpetually begun anew.

Notes

This essay was first presented in a different form in the winter of 1983 as a part of the Irvine Focused Research Program in Contemporary Critical Theory. In that version, the sections on Lyotard were greatly reduced and served only to introduce a more extensive analysis of Bakhtin. Under the title "The Alterity of Discourse: Form, History, and the Question of the Political in M. M. Bakhtin," the original essay appeared in *Diacritics* (Summer 1983), vol. 13, no. 2. The present text extends the "dialogue" between Lyotard and Bakhtin suggested in the earlier version and develops at much greater length the analysis of Lyotard's position on narrative. The analysis of Bakhtin included here is a modified version of one section of the previously published essay.

1. In *Instructions païennes* (Paris: Galilée, 1977), Lyotard gave the following reasons for the decline in the impact of metanarratives: "the reduction of official Marxist metanarratives, especially after the break of Peking with Moscow, the political decline of the primary world power after its failure in Vietnam, the economic recovery of certain Third World countries due to the crisis in energy and primary materials, the discovery that progress has made a sterile dump of the world, the ostensibly artificial character of scientific procedures" (p. 25).

2. Jameson, "Foreword," to Jean-François Lyotard, *The Postmodern Condition*, Geoff Bennington and Brian Massumi, trs. (Minneapolis: University of Minnesota Press, 1984), p. xi.

3. See Lyotard's forceful analysis of his dispute with Marxism in his "Pierre Souyri: le marxisme qui n'a pas fini"—*Esprit* (Summer 1983), vol. 13, no. 2—which is much more than the "interesting memoir" Jameson qualifies it as being. See also his essay on Jameson, "The Unconscious, History, and Phrases: On *The Political Unconscious*," in *New Orleans Review* (Spring 1984), vol. 11. no. 1.

4. Lyotard, *Au juste* (Paris: Christian Bourgois, 1979), p. 113.

5. Lyotard, *Instructions païennes*, p. 11. The following quotations from Lyotard are from this volume.

6. M. M. Bakhtin, *The Dialogic Imagination*, Caryl Emerson and Michael Holquist, trs. (Austin: University of Texas Press, 1981), pp. 262–263.

7. Lyotard, *Le Différend* (Paris: Minuit, 1983), p. 228.

8. Bakhtin, The Dialogic Imagination, p. 411. The following quotations from Bakhtin are from this volume.

9. I am following Lyotard here and using "Idea" in the Kantian sense. As Lyotard argues, "This [Kant's] notion of an Idea should never be confused with the notion of a concept" (Au juste, p. 144). "For Kant, an Idea seems to have nothing to do with verisimilitude (le vraisemblable). It can even be completely invraisemblable. It does not rest on a given constituted either by accepted narratives or the names of those who are recognized by the public as being at the same time great and wise. On the contrary, it rests rather on something like a future devoted to searching" (pp. 145–156).

10. Lyotard says this about the relation between laughter and "the people": "The people are not the sovereign; they are the defenders of the différend against the sovereign. They laugh. Politics is tragedy for authority, comedy for the people" (Le Différend, p. 209).

11. Bakhtin, Rabelais and His World, Helene Iswolsky, tr. (Cambridge: MIT Press, 1968), p. 7.

12. Natalie Davis in her study of festive life, "The Reason of Misrule," supports this view: "I hope to show that rather than being a mere 'safety valve,' deflecting attention from social reality, festive life can on the one hand perpetuate certain values of the community (even guarantee its survival) and on the other hand criticize political order"—in Society and Culture in Early Modern France (Stanford: Stanford University Press, 1975), p. 97. See also Dominick LaCapra, "Bakhtin, Marxism, and the Carnivalesque," in his Rethinking Intellectual History: Texts, Contexts, Language (Ithaca, N.Y.: Cornell University Press, 1983).

13. D'Ans, Dit des vrais hommes (Paris: Editions 1018, 1978).

14. In a recent text, Lyotard develops his critique of the "totalitarian" aspects of the Cashinahua narratives: "The Cashinahua call themselves 'true men.' Whatever is exterior to this tradition, whether a natural or human element, if there is no name for it, it does not exist because it is not authorized (not 'true'). Authority is not represented in the modern sense; the Cashinahua people legislate through the transmission of their narratives, and in executing them (because names create obligations of all sorts), they exercise the executive power themselves. A politics is thus certainly in play in this narrative practice, but it is rooted in the totality of life instituted by the narratives, and in this sense it can be called 'totalitarian'"—in "Memorandum sur la légitimité," Le Postmoderne expliqué aux enfants (Paris: Galilée, 1986), p. 76.

15. Etienne Tassin, "La Déflexion des grands récits: Entretien avec Jean-François Lyotard," Intervention (novembre-décembre 1983, janvier 1984), no. 7, p. 52.

16. The difference between the origin and end is the difference between the identity of the Cashinahua "we" and the uncertainty of the republican "we": "In the republic there dominates by principle an incertitude concerning its ends, which is an incertitude concerning the identity of the we. . . . The Cashinahua narrative always answers that we must be what we are, Cashinahua. (And the Aryan narrative answers in the same way.) There are several narratives in the republic because there are several final identities possible, and only one possible in despotism because there is only one origin. . . . Different from myths, they [the narratives of the republic] do not find their legitimation in original, 'founding' acts but in a future still to be made, that is, in an Idea to be realized"—in "Memorandum sur la légitimité," pp. 81–82.

17. In another recent text, "Missive sur l'histoire universelle" (also published in Le Postmoderne expliqué aux enfants), Lyotard criticizes his privileging of the critical

function of narrative: "It is not right to give the narrative genre an absolute privilege over other genres of discourse in the analysis of human or in particular 'language' (ideological) phenomena, and even less in a philosophical approach. Certain of my previous reflections perhaps succumbed to this 'transcendental spectre'" (p. 45).

18. Lyotard characterizes his Idea of "the people" as "the name of heterogeneous phrases that contradict each other and are held together by their contrariety itself"—in Etienne Tassin, "La Déflexion des grand récits: Entretien avec Jean-François Lyotard," p. 57.

19. For example, since the notion of a citizen is a political ideal of the republic, no one has the right to proclaim himself or herself a citizen, and yet everyone is obliged to be one: "The republican subject is not empirical man but emancipated freedom; the citizen is a rational being. He/she is not describable as an actual reality; no one can give an example of a citizen, no one can call him/herself a citizen. It is a kind of ideal of political reason" (Tassin, p. 57).

20. As Lyotard says, "What must we be? What is our common end? It is not an empty 'You must' but a 'We must' that questions the nature of the we" (Tassin, p. 57).

3

FOUCAULT, POST-STRUCTURALISM, AND THE MODE OF INFORMATION

Mark Poster

IN the United States post-structuralism is commonly understood in the context of literary criticism, but in this paper I will treat it as a response to the crisis of Marxism. Post-structuralism is illuminated in a new way when it is seen in relation to the inability of classical Marxism to serve as a critical theory of advanced industrial society. The positions of post-structuralism are significant to the extent that they present a critique of Marxism and therefore indicate the paths that may be taken to get beyond its current theoretical impasses. My aim therefore is to take post-structuralism as far as it can go in the critique of Marxism and then to outline its own limitations as a critical theory. In this effort I will take Foucault's work as the main reference point since, of all the post-structuralists, he has been most concerned with the problems of historical materialism.

Marxism centers critical theory and it totalizes from that center. In the essay "The Jewish Question," Marx presents a critique of the liberal solution to the project of human emancipation. He argues that the liberal version of emancipation is flawed because it is limited to political emancipation. What is needed, he thinks, is a form of emancipation that encompasses civil society as well as politics, the private sphere as well as the public sphere. Only in that way can domination be thoroughly eliminated. He finds the key to human emancipation in the organization of labor and in the potential critical praxis of the working class. In short, the foundation of Marxism is a revised project for "total human emancipation" which is centered on the working class. It is a tribute to Marx's consistency that he never surrendered this project or compromised its integrity. From the 1844 Manuscripts through The German Ideology and Capital, the basic principle of social critique remained the same: only the working class can abolish capitalism and therefore abolish the distinction between the private and the public along with all the forms of domination that divide society into classes and prevent the formation of community. The totalization of critique at the locus of the working class remains the keystone of Marx's thinking through all the shifts of position or "breaks" that one may wish to locate in it.

Foucault and the post-structuralists take exception to the formal aspects of Marx's critique, to its centering and totalizing tendencies. For them critical theory cannot find its center in the working class and it should not busy itself with searching for a center in any case. The history of socialist and capitalist societies in the twentieth century provides all the evidence one could want to dispute the claim that the working class is the unique vanguard of "total emancipation." More important to the critique of Marx is the post-structuralist's admonition that centers of discourse serve to repress unwanted questions and to disqualify valid objections.

Foucault took two positions on this question. During the heyday of the "new philosophers" in the mid-1970s he gave more credence than was warranted to the anti-Gulag craze, flirting with a position that was barely distinguishable from anti-communism. At that point Foucault rejected Marx as a totalitarian thinker. But in other moments he acknowledged the critical force of Marxism if it could be understood as the special, not the general, theory of the working class and its wrongs.[1] The main thrust of Foucault's writings was to admit that capitalism exploited and alienated the proletariat but at the same time to insist that other social groups also suffered domination, that these forms of domination could not be understood from the perspective of the categories developed to reveal the domination of the working class, and finally that in the context of advanced capitalism, it was likely that forms of domination suffered by groups outside the workplace were better locations from which to initiate movements of revolution than was that of the factory.

The insane (in *Madness and Civilization*), prisoners (in *Discipline and Punish*), homosexuals (in *The History of Sexuality*) and women (in *The History of Sexuality* and *The Birth of the Clinic*) were all groups that were oppressed by modern society and whose oppression is obscured not illuminated by the theory of the mode of production. Indeed in the aftermath of May 1968 the momentum of radicalism had shifted away from the working class. The foci of protest in the 1970s were feminism, gay liberation, anti-psychiatry, prison reform—the groups addressed by Foucault's writings—as well as other challenges to capitalism that were equally at the margins of the theory of the mode of production (racial, ethnic, and regional protest, anti-nuclear movements, ecologists, and so forth). Thus post-structuralism argues for a plurality of radical critiques, placing in question the centering of critical theory in its proletarian site.

In a similar vein, post-structuralism disputed the tendency of Marxism to limit critical theory to a given center. The quest for a unique center was the bane of both Foucault and Derrida, though their intentions were quite distinct, if not at odds. For the post-structuralists, theories that relied on a center were burdened by the limitations of reductionism. In the *1844 Manuscripts* Marx recognized the difficulty quite sharply. He admonished against those thinkers who persist in positing questions of origin:

> If you ask about the creation of nature and man, you thus abstract from man and nature. You assert them as *non-*

existent and yet want me to prove them to you as *existing.* I
say to you: Give up your abstraction and you will also give
up your question. Or if you want to maintain your abstraction, be consistent and if you think of man and nature as
non-existent, think of yourself as non-existent as you too
are nature and man. Do not think, do not question me for as
soon as you think and question, your *abstraction* from the
existence of nature and man makes no sense.[2]

The question of origin or center exceeds the proper limits of
reason and is therefore fruitless. When a social theorist specifies an absolute origin he or she denies the differential forces at
play in all beginnings, forces which operate to relativize origins. The theorist posits a privileged status for him or herself as
well as for the object specified. This privilege is metaphysical.
Thus to maintain the question of origin is to inflate reason to a
degree that invalidates its critical function. And yet only two
years later, in *The German Ideology* of 1846, Marx proposed to
discover the origin of class society in the division of labor. The
division of labor "alienates" human beings from their universality or species being; they equate their particular position in
the division of labor with the general good, falsely identifying
their particular interests with the general interest. History begins as the alienation of species being in the division of labor
and will end only with the onset of communism which puts an
end to the division of labor. A center was thus proposed for
revolutionary theory—labor—and it would remain installed in
that theory through the nineteenth and twentieth centuries,
sitting there, the post-structuralists would say, in a disruptive
relationship with radicalism, functioning to limit the boundaries of critique.

    It is not a long step from the concept of the center to that
of totalization. Theories that maintain a center also totalize.
The problems introduced by totalizations are no less severe
than those of the center. Totalizations are always reductive. In
addition they have a feedback effect which positions the totalizing theorist in a stance of domination. Critical theory seeks to
assist the movement of revolution by providing a counter-

ideology that delegitimizes the ruling class. In a curious manner, however, revolutionary theory itself tends to become a point of domination in the historical field. In Leninism, for example, the locus of theory is the locus of leadership and eventually the locus of bureaucratic control. The totalizing tendency in Marxist thought thus slips into the totalitarian power of the Marxist state. I do not wish to assert a causal relationship between a feature of theory (totalization) and a social system (totalitarianism). The forces at work in the creation of the Soviet state apparatus were complex and overdetermined. Nevertheless the tendency toward totalization in theory does counteract the praxis of democratizing social movements. In these cases, theory becomes the point of certainty for the movement; the informing function of theory becomes a directing function.

The problem of totalization is not as easily eliminated from theory as the post-structuralists would imply. An aspect of totalization necessarily emerges in every effort to counter the prevailing ideology and appears to be necessary to the process of thought itself. Derrida's otherwise careful strategy of deconstruction, for example, which strives to posit nothing except rigorous textual analysis, becomes itself a totalization, excluding all other positions in spite of itself.[3] It appears that Sartre was on the right track in the opening pages of The Critique of Dialectical Reason when he attempted to present a social phenomenology of totalization.[4] Consciousness totalizes its field as surely as totalization inhibits the freedom of the totalizer. The act of formulating a problem implies the decision that other problems will not be addressed. In that sense a totalization has occurred of the field of possible problems to theorize. Contrary to the positions of the post-structuralists there is no antidote to totalization, no simple theoretical step that can be taken completely to eliminate its force and effects.[5]

Nonetheless much can be done to curtail and inhibit the limiting effects of totalizing thought. Along this line Foucault has proposed a distinction between the "universal" and the "specific" intellectual. In addition to the problem of totalizing theory, the figure of the universal intellectual is a subject of serious critique of Marx by the post-structuralists. Foucault argues that Marxist intellectuals may be termed "universal" in the sense that they claim to speak for humanity.[6] Marxists naturally do not speak for the bourgeoisie, but they claim that the proletariat embodies the interests of humanity and the hopes for a society without classes. This posture, Foucault contends, leads to severe difficulties for the movement of emancipation.

Since Foucault assumes a close connection between discourse and power, he finds a danger in the arrogation of power by the universal intellectual. Also the claim to speak for the universal can be troublesome because it denies the multifarious oppressions which Foucault assumes to be a feature of contemporary society. In place of the universal intellectual, Foucault discerns the "specific intellectual" emerging since the Second World War. Closely associated with a particular form of oppression in a particular institution, the specific intellectual is less likely to take control of the protest movement and less likely to reduce all forms of domination to that of his or her constituency.[7] In this way the pretensions of Marxist political parties to represent the entire left are undercut. Foucault recognizes the danger of pluralism and anarchism connected with the specific intellectual,[8] but at least the dangers of reductionism are minimized. A full evaluation of Foucault's concept of the specific intellectual requires an analysis of the social roles of intellectuals in the past few decades, an analysis that is beyond the scope of this essay.

The third challenge to Marxism presented by post-structuralism is one which I have developed as an elaboration of their position. It concerns changes in the nature of contemporary society that are reflected in the thought of Foucault and Derrida but which also in turn are illuminated by their thought. Like many other twentieth-century thinkers, Foucault and Derrida are centrally concerned with language. In Derrida's texts the category of écriture or writing is the point of departure for an entire critical position. While writing is but one form of language, Derrida sees certain features of it to be characteristic of all language. From the standpoint of this essay what is important is the preoccupation with language as opposed to action. And Derrida takes a certain structure he finds in writing as the basis for a critique of the "Western Philosophical Tradition," of the "logocentrism" which underlies thinking even in the revolutionary camp.

Foucault as well takes a certain view of language as the heart of critique, one that he calls "discourse." For him Western thought since Descartes has assumed the innocence of reason. By focusing on discourse instead of on ideas, Foucault demonstrates the linkage of knowledge and power. Without pursuing the subtleties of the post-structuralists' position any further, we can conclude that they ground their critiques in forms of linguistic experience, as opposed to forms of consciousness on the one hand or forms of action on the other. The focus on language constitutes an important shift in discursive strategy, one that raises the question of context. What are the conditions for this shift and how may they be understood?

If we inquire into the changes of linguistic experience in the recent past, it becomes apparent that beneath the philosophical project of the post-structuralists a new linguistic world has appeared in social life. For what characterizes advanced capitalism is precisely a sudden explosion of multiple types of linguistic experience at every point in daily life. The act of production, for one, is increasingly defined by computer regulated machines. The world of leisure, as well, increasingly concerns the manipulation of information processors. Social control systems are dependent on vast amounts of stored information and on organizations that can manipulate that information. Knowledge about the social world is transmitted from one person to another indirectly through the mediation of electronic devices. Science once stood outside the world of opinion; it represented the rational critique of ignorance and of the domination that ensued from it. Now science and reason are part of the machinery of society and participate in the systems of social control and domination.

These new linguistic experiences have very little precedence in the history of capitalist society. The new linguistic forms appear at ever increasing rates and impose new types of relationships. Telephone communications are two-way conversations without physical presence. Television communications are one-way conversations without physical presence. These linguistic experiences rely on traditional languages encoded and then decoded electronically. Still more remote from traditional linguistic expression is the computer, which contains an entirely new language or languages, languages that regulate with equal ease populations or things. Bureaucratic organizations, which increasingly characterize advanced capitalism, can be seen as primitive computers. With these new languages and linguistic experiences pervading everyday life it is not surprising that a position is developed which calls into question traditional language forms. And such is precisely the impact of post-structuralism. To avoid obsolescence, critical theory must account for the line of new languages that stretches from body signals, grunts, spoken language, and writing to print, the telegraph, radio, film, television, computers, and communication satellites. These new phenomena constitute a rupture with traditional linguistic experience and they make possible new forms of communicative relationships. It is reasonable to hypothesize that the network of social relations is being fundamentally altered at the present time by the new linguistic experiences.

The post-structuralists do not often reflect on the social world in which their positions are developed. But those positions are symptoms of the times and are useful in comprehending the emerging social formation. If Marx failed to develop a language theory when he analyzed the change from feudalism to capitalism, such an absence is no longer tolerable. The change from capitalism to late capitalism or from the mode of production to what I call the mode of information requires the reconstitution of critical theory, a reformulation which can unlock the forms of domination inherent in diverse linguistic experiences, reveal the significance of new forms of protest particular to the present conjuncture and imagine the shape of a democratic future that is possible as a transformation of the present situation.

Foucault's *Discipline and Punish* is exemplary of the advances and the hesitations of post-structuralism in relation to the mode of information. The book presents a detotalized view of the social field. It examines the formation of new mechanisms of punishment without ontologizing that mode of domination as the key to total freedom or the "riddle of history." *Discipline and Punish* traces the emergence of a new "technology of power" in the nineteenth century without claiming that it is a base upon which everything else rests, without consigning histories of other aspects of the nineteenth century to the status of epiphenomena or superstructures. Relations between the new technology of power (the Panopticon) and other social levels such as the economy are described without any hint of reductionism. Capitalism is not reduced to the Panopticon but the complex play of their interactions are given due recognition.

Metaphysics is kept at bay as well when Foucault traces the origins of the Panopticon. The new technology of punishment emerges in the nineteenth century out of a complex play of differential forces. The difference between the Panopticon and Torture (the earlier system of punishment) is not absolute. Unlike Marx in his analysis of the origins of the division of labor, Foucault does not present the birth of the prison as the institution of domination in human history, as the beginning of human alienation. Instead Foucault goes to great lengths to show that the torture system included a strong element of domination, so that the change to the Panopticon constitutes a substitution of one system of domination for another, a relative not an absolute transformation. At the same time he undermines the opposite metaphysical strategy, that of liberals who view the change as one from evil to good. For liberalism the birth of the prison signifies decisive progress in the dignity and freedom of man. The Panopticon abolished "cruel and unusual punishments" and was decisive proof that liberal society inaugurated the reign of freedom on Earth. On the contrary, Foucault indicates first, that while the torture system was certainly cruel (recall the dismemberment of Damiens), it was a coherent mechanism of social control, not the incarnation of evil. Similarly, the prison system, while it rid society of cruel spectacles of punishment, instituted a new mechanism of power that was efficient and effective in controlling populations. In this way Foucault presents an origin (the Panopticon was a genuinely new mechanism) that is free of metaphysics.

A third important feature of *Discipline and Punish* speaks to the advances of post-structuralism over traditional critical theory. In his analysis, Foucault integrates with critical theory the new sense of the importance of language. The depiction of the Panopticon includes not only an institutional framework and a system of practices but also a set of discourses. These discourses are composed of the Enlightenment reformers' tracts advocating the abolition of torture and the writings of Bentham and others proposing the basic form of the Panopticon. It includes as well the records kept by the administrators of the prisons and by the police. Especially interesting however is the role of the discourse of the new science of criminology in the legitimation of the Panopticon. Through a discussion of criminology Foucault demonstrates how the human sciences are implicated in systems of domination. He shows how discourses and practices are inextricably interwoven in the fabric of technologies of power, how science is not innocent of force. He offers the couplet discourse/practice to underscore the involvement of language with action. This sensitivity to the ability of language to shape practice is typical of the post-structuralists and exemplifies their rejection of the metaphysical dualism of mind and body, ideas and behavior, consciousness and action.

Yet with all of these advances Foucault and the post-structuralists do not take the next step in the deconstruction of traditional theory, a step that Marx himself pioneered. To avoid metaphysics at the level of epistemology, to prevent one's own discourse from being regarded as an absolute beginning, in other words as science, it is necessary to engage in the effort of self-reflection, to relativize one's status as a subject of knowledge. Foucault does entertain this line of thinking but he does so by refusing systematically to theorize. He chooses that strategy of deconstruction rather than the alternative of situating his discourse in its social-historical context. I will first analyze Foucault's effort at self-reflection and then offer an alternative, one that roots Foucault's discourse in the present conjuncture and thereby reveals a new level to its analytical power.

Like Nietzsche, Foucault introduces his categories in the midst of his text without a full elaboration or a systematic presentation of them. For example, the concept of "technology of power," a central theme of *Discipline and Punish*, appears first on page 23 with no explanation whatsoever. Foucault is at that point discussing the "four general rules" of the book. The third rule reads as follows:

> 3. Instead of treating the history of penal law and the history of the human sciences as two separate series whose overlapping appears to have had on one or the other, or perhaps on both, a disturbing or useful effect, according to one's point of view, see whether there is not some common matrix or whether they do not both derive from a single process of "epistemological-juridical" formation; in short, make the technology of power the very principle both of the humanization of the penal system and of the knowledge of man.[9]

In this off hand manner Foucault specifies the object of his study as "the technology of power" of the prison systems from the Old Regime to the present. But what does it mean to say that one will "make the technology of power" the principle of both the institution of the prison and the social science that studies it? Foucault employs the term "technology of power" dozens of times in the book; he also uses other terms as if they were identical to it in meaning ("micro-physics of power," "mechanisms of power," and so forth). At issue is not the game of finding all the meanings of the term "technology of power" in order to show a contradiction in Foucault's thought or simply to refine a formal definition of the term. The difficulty lies elsewhere: without a clearly enunciated systematic theory the limits of Foucault's project remain uncertain. It is impossible to indicate the parameters of the phenomenon of the technology of power, for instance, without a systematic elaboration of its conceptual basis. By the end of the book, the reader may have a pretty good notion of what Foucault means by the technology of power, but it will be very difficult indeed to determine if the category is compatible with other theories, such as Marxism, or if it can be the basis of studies of other institutional matrices. In fact, Foucault's tendency to totalize the concept "technology of power," going against the grain of his general position, can be attributed to his failure adequately to theorize it. There is a general tendency among post-structuralists to avoid formal theorizing. Derrida, much like Foucault, introduces new terms in each new book he writes. It may be retorted to my objection to the atheoretical strategy of the post-structuralists that they adopt such a strategy in order to avoid the very pitfalls of theorizing such as totalization that were addressed at the beginning of this essay. My response to that retort is that they have gone too far in the direction of anti-systematic thinking and that an intermediate strategy needs to be developed by which categories are systematically developed without embedding them in a closed, totalizing system.

For his part Foucault justifies his theoretical diffidence on the ground that it is required in order to develop a critique of the human sciences. He steadfastly rejects the traditional strategy of theoretical development and empirical verification that is practiced by liberal positivists and Marxists alike. In *The German Ideology* Marx insisted that the value of the theory of the mode of production could be determined only by empirical studies.[10] What Foucault finds objectionable in standard social science is the unacknowledged implication of the claim of knowledge, that is, the will to power. Like the Frankfurt School's critique of humanism in the *Dialectic of Enlightenment* and, of course, like Nietzsche in *Beyond Good and Evil*,[11]

Foucault argues that systematic social science, especially careful theoretical elaboration, itself inherently contains an element of domination or a technology of power. As was stated in the passage above where the term "technology of power" was introduced, the discourse of criminology is itself a form of power. Technologies of power consist of knowledge and practice intimately associated in the formation of social relations based on domination. Because social science is not neutral, above the fray of class struggles, the rational exercise of theoretical production is implicated in the problem of domination. And Marxism, with its oppressive state systems and hierarchical political parties is not different in principle from the behavioral sciences and public policy sciences of capitalism. Even if the theorist explicitly takes the side of the oppressed rather than hiding behind the mask of scientific neutrality, the function of domination associated with systematic theory is not eliminated.

In *Discipline and Punish* Foucault is by and large consistent in his theoretical asceticism. Many readers find the book frustrating and difficult because at the same time that the case is made against modern prison systems, nothing is offered by the author as a response to it. Some students of the book find in it deep despair,[12] when this impression is better attributed to the effect on the reader of the convincing genealogy of prisons without the utopian alternative that systematic theory provides. Foucault himself replies to the charge of pessimism as follows:

> My point is not that everything is bad, but that every-
> thing is dangerous, which is not exactly the same as bad. If
> everything is dangerous, then we always have something to
> do. So my position leads not to apathy but to a hyper- and
> pessimistic activism.[13]

This response to critics is inadequate not because it is untrue but because there is no ground in Foucault's text on which to base the conclusion of "hyper- and pessimistic activism." One may just as easily argue that the position emerging from *Disci-*

pline and Punish is pessimistic apathy, optimistic adventurism, or whatever. The reason that multiple, contradictory political conclusions are possible is that the concepts underlying the analysis of prison systems are theoretically inchoate. If the concept of the technology of power were fully elaborated at some point in the text a political stance of refusal would probably have to emerge as a clear conclusion. Forms of resistance to the technology of power, so underplayed by Foucault in the book (see his recognition of this problem in *Power/Knowledge*), are a necessary aspect of an analysis of the history of punishment systems from the perspective of critical theory.[14] Marx theorized a proletarian revolt against capitalism and liberals theorized resistance to monarchical despotism. But if such a theoretical turn were taken, Foucault contends, the concept of technology of power would return to the theorist and become an emanation of the reason of the author, Foucault himself. The author of the theory would be the commander of a new movement and would exercise domination over its followers. The intellectual would take his place at the head of the revolutionary column; his mind would be venerated by the oppressed as a source of power and they would be subject to oppression by him. Once again the scenario of the Western philosophical tradition would be enacted as Hegel's deity of reason would confirm His dialectical power of immanence. Foucault's refusal of systematic theory is thus the post-structuralist's rejection of reason as the center of being. And Foucault gives up much to maintain that stance. He insists that his books are only tools for the revolutionary deconstruction of the established apparatus.[15] Alternatively he would have us think of them as bombs for others to throw at the halls of power and wealth. The only systematic principle for this anti-systematic writer is his denial of system, denial of reason, and necessarily denial of authorship.[16] Yet even if one sympathizes with Foucault's predicament, the position he is in remains a predicament, one fraught with difficulties.[17]

Discipline and Punish cannot escape its fate as a form of communication. However much Foucault would hide from his text, withdraw his authorship, and however sound his reason for doing so, his text remains itself a discourse and as a discourse it retains its power effects. To deny them is not to make them go away. Foucault's confusion is therefore to think that his awareness of the limits of reason and systematic theory can result in a form of theory immune from those limits. In short, Foucault betrays an idealist assumption that an author's awareness of the dilemma of authorship by itself avoids the difficulties and sanctions a stance of non-authorship. In other words, Foucault implies that his mere awareness of the problem enables him, in his writing, to elude the technology of power inherent in writing. But it is clear that if the domination inherent in reason and authorship can be muted that would occur not through an author's awareness but through a change in the social system, through a new set of practices in which the audience and the system of publishing no longer conferred power on the author, a situation that has probably never existed and may never exist. For these reasons the discourse of the technology of power must be considered badly incomplete and therefore open to a kind of misinterpretation beyond that inherent in the dialogic process of citation and reported speech.

If the story ended at this point a fundamental aspect of Foucault's achievement would remain obscured, that is, the epistemological advance of his position contained in the notion of discourse itself and most importantly the relationship of the concept of discourse to the mode of information. Earlier in this essay I suggested that post-structuralism advances critical theory by raising the question of language, thereby opening the field of critical theory to the dramatic changes in linguistic experience that have so altered the social formation in the past few decades. At this point I will indicate how the post-structuralist position may be elaborated to account for the mode of information.

Critical theory has in general not looked favorably on positions rooted in theories of language, such as Foucault's concept of discourse. In *The German Ideology* Marx relegated language to an insignificant place in social theory:

> From the start the "spirit" bears the curse of being "burdened" with matter which makes its appearance in the form of agitated layers of air, sounds, in short, in the form of language. Language is as old as consciousness. It *is* practical consciousness which exists also for other men and hence exists for me personally as well. Language, like consciousness, only arises from the need and necessity of relationships with other men.[18]

This passage, one of the few where Marx directly speaks of language, has been interpreted in a manner that credits Marx with an awareness of the importance of language in society. He writes after all that language is "practical consciousness." Against this view I argue that in fact Marx is here dismissing the problematic aspect of language for critical theory. The emphasis in the passage, as I read it, is that language is determined by social relationships, that action precedes language. Support for my reading of the passage is found in the vast body of Marxist literature which with few exceptions ignores the structuring features of language, or at best treats language in the form of ideology as part of the superstructure. For Marx the object of critical theory is praxis and in particular labor. The act of labor is the focus of social critique and domination is revealed by him in the forms of the alienation and exploitation of the labor act. Even though praxis includes a moment of consciousness, the critique of domination focuses on the activity of labor. In fact the central object of the liberal tradition of the critique of domination also concerned a form of praxis. From John Locke onward the main force of liberal criticism was brought to bear on arbitrary power, especially that of the monarch. The acts of kings, nobles, and clerics were the source of the limits of freedom, in the liberal account. In both liberal and Marxist traditions emancipatory theory was grounded in the critique of action. Ironically it was not until Stalin, a great tyrant and exploiter on his own, that Marxism began to consider language outside the framework of the superstructure.

Recently Habermas and Baudrillard have attempted to base critical theory on forms of linguistic experience.[19] Haber-

mas' concept of the ideal speech situation grounds the democratizing movement in an egalitarian context of public discussion in which reason may emerge. But "distorted
communication," for Habermas, remains a product of the social
relations of the speakers. His critique of domination does not
yield categories for the analysis of the linguistic modes by
which to reveal how language patterns are themselves sources
of domination. Baudrillard's early work, especially *Towards a
Critique of the Political Economy of the Sign* (1972), *The System of Objects* (1968), *Consumer Society* (1970), and *The Mirror
of Production* (1973) move closer to a materialist theory of
language.[20] His theory of the mode of signification was an effort
to employ a variety of semiotic categories to disclose the domination inherent in linguistic forms in different epochs. Like
Habermas, Baudrillard ran into difficulty over the question of
utopia. He posited one linguistic form, that of the symbol, that
promised liberation from the semiotic horrors of the code.
Unlike Habermas, however, Baudrillard began the serious examination of contemporary modes of communication and
opened up significantly the field of the semiology of everyday
life.

Foucault's concept of discourse must be viewed in relation to this theoretical tradition if its advantages are to be
grasped. First, Foucault rejected the split between knowledge
and power, discourse and practice. Since, as Nietzsche had
shown, knowledge was a form of power and since power created and shaped practice rather than limiting it, discourse was
deeply implicated in the critique of domination. This strategy
required that discourse be analyzed not as a form of consciousness, not as an expression of the subject, but as a form of
positivity. The rejection of the subjectivity of discourse led
Foucault in *The Archaeology of Knowledge* to elaborate a new
set of categories that would allow discourse to stand on its own
as a form of power.

> I shall abandon any attempt . . . to see discourse as a
> phenomenon of expression—the verbal translation of a

previously established synthesis; instead, I shall look for a
field of regularity for various positions of subjectivity.
Thus conceived, discourse is not the majestically unfolding manifestation of a thinking, knowing, speaking subject,
but, on the contrary, a totality, in which the dispersion of
the subject, and his discontinuity with himself may be
determined.[21]

This passage contains the rudiments of a concept of language,
in the form of discourse, appropriate to a critical theory of the
mode of information, one that, properly understood, remains
materialist because it points to the analysis of modes of domination in the contemporary social field. Historical materialism
is based on the conviction that the object of historical knowledge cannot be ideas because the ideas that people hold about
social existence do not determine their existence. Marx formulated this salutary principle of interpretation at a time when
historical thinking, especially in Germany, was indeed idealist.
At that time, however, in the mid-nineteenth century, vast
social changes were occurring in the organization of political
and economic action. A theory grounded in idealism was particularly unsuited to lay bare the structures of these political
and economic transformations.

But what must become of historical materialism at a time
when the structures of linguistic experience are undergoing
drastic change—when bureaucracies accumulate extensive
files on the population; when visual and aural electronic impulses (TV, telephone, radio, film) constitute significant por-
tions of the communications in everyday life; when commodities are produced through the mediation of computers and
sold through the mediation of clusters of meanings generated
by advertising teams; when political processes are shaped by
mass communication devices; when surveillance by the digital
logic of the computer threatens to extend itself into every cor-
ner of the social world; when the human sciences and the
natural sciences are integrated into the systems of social control
and reproduction? In this context, which I have given the tentative label "mode of information," historical materialism must

do more than calculate rates of exploitation and declining surplus value. It must do more than demonstrate the alienated
conditions of the act of labor. Indeed it must take into account
these new forms of language; it must develop categories for the
analysis of the patterns of domination and distortion inherent
in their contemporary usage; and it must examine the historical
stages of their development.

Employing only the traditional categories of Marxism
(perhaps adjusted by the traditions of Western Marxism), one
would learn how the new systems of language serve the ruling
class and are controlled to some degree by them.[22] While that is
a valid enterprise, it is not by itself adequate for the analysis of
the mode of information. Foucault's recent work is useful precisely on that account. *Discipline and Punish* avoids centering
critical theory on a totalizing concept of labor. It grasps structures of domination in their specificity and, while relating
different patterns of domination to each other, resists the temptation to reduce one to another. In addition, the book employs a
notion of discourse, elaborated further in *The History of Sexuality*, which sanctions the analysis of language yet avoids
grounding it in subjectivity. Critical theory thus has an example
of an examination of a structure of domination in language that
is not rooted in idealist assumptions. For these reasons aspects
of Foucault's methodology are valuable for a critical theory of
the mode of information. Post-structuralism has come to the aid
of critical theory not so much in the theory of writing but in
connection with the analysis of a digital logic that may relegate
writing to past epochs of signifying practices.

Foucault himself did not situate his thought in relation
to the new conjuncture. He did not define the present situation
in terms of a new social formation, much less in terms of a mode
of information or anything equivalent to it. As a result the impact of his texts are less than they might be and for several reasons. First, at the epistemological level, he substitutes a strategy
of evasion of authorial presence for that of situating his position
in its historical conditions. Both strategies have the same in-
tent: to undermine the absoluteness of the author as subject and

origin of the text. But the former strategy, Foucault's, merely creates ambiguity over the interpretation of the text, while the latter, the one I am suggesting, defines more clearly the direction of political intervention that the text proposes. On this score Foucault's tendency was to discuss his political positions in occasional pieces, interviews, and the like, not in his major texts.

Second, if Foucault were to specify those aspects of the social formation that provide the framework of the questions he poses, those questions and the works he develops to answer them could be more systematically developed into a critical theory. His texts would be part of a larger project and would not stand on their own, inviting critics to respond to them in terms of the star system of intellectuals. At the same time, to insert *Discipline and Punish* and the other recent works into a theory of the mode of information would immeasurably clarify their conceptual underpinnings. Notions like discourse/practice and technology of power would become specified in relation to particular levels of the social formation. By elaborating above the concept of the mode of information in terms of new linguistic experiences I have indicated the lines for this theoretical development. More work needs to be done in clarifying the concept of the mode of information with particular attention to the question of avoiding totalization.

Third, and by way of illustration, I will explore the analysis of the Panopticon as presented in *Discipline and Punish* in relation to the mode of information. As a means of punishment and reform of criminals the Panopticon was a failure. As a means of the control and discipline of a population it was a success. Foucault therefore does not evaluate it in relation to juridical norms, as liberalism does, nor in relation to the mode of production, as Marxism does. He treats it as a new technology of power, one peculiar to modern society. Its success as a tool of the administration of large institutions insured its widespread use in schools, asylums, workplaces, the military, and so forth. The problem with Foucault's presentation is that it does not specify the characteristics of the social formation into which the Panopticon is differentially inserted. For that reason his analysis gets unhinged at points and he takes positions which go against his own theoretical strategies. For example, at one point in the text he totalizes the Panopticon as the general technology of power in modern society.[23] His refusal to specify the social formation derives from his reluctance to insert his writing in liberal or Marxist contexts, contexts which would undermine the force of his analysis of the Panopticon. But the alternative he takes, failure to specify the social formation, leads only to confusion.

He might have chosen a Weberian frame for his work.[24] After all Weber is the theorist of bureaucratic society, one in which the main issue of social control concerns the management of large populations. In addition Weber presented a critique of the form of rationality associated with bureaucratic institutions and was the first major thinker, after Nietzsche, to associate reason (in the form of instrumental rationality) with domination, a strategy that Foucault himself admires a great deal. The chief drawback in Weber's position and the reason why Foucault was prudent to avoid his standpoint is that Weber fails to develop his position in relation to a theory of language, limiting himself to a theory of action. Weber's discourse remains rooted in the humanist dualism of reason and action. It is therefore unsuited to the task of reconstituting critical theory.

The only viable path open to Foucault is to develop his own sense of the social formation. Had he done so he might have recognized the extraordinary relevance of the discourse/ practice of the Panopticon in revealing new modes of domination. The Panopticon's effectiveness was based on its ability to instill in each member of the subject population the sense that they were always open to observation or surveillance by the administrative authorities. In the prison system of the nineteenth century this was accomplished largely by architectural means. A guard was positioned in a central tower with a complete circular view. Around him the cells were built so that the guard was able to see into them at his pleasure but the prisoners were not able to ascertain whether they were being observed.

The goal of the system was to so alter the prisoners' awareness that they were to become continuously oriented to the prison authorities. One can easily imagine how this system might be effective not only in prisons but in other settings as well.

What Foucault apparently did not notice is that the same panoptical system has been perfectly and widely extended in the second half of the twentieth century by dint of the information gathering and storing ability of the computer. It is now possible to monitor large populations without the material apparatus of the nineteenth-century prison. Electronic monitoring of the population occurs silently, continuously, and automatically as the transactions of everyday life occur. Under the domain of the super-Panopticon the population need not be gathered in institutions to be observed. In the mundane affairs of private life as well as in public life the population is under the gaze of the corporate and state bureaucracies. Market behavior, personal preferences, credit status, vacation decisions, health profiles—every conceivable aspect of ordinary activity leaves a trace in the memory banks of machines, traces that are available instantaneously should the occasion arise. The celebrated distinction, so dear to liberals, between private life and public life is being effectively abolished not by a communist revolution but by the extension of the Panopticon as a technology of power.

Surveillance by the super-Panopticon is made possible only by the mode of information. The new technology of power relies upon certain configurations of *linguistic* experience. Nothing illustrates better than the super-Panopticon the interrelation of discourse and practice. Contemporary surveillance is a product of new methods of *information* processing, not brute force. What is needed then is a full analysis of new modes of linguistic experience in a manner that reveals the extent to which they constitute new modes of domination. It is difficult to see how critical theory can proceed without such an analysis. At the same time cautions must be taken to avoid totalizing the new theoretical direction. The aim must be to develop theoretically and specify analytically the types of domination inherent in the mode of information.

Foucault's discussion of the Panopticon leads directly into this theoretical line of inquiry, but falls short of taking the important next steps. Post-structuralism has cleared the way for critical theory to incorporate the question of language. Only its undue suspicion of systematic theory and inadequate self-reflexivity prevents it from a major theoretical breakthrough.

Notes

I wish to thank David Carroll and Michael Clark for their helpful comments on this paper. I am also grateful for the comments and the grant support given to me by the Focused Research Program in Contemporary Critical Theory at the University of California, Irvine. Parts of the manuscript have appeared in an earlier form in my book, *Foucault, Marxism and History* (London: Blackwell's, 1984).

1. See, for example, the interview "Prison Talk," translated in *Power/Knowledge: Selected Interviews and Other Writings, 1972–1977*, Colin Gordon, ed. (New York: Pantheon, 1980), pp. 37–54.

2. *Writings of the Young Marx on Philosophy and Society*, Lloyd Easton and Kurt Guddat, eds. and trs. (New York: Anchor, 1967), pp. 313–314.

3. See, for example, Jacques Derrida, *Of Grammatology*, G. Spivak, tr. (Baltimore: Johns Hopkins University Press, 1976).

4. Jean-Paul Sartre, *Critique of Dialectical Reason*, Alan Sheridan-Smith, tr. (London: New Left Books, 1976), pp. 45–48.

5. On the importance of the concept of totality to Western Marxism see Martin Jay, *Marxism and Totality* (Berkeley: University of California Press, 1984).

6. *Power/Knowledge*, pp. 126ff.

7. Foucault's categories are different from those of Antonio Gramsci who distinguishes between organic and traditional intellectuals.

8. *Power/Knowledge*, p. 130.

9. *Discipline and Punish: The Birth of the Prison*, Alan Sheridan, tr. (New York: Pantheon, 1977), p. 23.

10. Easton and Guddat, *Writings of the Young Marx*, p. 431.

11. Theodor Adorno and Max Horkheimer, *Dialectic of Enlightenment*, John Cumming, tr. (1944; New York: Continuum, 1972). Friedrich Nietzsche, *Beyond Good and Evil: Prelude to a Philosophy of the Future*, Walter Kaufmann, tr. (New York: Vintage, 1966).

12. See, for example, Edward Said, "Travelling Theory," *Raritan* (Winter 1982), pp. 41–67.

13. "How We Behave," interview with Michael Foucault, *Vanity Fair* (November 1983), p. 62.

14. For an attempt at a general theory of resistance see Michel de Certeau, *L'Invention du quotidien: I. Arts de faire* (Paris: 10/18, 1980).

15. *M. Foucault: Power, Truth, Strategy*, M. Morris and Paul Patton, eds. (Sydney: Working Papers, 1979), p. 57.

16. "What is an Author?" in *Language, Counter-Memory, Practice*, Donald Bouchard, ed. (Ithaca, N.Y.: Cornell University Press, 1977), pp. 113–138.

17. See the treatment of this problem by David Carroll, "The Subject of Archeology of the Sovereignty of the Episteme," *Modern Language Notes* (1978), 93:695–722.

18. Easton and Guddat, p. 421.

19. For a more complete discussion of Baudrillard and Habermas on this question, see my "Technology and Culture in Habermas and Baudrillard," *Journal of Contemporary Literature* (1981), 22(4):456–476. See also V. N. Voloshinov, *Marxism and the Philosophy of Language*, L. Matejka and I. Titunik, trs. (New York: Seminar Press, 1973).

20. For a fuller exploration of this topic see Rosalind Coward and John Ellis, *Language and Materialism* (London: Routledge & Kegan Paul, 1977).

21. *The Archaeology of Knowledge*, A. M. Sheridan-Smith, tr. (New York: Harper, 1972), p. 55.

22. Herbert Schiller, *Who Knows: Information in the Age of the Fortune 500* (New York: Ablex, 1981).

23. *Discipline and Punish*, pp. 216–217.

24. He mentions and then rejects this path in a recent interview. See "A Discussion of the Work of Michel Foucault," *Skyline* (March 1982), p. 18.

4

SURPLUS ECONOMIES: DECONSTRUCTION, IDEOLOGY, AND THE HUMANITIES

John Carlos Rowe

If the police is always waiting in the wings, it is because conventions are by essence violable and precarious, *in themselves* and by the fictionality that constitutes them, even before there has been any overt transgression, in the "first sense" of *to pretend.*

—Derrida, *Limited Inc abc . . .*

THE epigraph conventionally serves the scholarly essay as a sort of literary image, in which the subsequent argument is condensed and glossed. At the same time, the epigraph notes in shorthand the particular tradition to which the essay belongs. My work has followed that of Derrida's, and my work has succumbed at times (almost inevitably) to the aestheticist implications in deconstruction that have come to characterize much Anglo-American post-structuralist theory in the humanities. Having confessed this much, I want to begin again by saying that my purpose in this paper—and several others I have written on related subjects in the past two years—is an understanding of some of the motives for this aestheticist impulse in deconstruction, in order to overcome its inherent limitations. The task is not so easy as it might first appear. Using my epigraph in an antithetical manner, then, I would contend that Derrida already has indicated one of those motives, and it is one that is by no means restricted to the particular interpretative strategies (often quite diverse) gathered under the merely notational headings of "deconstruction" and "post-structuralism." In this passage—one of the occasional moments (and thus all the more frequently quoted) in which Derrida directly employs political metaphors—ideological forces are already modeled after literature. Social conventions are essentially and inherently "violable and precarious," because those conventions are "fictions." To recognize them as fictions is already to acknowledge their transgression of their contrived origins (their origins *as* contrivance or pretense) in their conventional acceptance, in their uses as part of social reality—that is, in the constitution of a "reality-principle." The statement is unremarkable in itself, except when we consider how often theories of social fictionality derive from the presumed paradigm of literary or philosophical fictions. Derrida considers the duplicity of social conventions to make them inherently "violable and precarious," because such duplicity in literary or philosophical discourses most often functions in this manner, seemingly unsupported by other resources or foundations and thus doomed ultimately to the enveloping "fictionality" or "ideality" in which philosophy and literature continue to inscribe themselves as disciplines.

Ideological conventions are not as violable and precarious as Derrida and others would have us believe; we mistake their uncanny powers of disguise, displacement, reproduction, and appropriation when we assume that they "follow" our inadequate literary and philosophical paradigms for fictionality. Here, by way of digression, I would argue that Derrida's principal concern with the history of philosophy is misplaced. Others have criticized this narrowness, setting it explicitly against more encompassing interdisciplinary efforts by Foucault.[1] My objection, however, is somewhat different from those who consider Foucault's method as a cure. Concentrating on the philosophic and literary, Derrida unwittingly transforms these discourses into founding structures (or rhetorics) for politics, economics, society in general, even as Derrida's own theories acknowledge the reverse: the emergence of conceptual and metaphoric forces as a consequence of very particular socioeconomic and historical repressions. In aesthetic terms, the transparency of the fictionality Derrida finds in ideological conventions carries with it an implicit value judgment. "Bad art" is that which too readily gives the lie to its "naturalness" by exposing its artifice. Kant's dictum that "art can only be called beautiful if we are conscious of it as art while yet it looks like Nature" has considerably more persistence in modern aesthetics than we might at first wish to believe.[2] Notions of "Nature" may change dramatically, but the relation of "art" and "Nature," of "form" and "reality," of "inside" and "outside" continue to reinforce this basic Kantian premise. I would be tempted to exclude Derrida from this charge, insofar as his own work has been devoted so carefully to the deconstruction of such binaries, but in my epigraph, at least, Derrida has implicitly evoked the Kantian hierarchy for judging successful fictions: "*Genius is the innate mental aptitude (ingenium) through which* nature gives the rule to art" (#46, p. 168). Insofar as Derrida conceives social conventions to expose their artificiality and contrivance, he implicitly judges them inferior to, weaker than, fictions capable of "naturalizing" their fictionality. Modern aesthetic and philosophic theories accomplish the work of naturalizing most often by hypostasizing "fictionality" itself, in a move that seems to me to follow quite directly and historically from the arguments of the Romantic Idealists: the ideality of the world, its constructed "nature," makes fiction the only proper domain for truth and knowledge. Such "insight" requires that peculiar form of humanistic "reflection" or "self-consciousness" that transcends the ordinary commerce of social behavior. The social convention is "stupid," clumsy, simple; the philosophical concept is reflective, transcendental, complex. The former reveals itself and requires

the "police" to protect its rule; the latter hides itself by subordinating itself to its own invented truth and thus "polices"
itself.

For strategic reasons that are ultimately defensive and
virtual admissions of our political impotence, we humanists
insist upon trivializing the power and complexity of the dominant ideology's "artistry." In the same manner that we are fond
of speaking of "science" and "technology" in the vaguest and
most uninformed ways (e.g., imagining that modern science is
still some version of Newtonian physics), we caricature the
complex arts involved in the formation of social values. Like
most willful misreadings, our casual analyses of these social
arts are designed to preserve our disciplines and our discourses
from the historical constraints governing the more material
processes of the culture. I need not analyze for you how such a
"will-to-freedom" in the humanities involves a narcissism that
contributes to the present debility and neglect of our work.
Given the self-evident and transparent *legerdemain* or jugglery
we presume to operate in ideological conventions, we are all
the more inclined to find the subtleties and complexities of art
and philosophy to constitute proper "counter-forces," correc-
tives, or cures for the silly vaudeville antics we imagine are
performed daily in the theaters of politics, economics, and the
law.

One of our apparent values in this self-styled division of
the world into "good" and "bad" fictions (to persist in a crude
terminology to parody the rough distinction made by humanists) is the "self-consciousness" involved in such fictionality.
The figurative characteristics of literature would seem to call
constant attention to the fact that "we are conscious of its being
art, while yet it has the appearance of nature." The coin of the
realm erases its figure, Derrida tells us; social convention works
to obliterate its figurative origins, in order to masquerade as a
signifier with some natural signified, with some semantic horizon determined by (rather than *constituting*) Nature.[3] Literary
self-consciousness is characterized more often than not by its
recognition of what exceeds it, of that "surplus" or "excess"

that figuration cannot master: the unconscious that self-consciousness can never make fully present to itself. Whether existential in the manner of Sartre's conception of the sheer plenitude of existents (*de trop*) or formalist in the manner of Geoffrey Hartman's notion of literature's infinite figurative potential, such "self-consciousness" is often an admission of inadequacy that nevertheless *defines* all that exceeds it. The very formulation of these excesses and surpluses as constituting the boundaries of our rhetorical or analytical concepts would seem to distinguish our discourses from those of the dominant ideology, in which the convention would appear to work to constrain such excess, to keep it utterly "within bounds," as a skilled player does in a soccer match. Indeed, the "metaphysics of presence," "logocentrism"—these notions criticized by deconstruction are based on a similar assumption about the "economy" of social conventions, which functions to repress as fully as possible all those differences that exceed the form of such conventionality in the interests of perpetuating such convention as the reproduction of the selfsame.

I shall not at this moment call for "common sense"; my audience knows, I hope, the trap and desperation of such an appeal. I shall turn instead to the persistence and power of social conventions in modern bourgeois societies (I am thinking particularly of American society), and ask why the humanities have been so incapable of transforming, of transvaluing those conventions that would appear to be so inherently fragile, so subject to transgression (especially those "transgressions" we consider constitutive of *literary* function). Although he understood well, I think, the complexities of these social arts, Marx himself was perhaps too convinced that the internal contradictions of capitalism would transform powerful conventions into fragile fictions, that the cynicism of capitalism would prepare for its own transvaluation by the inevitable (that is, *historical*) revelation of just such cynicism and contradiction. And there persists in Marx's text as well some of the same romanticism concerning the exclusion of certain forms of discourse from the economics of capitalism, as I think Marx's remarks regarding "productive" and "unproductive" labor indicate.[4]

My assumption is that the social arts that serve the production and reproduction of social conventions are far more complicated than we have been willing to acknowledge. Rather than the paradigms of literature and philosophy providing us with "measures" or even subversive "levers" for understanding these arts, I would argue that the complex methods informing and sustaining social values ought to be models (albeit very troublesome models, given their origins) for understanding literary and philosophic formations and concepts. If we are concerned with the ways in which representations assume power in culture—rather than with the discrete "meanings" of those representations as they might be abstracted from concrete historical situations, then our best, even when antithetical, models for such power structures ought to be drawn from those social forces that have demonstrably succeeded in preserving themselves, even when and perhaps *because* they appear to be so "fragile" and "precarious." And if we are concerned that deconstruction assume political force in both our genealogical understanding of cultural formations and in our efforts to transvalue powerful cultural values, then we would do well to study more carefully the ways in which our own methods and humanistic values are implicated in the artistry by which social conventions preserve and duplicate themselves. Such study would constitute at once an internal questioning of our motives and methods as part of historical actuality and make possible the development of more powerful humanistic discourses capable of engaging social conventionality in terms of its complex internal workings, not merely its superficial manifestations.

The principal function of social conventions is the preservation and reproduction of the dominant ideology. Those who have attempted to deconstruct logocentrism have reductively transformed the ideology into a simple set of "concepts" that might be arrayed as its predicates: teleology, univocity, strict and unilateral referentiality, intentionality, the reduction of differences in an economy of presence. These predicates operate within a capitalist society principally to disguise the contradictions within the value system of that society. These contradictions, however, are not simply the means to debilitate ultimately that ideology, they also constitute the essence of the ideology in its motive power. Marx's great insight into the workings of capitalism was his formulation of the *concept* of surplus value—that is, both the origin and nature of surplus value in capitalist economics. Marx acknowledges that Ricardo and others understood "relative surplus value," which is to say that previous economists had studied the role of surplus value (Ricardo's mistaken term for "profits") in the economic system; Marx claims as his own task the analysis and understanding of "surplus value" as the founding concept and preserving agent of the system: "Ricardo never concerns himself with the origin of surplus-value. He treats it as an entity inherent in the capitalist mode of production, and in his eyes the latter is the natural form of social production. Whenever he discusses the productivity of labour, he seeks in it not the cause of the existence of surplus-value, but the cause that determines the magnitude of that value."[5] Marx's concept of surplus value in itself threatens to expose the naiveté of any social critique that would take the univocity, formalism, and economy of presence in social conventions at mere face value. The difference, excess, or "reserve" that they disguise in their own appearances may well be precisely what they are designed to protect: not the fundamental "*différence*" of language or the ontic-ontological "difference" of Heideggerian metaphysics, but that founding "surplus" (economic, libidinal, hermeneutic) that is at once the originating contradiction of the system. Rather than "discovering" behind the "illusion" of social coherence the authentic heterogeneity that the culture thinly veils, the deconstructor may be merely uncovering that "surplus" by which the cultural hierarchy is preserved. And by acknowledging "surplus" to exceed the control of the culture, the deconstructor is serving that basic impulse of capitalism: the *naturalization* of its own contradictions.

To remain for a moment within this crudely sketched

economic rhetoric, which I confess to have appropriated from
Marx for my own purposes, the principal labor of social conventions would be the preservation and reproduction of that
founding concept of surplus value. It is only by virtue of the
"appropriation" of a portion of the labor force, of course, that
"surplus value" may constitute itself. The potential material
production of the labor force must be *transformed* into such a
surplus, and it is that transformation which is at once effected
and disguised by the arts of social conventions, by ideology. In
a cynical manner, then, one might argue that there is some
"labor" exercised by the capitalist in the production of surplus
value: such labor would be, of course, the artistry whereby the
concept of surplus value is perpetually disguised by the customary means of repression: condensation, transference, displacement, projection. Marx considers the transformation of
labor force into surplus value to follow the model of the "primitive accumulation of capital," insofar as that metamorphosis
involves a fundamental act of violence, whose very exposure as
such requires supplementary accommodations that assume the
forms of law, science, government and—in our context—art,
philosophy, and the rest of the "humanities."[6] These forces of
the superstructure are not just mechanical agents of the basic
economic force of surplus value—indeed, the very origin and
nature of surplus value already implicate these other forces in
its very constitution as the essence of capitalism. At the most
elementary level, of course, the "arts" whereby surplus value is
extracted are operative in basic processes within capitalist economics: the seeming naturalness of the time of the workday; the
presumed equivalence of the exchange of labor force for wages
(in which the compulsion of the worker and the arbitrary
choice of the capitalist are forgotten); the natural "organicism"
of capital itself—its "will-to-grow" represented in terms of
natural laws.[7] Even these basic transformations of subjective
relations into apparently objective economic laws might be
said to employ *rhetorical* strategies developed in purer and
more complex forms in the various discourses of the superstructure: from the bureaucracy to the academy.

It is fair to conclude as Michael Ryan has that such a system "will always contain a potentially dispersive, disruptive, and heterogeneous force pushing against its bounds and limits, simply because the system is established as a repressive homogenization; where there is coercion, there will be resistance; where there is forced closure, there is the possibility of rupture."[8] For some of these very reasons, however, the system *employs* heterogeneity in the very course of its reductive will toward homogenization, normalization, or conventionalization. Before we rush too hastily to fetishize the heterogeneity, difference, marginality, supplementarity, "openness," or "otherness" produced unwittingly by the contradictions of bourgeois society and thereby serving as its proper alternatives, we ought to understand more clearly the ways in which that society employs a certain heterogeneity and difference for the sake of its own founding surpluses.

Taking the capitalist surplus, then, in this broader framework, we may describe it as that which grounds the laws of the culture while presuming to escape the constraints of those laws. By giving the laws, it presumes to be above those laws, very much in the sense that Derrida has defined the "center" in classical structures: "Thus it has always been thought that the center, which is by definition unique, constituted the very thing within a structure which governs structure, while escaping structurality."[9] Even within a capitalist economy's values, such a definition could be judged valid for surplus value: the "objectification" of surplus value as "wages" nevertheless requires a transformation of that surplus. As Marx understood, the capitalist means of transformation in this presumed exchange is precisely what serves to disguise the surplus as such: "In wage-labour . . . even surplus labour, or unpaid labour, appears as paid. . . . The money-relation conceals the uncompensated labour of the wage-labourer."[10] In one regard, the surplus value in its relentless will-to-grow is, like Hegel's *Geist*, always "ahead" of the law, governing the formation of social values and conventions just insofar as it remains evasive: "itself" defined by its perpetual futurity, ideality, or what the capitalist might term its ultimate "reinvestment." Like Heidegger's "Being of beings," it is recognized only as it is other, thus essentialized in its very "self-concealedness."[11] In such a tradition, then, it assumes the appearance of a constitutive difference motivating the inadequate representations (in economics, read: "objectifications") of the society and prompting the sort of romantic "striving" inherent to a capitalist economy and its class structure. Another way to conceive of such a difference or heterogeneity, of course, would be to recognize it as an "effect," the consequence of the repressions required for the social code to preserve its authority by projecting its internal contradictions as problems to be overcome, always in the course of *Aufhebung*.

The essential and founding concept of "surplus" may be disguised by means of *condensation*, in which its heterogeneity is repressed by those conventions that would resolve its difference. It may also be hidden by means of a strategic *deferral*, whereby its structural conceptuality permits it to remain always above and beyond its historical manifestations, always at the "end" of history. Yet it may also work its "arts" by virtue of *transference* and *projection*, inventing spurious, extemporized "surpluses" and excesses to deflect attention from itself. It is this function of *transference* that most interests me, especially when we consider those presumed "marginalities" and "othernesses" that the deconstructor would mark as the sites of a contrary, transvaluing cultural movement. Themselves the product of repression by the dominant ideology, they would appear to assume independent forms by virtue of their exclusion. As products or effects of repression, however, they still carry the traces of that displacement. In this context, "exclusion" is an inadequate term, insofar as their exclusion is not absolute but only *provisional*. Such marginalities and excesses are *permitted to exist* by the dominant ideology, insofar as they preserve their eccentric relations to the center. As such they may serve very concrete purposes in the preservation of the dominant ideology, diverting public attention from that founding surplus on which the ideology draws to reproduce itself in the interests of "growth" and "development." In such a manner does a society perpetuate xenophobia, for example, through which it projects and transfers its internal contradictions to assume forms of "external" aggression. Out of this crude paradigm of xenophobia, we might develop more particular notions of imperialism, as well as attitudes toward ethnic or sexual minorities that argue for their otherness to the norms of society. In an analogous sense, the marginalized discourses of the humanities, especially marked in Western bourgeois culture on account of their demonstrable impotence and their contrary threat as "subversive," may well be subject to similar appropriation to those other margins invented to "frame" the culture and thereby deflect the gaze from the central artifice.

Kant's "aesthetic judgment" may be considered an instance of this sort of transference, and it is an especially important example because it has attracted Derrida's own attention. Because Derrida's "Economimesis" (1975) and "The Parergon" (1974–1978) deconstruct Kant's *Critique of Judgment* according to the ways in which the philosophical and social excesses of "taste," "aesthetic pleasure," "beauty," and "mimesis" secretly function in service of a social hierarchy and its epistemological laws, these works should help us measure the extent to which Derrida's own notions of marginality and supplementarity succumb to or resist such appropriation by the dominant ideology.[12] Given the rigor of Kant's transcendental deduction in the *Critique of Pure Reason* and its practical consequences in the second *Critique*, the "subjective universals" governing aesthetic judgment and the waywardness of figurative language with which Kant must work in the third *Critique* would seem to argue for that work as a sort of appendix to the system, an "afterthought" suggestive of analogies to other forms of reason and understanding developed with more certainty in the first two critiques. Kant's third *Critique* thus would appear to be doubly marginal: first, as eccentric to the architectonics of the philosophical scheme; second, as eccentric to the normative discourse of the culture by virtue of its "aesthetic" and "philosophical" method.

Nevertheless, it is now generally accepted that the third *Critique* is the means by which Kant relates the laws of cognition with an ultimately unknowable nature—"das Ding an sich" whose bracketing is the indispensable first step in the transcendental deduction of the categories in the first *Critique*. Rather than serving merely as an appendix to the system, then, artistic representation is the means by which nature returns to that system, albeit by means of a shadowy and irreducibly metaphoric detour. The freedom that art couples with its disinterested contemplation—that intransitivity exceeding the animality of transitive appetites (*Lust*)—is not a particular freedom (such as the artistic harmony of imagination and understanding in a specific composition) but liberty in general, a natural liberty imitated in the productive processes (not the products themselves) of artistic representation. Whereas freedom (of *Genuss,* of artistic free play, etc.) functions in the judgment of taste as a consequence of that judgment's difference from a cognitive judgment—viz., that it "is not *grounded* on concepts, nor yet *intentionally directed* to them" (#5, p. 49), such freedom would appear closer to frivolity and license than to the concept of "liberty." In this regard it would certainly seem eccentric to the moral governance operative in the second *Critique*. Insofar as "the good is good for every rational being in general" (#5, p. 49) and thus governs the very concept of Reason, aesthetic judgment would seem to belong to a special class, subordinate to the rule of the Good (*Gut*) but not entirely circumscribed by its laws. The "subjective universality" of aesthetic judgments remains eccentric to the apparently demonstrable universality (the necessity) of the a priori categories; that "subjective universality" cannot be understood completely by transcendental deduction: "Since an aesthetic judgment is not an objective or cognitive judgment, this necessity is not derivable from definite concepts, and so is not apodictic" (#18, p. 81).

It is worth noting here that the "indeterminable" qualities of aesthetic judgment (viz., with reference to concepts) and of the function of genius are complements to those other indeterminacies that Kant finds generally in those schematizing functions mediating mind and nature, concept and sensible manifold, as in the following comment on the schematism of the pure concepts of the understanding in the first *Critique*: "This schematism of our understanding, in its application to appearances and their mere form, is an art concealed in the depths of the human soul, whose real modes of activity nature is hardly likely ever to allow us to discover, and to have open to our gaze."[13] Such indeterminacy belongs to the "excess" of nature itself, and for that reason needs to be analogized or symbolized in relation to those cognitive functions, unless we are to understand such functions as purely contingent, characteristics of a "monstrous" or "aberrant" humanity. The third *Critique* thus works to produce such analogies or symbolic relations, in order to assure some concordance between the productive laws of mind and those of nature, as well as between the liberty essential for moral judgment and the necessity of natural law.

In aesthetical judgments, "the cognitive powers . . . are here engaged in a free play, since no definite concept restricts them to a particular rule of cognition" (#9, p. 58). The subjective universality of beauty is based on the "harmonious activity" of this "free play" of imagination and understanding: "The quickening of both faculties (imagination and understanding) to an indefinite, but yet, thanks to the given representation, harmonious activity, such as belongs to cognition generally, is the sensation whose universal communicability is postulated by the judgment of taste" (#9, p. 60). In a sense, aesthetical judgment serves as a "test" of the orderliness and harmony whereby our cognitive faculties function together with our processes of intuition (that is, perception). In this regard, the criterion of "purposiveness without purpose" whose effect is "disinterested contemplation" of the beautiful would seem to have little to do with the cognitive orders, which are determined by their conceptual purposes. In fact, "purposiveness without purpose" is the "symbol" of an unknowable natural order that is presumed in the operation of ordinary cognition.

Kant distinguishes the "beautiful" from the "sublime"

with great care, but the effect of the dynamical sublime has clear affinities with one function of aesthetic ideas: "They furnish an *aesthetic idea,* which serves the above rational idea as a substitute for logical presentation, but with the proper function, however, of animating the mind by opening out for it a prospect into a field of kindred representations stretching beyond its ken" (#49, pp. 177–178). Indeed, this conception of aesthetic ideas helps gloss the very experience of the dynamic sublime. As Frederick Copleston has summarized its operation: "The dynamical sublime is experienced . . . when we are confronted with the spectacle of the terrible physical power of Nature but when at the same time we find in our mind and reason a superiority to this physical might."[14] "Superiority" may be a misleading term in this context, since what "aesthetic ideas" in their free play demonstrate for us is that the infinity of nature has its analogy in the mind—an infinity symbolized by the capacity of mind in aesthetic judgments to reproduce the "free play of imagination and understanding." It is this free play, in its reproductive power, that founds the subjective universal on which beauty is based:

> As the subjective universal communicability of the mode of representation in a judgment of taste is to subsist apart from the presupposition of any definite concept, it can be nothing else than the mental state present in the free play of imagination and understanding (so far as these are in mutual accord, as is requisite for *cognition in general*): for we are conscious that this subjective relation suitable for cognition in general must be just as valid for every one, and consequently as universally communicable, as is any determinate cognition, which always rests upon that relation as its subjective condition. (#9, p. 58)

It is insufficient merely to observe that the architectonics of the Kantian system meet the requirements of Derrida's classical, centered structure. The *infinity* of nature qualifies the necessity of its laws in a manner homologous with the ways that the "free play" of imagination and understanding in aesthetical judgments qualifies the logic of Kant's transcendental deduction to make moral freedom a necessary correlative (rather than mere contingency or additive). The indemonstrable conformity of natural and cognitive laws is symbolized not merely in aesthetic judgments but in the very form of Kant's method in the third *Critique*. I need only recall for you how the "four moments" in the Analytic of Beauty follow precisely the four logical forms of judgment (quality, quantity, relation, and modality); this is a formal symmetry that is in no way required by the Kantian system, since "beauty" has already been defined in terms eccentric to those cognitive forms of judgment. Derrida considers this symmetry to be the indication of how Kant must "force" his argument in order to disguise the formal artistry of the third *Critique* with the mask of philosophical order and coherence: "The frame of this analytic of the beautiful with its four moments was thus provided by the transcendental analytic for the single, unhappy reason that imagination, the essential resource in the relation of beauty, may *perhaps* be linked with understanding, that some understanding may perhaps still reside within it. The relation with understanding, which is neither certain nor essential, provides the frame for the entire discourse and, within it, for the discourse on the frame" (*P*, p. 31).

Thus the two critical surplus in Kant—art and nature— become the very props of the cognitive scheme, even as both clearly exceed the analytic critiera. "Purposiveness without purpose" might be read symbolically as an appropriate description of nature's function in and for itself: the active, willful, productive process whose only end is its reproduction of itself as such, and whose "infinity" assures that its perpetual differentiation might be contained within the bounds of such a conceptuality. The last word—"conceptuality"—recalls Derrida's detailed deconstruction of this system, insofar as "nature" appears within the Kantian text only by virtue of that conceptualization initiated by the "bracketing" of nature. The very moment in which "nature" is symbolized as that which exceeds the limits of a transcendental deduction, then the system begins a subtle and devious process of hierarchization, whose *telos* is the subordination of human reason, understanding, judgment, morality, and taste to an enveloping "natural" order.

In terms of the economic analogies we followed earlier, this process of "naturalization" may be said to have certain affinities with the naturalizing impulses in capitalism, insofar as the economic system must work to disguise its contradictions as natural processes. Derrida reads this impulse in the Kantian text in direct proportion to the "hierarchizing" we have noted above:

> Distinct from science, art in general (it is not yet a question of the "Beaux-Arts") is not reduced to trade (*Handwerk*). That which exchanges the value of its labor for wages is a mercenary art (*Lohnkunst*). Art proper is free and liberal (*freie*); its production ought not to enter the economic circle of commerce, of offer and demand: it ought not exchange itself. Liberal art and mercenary art thus do not form a binary opposition. The one is higher than the other, more "art" than the other; it has more value by not having a greater economic value. (*E/M*, p. 61)

The implication of this intransitivity in the "labor" of mimesis (expressed well in Derrida's catachresis, the neologism "*economimesis*") is quite clearly that: "The pure and free productivity ought to resemble that of nature" (*E/M*, p. 67). Carefully, strategically, in his own way playfully, Derrida demonstrates how an economics of "surplus value" always already governs the Kantian text, thus prompting Kant's counter-move to assert the "autonomy" of his philosophical investigation from any concrete historical situation. Thus Kant works to trivialize the use- and exchange-values operative in economic systems, virtually equating them as substitute gratifications that merely mime a more profound ontological need. This need to have and experience *being as such* (being human) may inform moral judgments, but it may be *thought* only in the symbolic form of aesthetic contemplation, which neither uses nor exchanges that which meets its desire.

The critical surplus in the Kantian system that we have called for convenience "intransitivity" is not merely the product or effect of "genius"; it is the essence of genius. Kant analyzes the two characteristics of genius as "spirit" and "originality." "Spirit" is that animation resulting from the harmonious play of imagination and understanding: tautologically, "the faculty of presenting *aesthetic ideas*" (#49, p. 175). The "originality" of genius causes Kant even greater problems, because it is defined by its very transgression of the conceptual limits of cognition: "Aesthetically it is free to furnish of its own accord, over and above that agreement with the concept, *a wealth of undeveloped material* for the understanding, to which the latter paid no regard in its concept, but which it can make use of, not so much objectively for cognition, as subjectively for quickening the cognitive faculties, and hence also indirectly for cognitions . . ." (#49, p. 179; my emphasis). Thus genius consists of an originality "which science cannot teach nor industry learn, enabling one to find out ideas for a given concept, and, besides, to hit upon the *expression* for them—the expression by means of which the subjective mental condition induced by the ideas as the concomitant of a concept may be communicated to others" (#49, pp. 179–80).

Quite predictably, Derrida emphasizes the indeterminacy of genius' originality, but this indeterminacy is clearly and explicitly part of Kant's system, rather than some uncanny appearance that escapes the constraints of the philosophy. This indeterminacy enables the Kantian text to appeal to an "outside," a nature, which now assumes the power of "inspiration" that grants to genius (and *through* genius) all that which is unavailable in the pure concept. Derrida's analysis makes explicit the relation between this "inspiration" and the "surplus value" that is the *conscious product* of the Kantian text:

> The poetic gift, contents and ability, wealth and act, is an ever-increasing giving as a giving by God to the poet, which transmits by permitting in that supplementary surplus-value [*plus-value*] the return to the infinite source: that which can't be lost. By definition, if one can speak of

infinity. All of which ought to occur by the voice. The ingenious [*ingenium* in Kant entangles "natural disposition" and "genius"] poet is the voice of God who gives him voice, who gives Himself and in giving Himself gives, gives himself that which gives, Himself gives the giving (*Gabe* and *es gibt* [*Gift/Presentation* and *there is/it gives*]), freely playing with himself, not breaking the infinite circle of contractual exchange that by making a contract with itself makes an infinite pact. As soon as the infinite gives itself (to thought), the opposition between the economy of limits and the general economy, between circulation and extravagant productivity tends to efface itself. (*E/M*, pp. 71–72)

Thus poetry (the highest form of the Beaux-Arts for Kant) employs its intricate ingenuity, in order to invent the supersensible realm to disguise, to conceptualize the very surplus, excess, or extravagance informing its discourse. Poetry "invigorates the mind by letting it feel its faculty—free, spontaneous, and independent of determination by nature—of regarding and estimating nature as phenomenon in the light of aspects which nature of itself does not afford us in experience, either for sense or understanding, and of employing it accordingly in behalf of, and as a sort of schema for, the supersensible. It plays with semblance, which it produces at will, but not as an instrument of deception; for its avowed pursuit is merely one of play, which, however, understanding may turn to good account and employ for its own purpose" (#53, pp. 191–192). Such "play" is not the product of deconstruction nor is it a "deceptive" illusion for Kant; declaring itself as such, it functions within the system and facilitates the "exercise" of the understanding. *Mere* play? *Self-conscious* fiction? *Metapoetic* awaiting its application by the understanding? Or already a transference of another sort of "play," the theatricality of the economic system in its specific substitutions of exchange for use? The capitalist surplus is at work here, *reinvested* for the sake of its reproduction as "poetry" and "philosophy," those systems whereby the hierarchy of the supersensible to the sensible, the transcendental to the material, is constructed and sustained. All by means of a most "natural" process, a process of "naturalization," which must ground such nature on the abstract concept of "infinity." This infinity escapes ordinary contracts—uses and exchanges—because its contract is that exchange which uses only its name, which is the perpetual telling of its name in those exchanges by which it circulates. Here I recur to the Heideggerian commentary that Derrida permits to contaminate his own interpretation of Kant, by way of explaining what Derrida considers the emergence from Kant (via Hegel) of that "surplus," that "most dangerous supplement," which will assume the intermediate form of the Heideggerian "*Sagen*": "*The moving force in Showing of Saying is Owning. It is what brings all present and absent beings each into their own, from which they show themselves in what they are, and where they abide according to their kind. This owning which brings them there, and which moves Saying as Showing in its showing we call Appropriation.*"[15]

Derrida recognizes how the metaphysics of the concept and consciousness, following the metaphysics of capitalism, carries over into a metaphysics of language, for which a similar deconstruction is necessary in the reading of the Heideggerian text. The implications of Derrida's reading of the poetic and ultimately metaphysical surplus in Kant is that "that most dangerous supplement" of language that threatens the will-to-truth, order, and coherence of logocentrism may also be turned, detoured into the service of that very logocentrism it would escape. Derrida's reading of Kant makes it clear that the indeterminate functions deliberately within that system, not as its unwitting by-product or unacknowledged contradiction. The task of locating indeterminacy and even "free play" within the third *Critique* is merely the ordinary labor of reading the text's own intentions. What makes Derrida's reading deconstructive, I think, is the extent to which he demonstrates the complicity of the "indeterminate" with notions of the "infinite," showing thereby how readily such a schema for the supersensible may carry a certain political force, serving the interests of ideology by subordinating material production to its "higher" law. At the same time, such a "higher law" operates in a discourse (philosophy, poetry, theory), whose very labor is to assure its exile from that material world. In this regard, such a discourse "saves" the capitalist surplus as a "concept" by situating it in a complex history whose end is the bracketing of the determining forces of material life. The capitalist surplus *hides* in this supersensible domain, disguised by that transference operating between different orders of discourse, each of which would have us understand its forms as discrete and autonomous. The forces of the dominant ideology may well effect the most skillful forms of *transcoding* and *intertextuality*.

When we imagine that the "reserve" "supplement," "margin," or "horizon" are terms descriptive of that which has been left out or excluded—unrecognized by the dominant ideology, we do so in an extremely naive manner, generally governed by a simple and mechanical model for social or psychic repression. The margin and the supplement ought not to be fetishized as alternative "concepts"; they are always the belated effects of the formation of powerful conventions. Shaped by that repression, carrying its traces in their very means and purposes, they often recuperate its values—and then *not*, as we might wish, in an inverted or negative form. If we set "heterogeneity" against the "homogeneity" apparently willed by logocentric culture, then we may end up affirming merely that secret heterogeneity, that production of a ruling "difference," whereby the authority of logocentrism preserves itself as "other," as "beyond the law."

In short, the cultural margin and surplus should not merely be extracted *analytically* from the dynamic relation of the manifest and latent forces of the social *code*. *Analytically, code*: these words indicate already how far removed from deconstruction such a method would be. The "location" of the margin and surplus must also involve a *transformation*, that deconstructive *estrangement* that would marginalize, rather than recenter, the margin of the dominant ideology. A certain *contamination* must be effected; this contamination may be a transgression of the apparently discrete boundaries of the different cultural discourses. Thus Derrida would expose the political and economic values governing Kant's philosophy, just as Marx would reveal the metaphysical and philosophical assumptions operating within the economic sphere. In "Economimesis," Derrida playfully transforms the indeterminacy that Kant freely acknowledges in the judgment of taste into an interplay of "taste/dislike" (goût/dégoût), an interplay already suggested in the relation Kant establishes between Beauty and the Sublime (Schöne/Erhabene), insofar as the genius that effects such beauty already relies on its "illimitable" qualities of spirit (Geist) and originality. All of this still belongs to the Kantian analysis and is not yet deconstructive, but Derrida transforms the surplus produced in the "higher" labor of art into just that which cannot be digested, cannot be mastered by the mouth (and thus, the voice), that which exceeds the "use" served by appetitive desire (Lust). Genuss is thus paradoxically entangled with the production of bodily wastes, of the body as waste: excretion or vomit in Derrida's deliberate confusion of the Freudian oral and anal: "The word 'vomit' arrests a vicarious dislike [dégoût]; it puts the thing in the mouth, substitutes, but only by example, the oral for the anal. It is determined by the system of beauty, 'symbol of morality,' as its other: it is thus for philosophy an elixir [like a 'paregoric,' in Derrida's play of 'parergon' and 'paregoric' earlier], in its very bad taste" (E/M, p. 93).

The governing concept of "surplus" in Kant and, implicitly, in capitalism is transformed by Derrida's own metaphoric jouissance into a "waste product," but this transformation occurs only by Derrida's manipulation of those terms he has drawn from the Kantian system (à vomir from sich zu erbrechen in section 21 of Kant's Anthropology, concerning the hierarchy of the senses). One might judge this merely clever "wordplay," if Derrida had remained exclusively within a philosophical order of discourse. In "Economimesis," however, Derrida's wordplays are designed to transgress the boundaries separating philosophy from economics, Kant from capitalism, by means of a method that crosses Derrida's characteristic deconstructive strategies with those of Marx. In these crossings (*catachreses*), Derrida has already begun the work of flushing out of hiding those forces of the dominant ideology which have taken cover in the "abstract," "impotent" discourses fixed on the supersensible: philosophy, poetry, theory. In this way, Derrida helps demonstrate how the very "powerlessness" of such humanistic discourses is in fact their most powerful resource, the means by which they serve the dominant ideology by protecting its founding concepts—in this context, the economic concept of "surplus value."

Such strategic supplementarity locates the margins and boundaries of its textual object by following the logic of its retentions and then by transgressing deliberately the determined and determining frame. To "marginalize" in deconstructive practice is always already to demonstrate how the center governs its own margins, which is to do no more perhaps than merely demonstrate a self-evident abstraction (albeit more complicated and far less self-evident in its actual historical manifestations): "A frame is in essence constructed and therefore fragile, this is the essence or the truth of the frame. If such a thing exists. But this 'truth' can no longer be a 'truth,' it defines neither the transcendent nor the contingent character of the frame. . . . Philosophy wants to examine this 'truth,' but never succeeds. That which produces and manipulates the frame sets everything in motion to efface its effect, most often by naturalizing it to infinity, in God's keeping (to be confirmed by Kant)" (*P*, p. 33). Only Derrida's insistence upon the "fragility" of the frame (the consequence of its "constructed" nature) deserves our renewed criticism. One of the means by which the ideology "sets everything in motion" to "efface" the "effect" of the frame is to construct other "frames," Potemkin margins, whereby the effect of *the constitutive frame* is disguised, displaced. Deconstruction, too, is thus always already a "reframing," despite its best efforts at lucidity (that is, vagrancy); it must therefore be especially wary that the means of its reframing inside and outside do not easily and readily serve the purposes of the ideology deconstruction would "put in question."

Deconstruction can avoid some of these dangers by insisting upon the transgression of the boundaries or the frames distinguishing material and immaterial forces, between the "sensible" and the "supersensible." The deconstructor's customary concern with philosophic or literary traditions need not result in charges of "formalism," if the deconstructor's purpose is to demonstrate how within the apparent "closure" of such an order other formations of political and historical power are at work. The task for deconstruction would thus be the rigorous examination of all such pretensions to closure and discreteness, in order to show how such claims work to disguise the material forces of culture, to demonstrate, for example, the political content of philosophy or literature. Such a method of reading would not fetishize "openness" or "anti-formalism" in and of itself—as some ideal alternative, but merely follow the lead or logic of "closure" to understand better the values it produces. Insofar as "intertextuality" concerns discourses already assumed by convention to belong within the "humanities" and thus concerned with values other than those operative in the political and economic spheres, then "intertextuality" merely reinforces the cohesion of the humanities in their apparent impotence and secret agency for the ideology. I would argue for an intertextuality that would transgress rather than reinforce the institutional coherence of the humanities, whether such intertextuality begins *internally* (as Derrida's functions in "Economimesis" and "Parergon") or takes the leap into the more explicitly material discourses of the culture. In this latter regard, then, we ought to be concerned, for example, with the ways in which certain "literary" strategies and "rhetorical" means inform the operation of certain economic processes, government institutions, and even technological activities (the metaphysics of technological research, production, and marketing, for example). Such intertextuality would avoid the repetition of the vague liberalism of the "interdisciplinary studies" so popular in America in the 1960s—studies that unwittingly reinforced a hermetic conception of the humanities and thus permitted the existing social order to continue virtually unchanged. It would also avoid repeating the illusion of "unified culture," in the liberal sense that the culture's forces constitute a simple "infrastructure" available to analysis, to transcendental deduction. Instead, such an intertextuality would demonstrate the ways in which multiple forces work diversely to preserve certain effects—effects demonstrable in concrete and historical experience, the results of a complex genealogy of the expressed and repressed, forces of determination and delimitation as well as of "freedom" and "choice."

For similar reasons, we ought to be careful not to valorize merely apparent forces of heterogeneity, supplementarity, and *différance*, until we have understood more precisely how similar forces may be made to do the work of the dominant ideology. Deconstruction ought to give way to a more demonstrable and aggressive sociopolitical practice, rather than remaining merely a strategy for reading the humanistic tradition. In this regard, I have great admiration for the courage of Michael Ryan and other recent theorists, who have attempted to sketch the implications of deconstruction for such a social practice. I find Ryan's proposal especially attractive:

> The displacement of instance into function would operate politically and economically as the replacement of privilege, bureaucratic control, autocracy, and hierarchically invested power by radical democracy and as the replacement of the instance of economic power by a social function of distribution, autonomous self-control, and dissemination, that is, production and circulation without exchange. It is for this reason that I would argue that deconstruction is a philosophical pretext for socialism that would be radically democratic and egalitarian in nature. The instances of conceptual or methodological power which Derrida attacks in metaphysical philosophy have always served political-economic interests.[16]

Even as we attempt to particularize a notion of this sort as a historical practice, we ought to be aware that the fetishization of heterogeneity, marginality, and supplementarity as governing concepts may well recuperate the powers we would transvalue. I do not mean by this merely that such valorization will replace one hierarchy with another: this is an old argument most often employed by liberals secretly afraid of revolutionary change. Rather, I would warn deconstruction to be careful to understand the extent to which the "margin" is always already constituted by its exclusion, by a powerful act of cultural repression. A revolutionary function for woman in western culture must not confuse itself with the "fragmentary, scattered remains" of that "sexuality" defined by its denial in patriarchal culture.[17] A revolutionary conception of American foreign policies regarding the Third World, for example, must avoid using the notion of "cultural differences" in the same ways that previous imperialistic efforts have done in order to disguise colonial enterprises as the interests of "self-determination." A revolutionary effort with regard to the liberation of ethnic minorities must avoid repeating those arguments concerning "difference" and "cultural plurality" that would offer the specious "liberty" of the autochthonous ghetto or barrio.[18]

In a similar sense, I would argue that the linguistic supplement or psychic reserve may well be a disguise for a surplus that has very practical and concrete consequences in capitalism. Such affinities are all the more dangerous, just in proportion as the "supplement" or "reserve" is imagined to symbolize a certain "infinity"—a linguistic or psychic *potentia*—that exists *outside* and *prior to* originating acts of social determination. I would also contend that the mystification of such potent deconstructive strategies may result from a "theorizing" that remains distinct from the practices of reading particular formations of historical power. Such "theory" that would remain aloof from such practice is all the more prone to transform very concrete forms of marginality, supplementarity, and difference into collective abstractions: those "concepts" that might be used to govern material functions. Compelled by his followers and critics into giving interviews, writing "position papers," and otherwise institutionalizing the diverse strategies of his readings, Derrida himself has often lapsed into this fetishism of interpretative strategies as concepts with discrete values. The labor of the present moment, then, should involve a searching critique of how such "concepts" have emerged from the traditions of the humanities (from their conventions) and how they continue to support the values of the dominant ideology. Such an interrogation of our deconstructive methods, given deconstruction's rejection of any naive "self-consciousness," would not be merely a reflective or meditative enterprise, in the manner of phenomenology's presumed "transcendentalism." Such questioning would further our understanding of the power and adaptability of cultural conventions, overcoming our crude paradigms for the ways in which fictions emerge and endure. Such a critique would also result in our renewed commitment to understand the functional relations between humanistic and political-economic discourses, and it would substitute an active and productive method of interpreting social reality for a reactive and narcissistic "theorizing" within the humanities.

Notes

1. Notably Edward Said, "The Problem of Textuality: Two Exemplary Positions," Critical Inquiry (Summer 1978), 4:673–714; Frank Lentricchia, After the New Criticism (Chicago: University of Chicago Press, 1980), pp. 188–210. Michael Ryan, Marxism and Deconstruction: A Critical Articulation (Baltimore: Johns Hopkins University Press, 1982), p. 35 and elsewhere, observes more generally that "deconstruction lacks a social theory and that this is not an extrinsic or accidental oversight but an intrinsic fault, because deconstruction points toward the possibility and necessity of such theory without ever providing one." Fredric Jameson, in The Prison-House of Language: A Critical Account of Structuralism and Russian Formalism (Princeton: Princeton University Press, 1972), Marxism and Form: Dialectical Theories of Literature (Princeton: Princeton University Press, 1971), and The Political Unconscious: Narrative as a Socially Symbolic Act (Ithaca, N.Y.: Cornell University Press, 1981), mounts the most sustained, sophisticated, and convincing of the attacks on deconstruction's failure to transcend its own humanistic boundaries.

2. Kant, Critique of Judgement, James Creed Meredith, tr. (Oxford: Oxford University Press, 1952), section 45, p. 167. Further references in the text by section number and page.

3. Derrida, "White Mythology: Metaphor in the Text of Philosophy," in Margins of Philosophy, Alan Bass, tr. (Chicago: University of Chicago Press, 1982), p. 210: "Abstract notions always hide a sensory figure. And the history of metaphysical language is said to be confused with the erasure of the efficacity of the sensory figure and the usure of its effigy. The word itself is not pronounced, but one may decipher the

double import of *usure*: erasure by rubbing, exhaustion, crumbling away, certainly; but also the supplementary product of a capital, the exchange which far from losing the original investment would fructify its initial wealth, would increase its return in the form of revenue, additional interest, linguistic surplus value, the two histories of the meaning of the word remaining indistinguishable."

4. Marx, *Theories of Surplus Value* (Moscow: Progress Publishers, 1975), 1:158, for example: "A writer is a productive labourer not in so far as he produces ideas, but in so far as he enriches the publisher who publishes his works, or if he is a wage-labourer for a capitalist."

5. Marx, *Capital: A Critique of Political Economy*, Ben Fowkes, tr. (New York: Random House, 1976), 1:651.

6. *Ibid.*, 1:915–916, in reference to the colonization of the Americas, Marx writes: "These methods depend in part on brute force, for instance the colonial system. But they will employ the power of the state, the concentrated and organized force of society, to hasten, as in a hothouse, the process of transformation of the feudal mode of production into a capitalist mode, and to shorten the transition. Force is the midwife of every old society which is pregnant with a new one. It is itself an economic power."

7. In his interpretation of Marx's *Grundrisse*, Michael Ryan in *Marxism and Deconstruction*, p. 58, observes: "Much of what passes for 'objective' materiality or 'natural' law in the economy is in fact a concretization of relations whose provenance is social and historical and which include a subjective component. This is the significance of defining constant or fixed capital as past objectified labor."

8. *Ibid.*, p. 95.

9. Derrida, "Structure, Sign, and Play in the Discourse of the Human Sciences," in *The Languages of Criticism and the Sciences of Man: The Structuralist Controversy*, Richard Macksey and Eugenio Donato, eds. (Baltimore, Md.: Johns Hopkins University Press, 1970), p. 248.

10. Marx, *Capital*, 1:680.

11. Heidegger's paradoxical formulation of the "measure" of Being as that which manifests itself as "concealed in its self-concealment" in "'... Poetically Man Dwells ...,'" *Poetry, Language, Thought*, Albert Hofstadter, tr. (New York: Harper and Row, 1971), p. 223, is given more explicit expression in the following passage from *An Introduction to Metaphysics*, Ralph Mannheim, tr. (Garden City, N.Y.: Doubleday, 1959), p. 66: "Thus the word 'being' is indefinite in meaning and yet we understand it definitely. 'Being' proves to be totally indeterminate and at the same time highly determinate. From the standpoint of the usual logic we have here an obvious contradiction. Something that contradicts itself cannot be. There is no such thing as a square circle. And yet we have this contradiction: determinate, wholly indeterminate being. If we decline to delude ourselves, and if we have a moment's time to spare amid all the activities and diversions of the day, we find ourselves standing in the very middle of this contradiction. And this 'stand' of ours is more real than just about anything else that we call real; it is more real than dogs and cats, automobiles and newspapers." It would be interesting to subject this claim for the "reality" of the contradiction of "being" to the sort of analysis I offer in the rest of this paper.

12. Derrida's "Economimesis" first appeared in *Mimesis des articulations*, in the series, "La Philosophie en effet," directed by Derrida, Sarah Kofman, Philippe Lacoue-Labarthe, Jean-Luc Nancy (Paris: Aubier-Flammarion, 1975), pp. 57–93. Further references included in the text as: *E/M*; English translations are my own. "Parergon" forms

the first part of *La Vérité en peinture* (Paris: Flammarion, 1978). The second section, "Le Parergon," has been translated into English by Craig Owens as "The Parergon," in *October* (1979), 9:3–40. Further references to the English translation are included in the text as: *P*.

13. Kant, *Critique of Pure Reason*, Norman Kemp Smith, tr. (New York: St. Martin's Press, 1929), p. 183.

14. Frederick Copleston, S. J., *Modern Philosophy, Part II: Kant*, vol. 7 in *A History of Philosophy*, 8 vols. (Garden City, N.Y.: Doubleday, 1960), p. 156.

15. Heidegger, "The Way to Language," *On the Way to Language*, Peter D. Hertz, tr. (New York: Harper and Row, 1971), p. 127. Given the particular verbal subtleties on which this passage turns, I quote here the original German from *Unterwegs zur Sprache* (Pfullingen: Günther Neske, 1959), p. 258:

> *Das Regende im Zeigen der Sage ist das Eignen.*
> Es erbringt das An- und Abwesende in sein jeweilig Eigenes, aus dem dieses sich an ihm selbst zeigt und nach seiner Art verweilt. Das erbringende Eignen, das die Sage also die Zeige in ihrem Zeigen regt, heisse das Ereignen.

16. Ryan, *Marxism and Deconstruction*, pp. 42–43.

17. Luce Irigaray, from *Ce sexe qui n'en est pas un*, in *New French Feminisms*, Elaine Marks and Isabelle de Courtivron, eds., Claudia Reeder, tr. (New York: Schocken, 1981), p. 104.

18. I have a similar argument concerning the marginal conception of woman in the work of Luce Irigaray, the Third World and Orient in Said, and literature itself in the writings of Geoffrey Hartman in " 'To Live Outside the Law You Must Be Honest': The Authority of the Margin in Contemporary Theory," *Cultural Critique* (Winter 1985–1986), 1:35–68.

5

ACTION, SUBJECTIVITY, AND THE CONSTITUTION OF MEANING

Anthony Giddens

THE three parts of the title accurately indicate the content of the lecture. I propose to discuss each separately, then show how they interconnect. First, the problem of action is a fundamental one for sociology. A cluster of problems quite crucial to social analysis are concerned with interpretation of what it is to be a human agent, of the sorts of activity appropriate to human conduct and how these might be linked to institutions.[1]

Considerations raised under the first category lead to a confrontation with literature which largely stands outside of sociology, but which has recently been extensively discussed by social scientists: structuralism and post-structuralism. Third, these in turn raise questions of the nature of meaning, questions which have a broad significance stretching from social analysis right through to literary criticism and the theory of the text.

Although it used to be true that most of those working in the social sciences either felt themselves at a great distance from such areas of interest, or perhaps knew nothing of them at all, in more recent times it has become the case that controversies in social theory connect social analysis in a very direct way with issues belonging to those other areas.

First, then, the problem of action. In respect of the concerns of sociologists the issue of the nature of human action has to be understood in the context of a traditional division in social theory. This is a dichotomy between on the one hand what could be called "objectivism" and on the other "subjectivism." By the former of these notions I mean that perspective in social theory according to which the social object, that is society, has priority over the individual agent, and in which social institutions are regarded as the core component of interest to social analysis. Subjectivism essentially means its opposite. According to this standpoint, the human agent is treated as the prime center for social analysis. That is to say, in this view the main concern of the social sciences should be with study of the purposeful, reasoning actor. Each of these standpoints in social theory has its attractions. On the one hand, those who belong to objectivist traditions have surely been correct in arguing that society or social institutions in some sense are more enduring and are wider in scale than the concerns of the individual members of society. They have been good at analyzing problems of history, problems of large-scale social transformation, and in analyzing conflict and change generally. Those who belong on the subjectivist side have quite rightly seen us, as human agents, as beings capable of understanding the conditions of our own action, of acting intentionally, and having reasons for what we do. In this, the subjectivists are surely correct. However, if each perspective has its attractions, each also has its fundamental shortcomings. On the one hand, the objectivists are, as it were, strong on institutions but weak on action. That is to say those who belong in this kind of perspective, to which I would link authors associated with functionalism in the social sciences and with structuralism in the social sciences and in areas of literary criticism, have typically not been very adept at demonstrating the qualities which I think quite rightly have to be attributed to human agents: that is to say, self-understanding, intentionality, acting for reasons.

Those on the subjectivist side of the fence, on the other hand, have failed adequately to analyze just those phenomena which the objectivists see as so essential in the study of human conduct. Subjectivism—in which I will include the analytical philosophy of action and symbolic interactionism, among other traditions—has tended to skirt issues concerned with the long-term processes of change which occur in history and the large scale organization of institutions.[2]

The dualism between objectivism and subjectivism is deeply embedded in social analysis, and I hold it to be the case that many of the controversies which dominate social theory turn upon issues raised by this division. In the approach to social theory which I have worked out over the past five or six years, which I call structuration theory, I have proposed the argument that this seeming opposition of perspectives actually disguises a complementarity which they display. That is to say this dualism should actually be represented as a duality, a duality that I call "the duality of structure."[3] In order to understand the importance of the notion of the duality of structure in social theory it is essential to look at the concepts of both structure and action. In those approaches which treat human agents as purposive, reasoning beings, the notion of action is often understood as though it were composed of an aggregation of intentions. That is to say, the agent is not placed in the unfolding of the routines which constitute day-to-day life. This unfolding is a duration, as Schutz put it, a continuity which persists throughout the waking life of the individual. Action in other words has an essential temporality which is part of its constitution.[4]

Interpreting agency within the context of its duration is one aspect which helps link the notion of action to those concepts, that is structure, institutions, and so on, which have been so important to objectivist social scientists. To see how these connections might be made, we have however to look at the concept of structure. Among English-speaking social scientists, the concept of structure has ordinarily been understood as a received notion. In contrast, for example, to the concept of function, the idea of structure has received remarkably little discussion. Why should this be so? The reason, I think, is that most English-speaking social scientists have had a clear idea of what the concept of structure should be understood as referring to. When they talk of structure, or of "the structural properties of institutions," they have in mind a sort of visual analogy. They see the structural properties of institutions as like the girders of a building, or the anatomy of a body. Structure consists of the patterns of relationships observable in a diversity of social contexts. Now this notion of structure needs looking at, just as much as the idea of action. In the traditions of structuralism and post-structuralism, which still remain fairly alien to most of those working in the social sciences in the English-speaking countries, particularly in sociology, the concept of structure is used in a fashion quite divergent from that characteristic of Anglo-Saxon social science. The easiest way to indicate this is still by reference to Saussure's classic discussion of the structural qualities of language. Structural features of language do not exist as patterns situated in time and space, like patterns of social relationships; they consist of relationships of absences and presences embedded in instantiation of language, in speech, or in text.[5]

Structure here presumes the idea of an absent totality. To understand the sentence which the speaker utters means knowing an enormous range of rules of a syntactical and semantical kind, which are not contained within the speech act, but are nevertheless fundamental to understanding it, or to producing it. It is a parallel idea of structure (as an absent totality) which I hold to be important as a concept for the social sciences as a whole, and as basic to the notion of duality of structure. The problem with conceptualizing structure as a set of relations of presences is that structure then appears as a constraint which is "external" to action. In objectivist social science, for example the version of functionalism worked out by Durkheim, this notion of structure as constraint is quite clear and consciously elaborated.[6] But if we do conceive of structure in this fashion, it is not surprising that action appears to be limited by structural constraints which have essentially nothing to do with it. For structures limit behavior, although within those bounds—so one would have to presume—the agent is capable of acting freely. According to the notion of the duality of structure, by contrast, structure is not as such external to human action, and is not identified solely with constraint. Structure is both the medium and the outcome of the human activities which it recursively organizes. By the recursive character of social life I mean that social activity in respect of its structural properties exists in and through the use of the resources which agents make in constituting their action which at the same time reconstitutes those structural properties as qualities of the systems in question.

Institutions, or large-scale societies, have structural properties in virtue of the continuity of the actions of their component members; but those members of society are only able to carry out their day-to-day activities in virtue of their capability of instantiating those structural properties. The best way to illustrate this is by reverting to the linguistic example of Saussure, although one must be clear that such linguistic illustrations have various dangers and I do not mean to argue that society is, as structuralism proposes, like a language. When a speaker utters his sentence, he or she draws upon the range of syntactical and other rules in order to do so. But the very process of drawing upon those rules, or structural properties, serves to reproduce the overall totality which is the language. Language exists only insofar as it is produced and reproduced in contingent contexts of social life in this fashion. This I hold also to be true of social life in its generality. This is not, to repeat, because social life is like a language; it is because language is such an important feature of social activity that it expresses some of its most generic qualities. If there is any validity to them, these ideas have clear connections which bear upon the theme of the "de-centering of the subject" in structuralism and post-structuralism.

One of the problems with subjectivist approaches in the social sciences and elsewhere is that subjectivity is taken as a given. It is not regarded as a phenomenon to be explicated but is taken to be the basis of what it is to be a human agent. In structuration theory, the agent is not understood as preconstituted subjectively. In this respect, I accept the fundamental importance of the critique of subjectivism developed in structuralism and post-structuralism. However, the decentering of the subject in structuralism and post-structuralism leads to the insertion of the subject in language, conceived of in a particular way—signs constituted through difference. This methodological tactic follows very directly from the premises introduced by Saussure and accepted even by many subsequent writers who were critical of that author. Structuralism and post-structuralism promote a "retreat into the code." For example, it is pointed out that the term "I," while it seems to refer to the most essential conditions of human subjectivity, is in fact a linguistic term like any other, which therefore has to be understood in relation to the remainder of the terminology built into the language. The "I" is in linguistic terms a shifter, which has no content in relation to its referent any more than the term "tree" has in relation to the object which it "stands for."

Now this critique of object theories of meaning or theories of ostensive reference is certainly in its main lines valid. However, what tends to occur in structuralist and post-structuralist traditions of thought is the disappearance of the referent altogether. Because the meaning is not the referent, any account of how one moves from the connotation of the terms within language to their extentional properties as designating, or in some way relating to, aspects of the external world becomes lost. As regards the terminology of human subjectivity, it is essential to understand that the fact that the "I" is constituted in language, and does not "mean" the body or the acting self to which the "I" refers, should not lead to a methodological disappearance of the agent. Terms like "I" and "me" may not have as their meaning the object (the body) to which they relate, but they nevertheless gain their significance from the context of activities in which human agents are implicated. They are part of the practical mastery of social relations, and of the continuity of social context which human agents display.[7]

The theme of the decentering of the subject, therefore, should not lead to the disappearance of the self as agent. This also has implications for how one understands the relation between subjectivity as consciousness and the unconscious in human conduct. According to the characteristic view of post-structuralism, the relation between the conscious and unconscious expresses, as it were, the two faces of language. The unconscious is the other side of language—what cannot be put into words because it is the organizing system through which those words derive their significance, and whereby they can be incorporated into the conscious awareness of the actor. Now there is no doubt that such discussion of the nature of the conscious/unconscious relation has proved in some respects highly illuminating. It does make some sense to say that the unconscious is "structured like a language." However, at the same time this conception obscures completely one of the most important areas of human action relating to consciousness and to unconsciousness.

I want to argue that there are two basic shortcomings in relation to the post-structuralist account of agency and the unconscious: (a) no account can be provided of what I call "practical consciousness"; (b) it is not possible to generate an interpretation of meaning as the use of "methods" embedded in practical consciousness. It is to ordinary language philosophy and to phenomenology that we owe an analysis of the significance of practical consciousness in human day-to-day affairs. Intentions and reasons which agents have for what they do are sometimes capable of being expressed in what they can say about the conditions of their action. In other words, agents can in some degree—fluctuating according to historically given social circumstances—give a discursive account of the circumstances of their action. But this by no means exhausts what they know about why they act as they do. Many of the most subtle and dazzlingly intricate forms of knowledge embedded in, or constitutive of, the actions we carry out are done in and through the practices which we enact. They are done knowledgeably, but they are not necessarily available to the discursive awareness of the actor. To speak a language an individual needs to know an enormously complicated range of rules, strategies, and tactics involved in language use. However, if the individual were asked to give a discursive account of what it is that he or she knows in knowing these rules, strategies, and tactics, he or she would find it very difficult indeed. The chances are that only a very trivial account would be given discursively of what is known in order to speak a language.

It is not a paradox to say that linguists spend the whole of their careers trying to find out things we already know. They are not only things we already know, in a contingent way, they are things we must know in order to be able to speak. We do not, however, know these things at a discursive level, any more than is the case in the multiple forms of practice which constitute day-to-day social activity. Any kind of account of social activity which eliminates the significance of practical consciousness is therefore massively deficient in respect of identifying the forms of knowledgeability that human agents display in the context of social life. I would include all variants of objectivism in this category. In these schools of thought human beings appear as opaque to themselves, precisely because what they know about the conditions of their action is assumed to be limited to what they can discursively say about them. All the rest is either (for functionalism) the result of forces operating in society; or (in structuralism and post-structuralism) the result of the unconscious.

Practical consciousness is in a certain sense unconscious. That is to say, it consists of forms of knowledge immediately available to discourse. But it is not unconscious in the sense in which symbols and modes of cognition which are subjects of repression are unconscious. For these latter forms of cognition cannot be translated into discourse without the influence of some kind of distorting mechanism, which depends upon (the bar of) repression which is placed upon them. I do wish to accept that the unconscious has a fundamental role in human social activity, and I think it reasonable to argue that one can at least make considerable headway in understanding what the unconscious is by following the line of thought which holds that the unconscious "is structured like a language." But intervening between the unconscious and the conscious is practical consciousness, the underlined center of human practical activity. Here there is a set of ties not just between discourse and "the other side of language," but between the individual as an agent and the institutions which the individual constitutes and reconstitutes in the course of the duration of day-to-day activity. A good deal of what we do is organized knowledgeably in and through practical consciousness; it follows that the way in which we make sense of our own actions and the actions of others and the ways in which we generate meaning in the world are in an elemental sense methodological. What I mean by this is that the sense of words and the sense of actions does not derive solely from the differences created by sign codes, or more generically by language. It derives in a more basic way from the methods which speakers and agents use in the course of practical action, to reach "interpretations" of what they and others do.

To say that all social activity, and indeed all interpretation of meaning, is methodological is to accept the significance of ethno-methods in social life.[8] The origins of meaning are not to be traced to the referent, and not to the system of differences that constitutes language as a semiotic system, but to the methodological apparatus embedded in a practical consciousness of the routines of day-to-day social life.

It is in this sense, as I have argued in my book *Central Problems in Social Theory*,[9] that Wittgenstein is more important than Derrida. For Derrida signification derives from the play of difference in the temporal and spatial constitution of language and action. It is for this reason that, according to him, writing is the most basic form of language, because in writing we see displayed the time/space organization of differences. In Wittgenstein also, however, there is a great deal about the timing and spacing of language. But according to this second thinker, such timing and spacing, as a property of language, has to be understood in the broader contexts of the timing and spacing of the mundane activities of day-to-day life. It is in the

time/space settings which agents make use of in order to organize their day-to-day social activities that we find the origins
and the nature of meaning. This is a theorem which in a basic
sense I take to be significant for the problems under discussion.
What Wittgenstein provides is essentially a theory of praxis,
elucidated in the context of the use of ordinary language on the
one hand, and the enactment of the ordinary practices of day-
to-day social life on the other. The differences which constitute
the code, for Wittgenstein, are interpolated within all the manifold things that one can do through language. Language is the
medium of social practice, and it therefore follows that there is
no essence to what language is—even if one should seek this
essence in the differences which constitute a code.

Let me sum up so far. I think it necessary to accept the
importance of certain of the insights of structuralism, and particularly post-structuralism, for a conception of the relation
between the conscious and the unconscious in agency. Subjectivity does indeed hinge upon the use of the deictic termi-
nologies of "I," "me," etc., as linguistic shifters. It is also important to hold that the unconscious can profitably be regarded as
the other side of language—what cannot be said in language
because it is the foundation of linguistic usage. But there is
another sense of what cannot be said, and that is what has to be
done. There is a massive conceptual arena here for the re-
introduction of the skilled knowledgeable subject, whose activities are geared into the continuities of day-to-day social life,
and whose knowledgeability is expressed in practice.

The forms of knowledgeability and symbolism built into
practical consciousness are crucial to the constitution of the
agent, and also probably to the stability of personality. One of
the best demonstrations of this, I think, is still to be found in
Garfinkel's so-called "experiments with trust."[10] What Garfinkel did was to disturb, in what seems to be a very minor way,
some of the somewhat more apparently trivial features of day-
to-day conversation. Although seemingly so minor, such inter-
ruptions of the taken-for-granted ordering of practical consciousness have major consequences for the affectivity of

agents. The interesting thing about Garfinkel's experiments—
or one of the interesting things—is that those who had to cope
with the dislocations of speech produced by others very rapidly
displayed extraordinary anxiety in the face of what appeared to
them to be a significant departure from the expected routines of
conversation. What is thereby demonstrated is the extraordinary moral and emotional fixity which is invested in apparently trivial characteristics of day-to-day life, as well as the
methodological basis upon which they are founded.

Let me at this point move to my third theme, the implications of this analysis for the understanding of meaning. As I
have indicated previously, in structuralism as well as in post-
structuralism, meaning is understood essentially in terms of
the play of difference within linguistically constituted codes.
Meaning is to be located in a system of signs, syntagmatically
organized in the flow of context of language use, and paradig-
matically organized in terms of their association within language as a whole. Here, in spite of the divergencies, we find a
quite direct line of continuity from Saussure to Derrida. But if
meaning is (a) contextual, (b) methodological, then a quite
distinct conception of it emerges. There is a contrast between
the "fuzzy" nature of ordinary language terms and their precision in use. Words when taken in isolation—or concepts—
seem to have only a vague significance as utilized in day-to-day
discourse. In fact, if we examine sequences of talk we find that
the meaning embedded in such talk is quite precise. The participants in a conversation are able to follow what each says and
relate what is said to the referential properties which are involved. This precision is impossible to understand without
grasping the significance of practical consciousness as a medium of the constitution and re-constitution of meaning in the
day-to-day context of activity, and without accepting the methodological nature of the knowledge which it involves.

This means a basic revision of some of the major connotations of the approach deriving from structuralist and post-
structuralist thought. This type of tradition of thought inevitably leads toward the text, or more generically toward writing,

for reasons which have already been identified. If meaning is constituted through difference, and difference derives from the overall nature of the code, then the text, in which differences are most directly displayed in a sort of visual sense, appears to be the prime vehicle of meaning. It was, therefore, quite logical for Derrida to take the step of regarding writing as the prime modality of signification. However, if the approach I have suggested here is correct, we have to accept that it is *temporally and spatially situated conversation*, not the text, and not writing, which is most essential to explaining what language and meaning are. The consequences of this for social theory, I think, are very important. They essentially involve rescuing the knowledgeable agent as the conceptual center for social analysis, and situating what "knowledgeability" is in the context of the ongoing practices of social life. Social life does then not appear as a phenomenon external to agency, but is contingently produced and reproduced in the moments of social activity stretching across the time/space context of action.

This is not the same as a relapse into subjectivism, because it does not involve taking intentions or reasons as given phenomena, and it does not involve treating social life as the outcome of what pre-constituted agents do. On the other hand, it is not a form of objectivism, because according to the perspective of structuration theory, the structural properties of social systems exist only in their instantiation in specific forms of human conduct. Rather, however, than pursuing further problems of social theory as such, I shall attempt to trace out some of the implications for the theory of the text. There are four major implications which I wish to draw.

First, in respect of discussions of the nature of texts, something of a similar dualism to that which I have sketched in social theory in general can be found. On the one side, we find again structuralist and post-structuralist theories, which emphasize the autonomy of the text and its separation from the intentions which authors might put into it. According to this standpoint, the nature of texts should be explicated in terms of the play of signifiers within the code which the text forms. On the other side, there are so-called "intentionalist" theories of the text, which emphasize that to understand the significance of a particular text, or to explicate it thoroughly, one must know the intentions of the author who wrote it. It is interesting to note that this division in respect of theories of the text has a direct linkage with social theory more generally via debates in the history of ideas. On the one hand, there are writers such as Quentin Skinner, who emphasize that it is necessary to grasp the intentions of the authors of historical texts in order to make sense of the text.[11] One has to reconstruct the author's intentions and the context in which the writings in question were originally produced, because they were aimed at particular audiences and written within a particular framework.

On the other hand, opponents of this type of standpoint in the history of ideas tend to treat texts as autonomous, in the sense in which they will regard, say, Plato's writings as capable of being read without any notion of the background against which they were written. According to this second school of thought there are, so to speak, "classical texts" whose character exists very largely independently of the media in which they were originally produced. In these debates, however, the sorts of views which I have criticized earlier reappear rather plainly. Each side tends to suppose that individuals who produce texts, or indeed other works of plastic art, have a discrete set of intentions which are then somehow embodied into the text or the cultural product. Whereas one side then goes on to argue that these intentions become irrelevant to the nature of what is produced, the contrary view holds that it is necessary to retrieve these original intentions in order to grasp the significance of the phenomenon to be understood.

But according to the standpoint I have suggested, intentional human action is much more complicated than this; and is grounded in practical consciousness, not just in a discrete set or aggregate of purposes that can be simply identified. It is therefore much more appropriate to treat the production of a text as something like the ordinary day-to-day activity in which individuals participate—that is, as a process of reflexive monitoring which has a duration. There is not a single set of discrete intentions built into any cultural product; there is a context of intentionality and practice which saturates that product. I would want to argue that intentionality is necessarily relevant to the understanding or explication of texts, although it does not exhaust them; but I would want to propose that the understanding of what intentionality means here has to be recast in the form I have attempted to analyze.

Second, we can grasp what is involved here by considering Ricoeur's notion that a text or a cultural product is above all a *work*, with all that that implies.[12] The reflexive monitoring of day-to-day conduct is a taken-for-granted part of human agency, and is casually organized by lay actors in the course of their activity. It is its routine, seemingly effortless production which is most impressive about practical consciousness. Now a text which has a particular form—for example a novel, a play, a poem, or a painting—in contrast to casual talk is a phenomenon into which an individual pours effort in order to achieve form. It is not just that the producer puts effort into what is produced that distinguishes a work from a casually produced outcome of mundane day-to-day activity. It is that *the creation of form is known to the agent to be constitutive of what the work is.* This, of course, does not in itself supply aesthetic value and is not relevant to the evaluation of the aesthetic properties of the work in question. But it is crucial to understanding the nature of what makes something a work.

In this respect, for instance, there is a major set of discrepancies between a novel and, say, myths, which are produced through repetitive oral communication, and may have no individual author who lays claim to the prime role in the production of the story. A novel has "an author" and this is known to those who produce novels, who do so in the light of such knowledge as part of their generalized cultural experience. Although there is no doubt, therefore, that what it is to be "an author" is culturally variable, this does not mean it is not relevant to the explication of texts to enquire into the differences in the context of authorship or production in relation to texts or materials or other cultural products.

Third, it should be stressed that—again as Ricoeur says—texts become distanciated from their authors. The concept of textual distanciation can be usefully substituted, in most respects, for that of the autonomy of the text. What this means, I take it at any rate, is that texts have a relative autonomy from the context of their production; but that there is a two-way relation of interpretation which needs to be accomplished between the analysis of the conditions of their original production and the meanings which can be gleaned from them in other conditions. It is only, of course, in such a manner that we can speak of "distanciation" at all, since this presumes that we have some notion of the "distance" which a text has traveled from the initial conditions of its generation.

But it is important to recognize that in a general way there is nothing distinctive to texts here. It is a characteristic of social life generally that its products escape the intentional input of its creators. In other words, one of the most distinctive qualities of social activity concerns the significance of the unintended consequences of action.

Fourth, a theory of meaning and interpretation must be grounded in an account of practical consciousness. To grasp the meanings of a text as they might have been understood by those who produced it involves investigating the conditions of their knowledgeability. What I mean by this is that textual interpretation is simultaneously an exploration of the relations between practical consciousness, discourse, and the unconscious. The text is not an objectified expression of discourse, any more than a social institution is an objectified expression of the subjectivity of the individuals who produce and reproduce it in the course of their activity. It has often been pointed out that the terms "text" and "context" have more than an accidental similarity to one another. If the interpretation I have suggested here is correct, it follows that we should develop a new understanding of what "context" means if we are to enrich the theory of textual materials.

Finally, as an implication of the whole of this lecture, I would like to argue for promoting a convergence of social and literary theory. In the days in which the social sciences were dominated by objectivism, particularly those versions which associated themselves closely with the ideals of natural science, literary theory seemed quite irrelevant to the concerns of social science. This is, of course, as I pointed out in the beginning, why many social scientists have very little acquaintance with issues to do with literary criticism and textual theory. With an appreciation of the partial character of objectivism— coupled to an understanding of the limitations of naturalistic models of social science—it becomes increasingly clear that there are interpretive issues which bind problems of literary theory closely to issues of social analysis. I do not hold, as Ricoeur does, that social action can be treated as a text. But I do believe that problems of agency, subjectivity, and meaning are shared in common by both sets of endeavors.

Notes

1. See Anthony Giddens, *The Constitution of Society* (Cambridge: Polity Press, 1984), ch. 1 and *passim*.

2. For further development of the above points, see my *Central Problems in Social Theory* (London: Macmillan, 1979), ch. 1.

3. *Ibid.*, ch. 2.

4. Alfred Schutz, *The Phenomenology of the Social World* (London: Heinemann, 1972).

5. Ferdinand de Saussure, *Course in General Linguistics* (London: Fontana, 1974).

6. Emile Durkheim, *The Rules of Sociological Method* (London: Macmillan, 1982).

7. Giddens, *The Constitution of Society*, ch. 2.

8. Harold Garfinkel, *Studies in Ethnomethodology* (Cambridge: Polity Press, 1984).

9. *Central Problems*, ch. 1.

10. Garfinkel, "A Conception of, and Experiments with 'Trust' as a Condition of Stable Concerted Actions," in O. J. Harvey, *Motivation and Social Interaction* (New York: Ronald Press, 1963).

11. Quentin Skinner, "Meaning and Understanding in the History of Ideas," *History and Theory*, 1969, vol. 8.

12. Paul Ricoeur, *Hermeneutics and the Human Sciences* (Cambridge: Cambridge University Press, 1981).

6

HISTORY, APPROPRIATION, AND THE USES OF REPRESENTATION IN MODERN NARRATIVE

Robert Weimann

TO postulate "aims of representation" and to suggest, through a colon, that these relate to "subject, text, history" is in itself already a philosophical decision and as such can be read to help control, define, limit, or extend the relations between the text and the world. At the same time, this postulate involves a theoretical provocation which resides in the expressed need for a reconsideration of "representation" in a historical frame of reference broad enough to encompass both textual and extra-textual dimensions, both the text itself and the subject (in whichever form subjective activities may be thought to relate to the process of writing and reading). So the question, which is one of control and opening, at last is raised: How, and in which respect, is it possible to historicize the issue of representation? How can historical activity be viewed as constitutive of the uses of "representation" without (let us hasten to add) falling back on either idealist methodologies of closure and homogeneity or the antirepresentational dogma of the autonomy of the signifier? Even to ask these questions is right at the outset to admit that we still need a good deal of knowledge and thought about the actual modes and functions of representation, especially after it was first uncritically taken for granted for so long and then so quickly proscribed almost out of existence. As against these positions of the distant and the most recent past let me submit that a more profound understanding of representational activity (including representational discourse) as radically historical is impossible on the presuppositions of either the hegemony of the subject or that of discourse itself and that neither the premises of a naively referential nor those of a purely nonreferential approach to meaning can be helpful in such a project.

From the point of view of a historicizing approach both these positions, although apparently irreconcilable, would appear equally unsatisfactory: The post-structuralist view of the ultimate hegemony of discourse stipulates some highly abstract scheme of the rise and decline of representation, which leaves a lot of representational practice out of account, in fact, almost as much as does the traditionally mimetic approach which, in the work of Erich Auerbach or Georg Lukács, continues to be associated with classical concepts of mimesis and the subject. Even more important, both these quite different approaches may be said to appear overdeterministic in that the gaps and links between what is representing and what is represented are viewed monistically, *either* in terms of rupture *or* in terms of closure. But as we shall proceed to glance at some representational strategies in the modern period (I must confine myself to some American texts between the early mid-nineteenth and the early twentieth century), it becomes obvious that it is precisely in these gaps and links, and in the way in which, simultaneously, the gaps are closed and the links are broken up, that historical activity can be seen to assert itself.

To situate historical activity within the (dis)integrating process and the (un)unified products of representation itself is to assume historicity not only on the level of what is represented (which would reduce this project to either a referential history of mimesis or some genealogy of the signified) but also on the level of what is representing. What this involves is a concept of history as a constellation of discursive as well as nondiscursive activities, a changeful conglomerate of social energies and conflicting interests which are taken to assert themselves within and without the text. To correlate the historiography within the text to the social history without the text is, at the crossroads of performance and function, to acknowledge the politics of representation as nothing external. Rather, the existential dimension (as involved in the legitimation or subversion of power, the appropriation of alienation of social relationships in and through writing) must be seen to inform the strategies of rupture as well as those of integration. Even more important, the semiotic perspective on signification can then connect with a sociocultural history of representation in which the extratextual dimension of representativity involves changeful relationships of individual writing and social reproduction. In this view, the use of signs, the instability in the relation between signifier and signified, although never reducible to a referential function, must be reconsidered with the view to establishing potential points of (dis)connection with whatever historical activity is represented, mimetically or otherwise, in the text.

This, of course, is a highly provisional and greatly oversimplifying chart of theory, but even so may perhaps suffice to motivate my critique of those post-structuralist positions which, since they proscribe the question of the subject, have tended to create some new areas of theoretical enclosure or silence. For as soon as language is viewed as annihilating the subject, as soon as the subject is viewed purely as a function of discourse but discourse not, simultaneously, as a function of the subject, the whole question of representation cannot be reconsidered at the crossroads of structure and event, system and history. As David Carroll notes in his recent book *The Subject in Question*, "To chase away the 'ideology of representation' only to replace it with what could be called an idealism of the signifier is in fact to remain within the same metaphysical enclosure. Representation, the text as the expression of a sub-

ject's relation to the real, and formalism, the text as an autonomous, closed, centered system, are two sides of the same
coin."[1] It is not enough to refuse to textualize discourse; discourse itself must be defined in relation to the temporality
which, since it involves both the emitter and the receiver, is
inscribed into the dialogic form and communicative function of
each utterance. Such temporality is inseparable from those
socially determined acts of cooperation without which important uses of language would cease to be intelligible.

Temporality needs to be emphasized when, ironically,
the new mode of post-structuralist enclosure affects the most
highly influential and, indeed, formidable critique of representation, even as this critique transcends the textualized, ahistorical autonomy of the signifier. I am of course referring to Michel
Foucault's brilliant archaeology of the rise and decline of representation, which contains some unforeseen element of paradox, some unsuspected inversion of teleology, by which the
narrative of the undoubted crisis of representation is turned
into a privileged code conveying the virtual impossibility, today, of representational action.[2] But as we, even at the end of
the twentieth century, are again and again confronted with
what Stephen Greenblatt has called "the cunning of representation: the resiliency, brilliance, and resourcefulness" of its strategies,[3] the question may be asked: Do we not have ample reason
to be unsatisfied with an archaeological prophecy which remains so embarrassingly unfulfilled? Is there not a newly repressive *régime* at work in this discourse, paradoxically serving
the inversion (not the destruction) of presupposed hierarchies?
It is almost as if—in the teeth of its denial of teleology—
Foucault's archaeology of the scientific consciousness maps
out a cyclic movement (not to say progress) toward the *liberation* of language from its representational functions. Foucault
asks us "to admit that since language is here once more, man
will return to that serene non-existence in which he was for-
merly maintained by the imperious unity of Discourse."[4] What
is more, this "return" (which makes the movement cyclic) is
supposed to obey "the strict unfolding of Western culture in

accordance with the necessity it imposed upon itself at the beginning of the nineteenth century."[5] Is there, one is tempted to ask, such a thing as an "unfolding" principle by which culture enacts some "necessity it imposed upon itself"? Or is the underlying logic not a metaphysical one, especially when it is argued that "language, having been situated within represen- tation and, as it were, dissolved in it, freed itself from that situation at the cost of its own fragmentation?"[6]

To assume that culture like some organism *unfolds* itself according to a self-imposed necessity, to stipulate that language like a prisoner *frees* itself from representation, is not a helpful way to approach the problem of representation as a problem in history. If anything, this tends to obscure the heterogeneity of those particular social circumstances, involving communica- tion, appropriation, or alienation, which promote or obstruct representation in a historically given moment. And it is of course quite forgetful of those very real forces in modern his- tory, which Foucault, in a mere aside, alludes to when he mentions "the obscure but stubborn spirit of a people who talk, the violence and the endless effort of life, the hidden energy of needs."[7] May I suggest that it is in reference to such energies and needs that representation must be reconsidered when its aims and uses are to be viewed in relation to subject, text, and history?

This, of course, is not to deny Foucault's basic proposi- tion that the predeterminations of discursive usage vitally af- fect the function of language as a tool of knowledge; but al- though language never was or is a neutral reservoir of transpar- ent vehicles, it is still historical circumstance that accounts for the differing modes through which, at different times, language is appropriated in discourse, and predetermined patterns of discursive usage are reappropriated in new constellations of communicative action. In this connection, there is no way to shirk the paradox contained in the contradiction between the historical and the structural dimensions of language: On the one hand, discourse so involves the appropriation of language, that at least some types of discourse constitute themselves not through the repetition or transcription of preexisting relationships between signs, thoughts, and objects, but through a series of performative and inaugural acts of social imposition and appropriation. To be sure, these do not serve the free expression of subjectivity; rather, they themselves are made possible by and within the necessary predeterminations of discursive usage, by and within the discursive situations and structuring systems in which they occur. The historical assertion of meaning, the discursive performance and utterance of intentions, energies, and interests, presuppose a given system, but for a given synchronic system to be used, articulated, or understood involves some temporal kind of activity in which the speaker (the "I," the emitter) always already associates the receiver (the "other") in an act of socialization, appropriation, or alienation.

It is at such crossroads between history and system that the signifying process involved in representation must be projected onto differing planes of cultural activity. The tasks of such historiography, therefore, cannot be defined in terms of those binary "mythologies of universal script," which Jacques Derrida has defined between the two typological poles of "pictography" and "algebra," along the two opposite directions of either the "unrestrained consumption" or the reduced "expense" of the signifier.[8] Instead, restrained as well as unrestrained uses of the signifier must be seen to relate such historical circumstances where socially accepted and ideologically sanctioned systems of signification can, in certain types of fictional discourse, either be acknowledged and amplified or challenged and reduced. As my reading of some selected literary texts may suggest, the historicity of representational strategies can constitute itself in either the usability and closure, in Emerson, of such signifiers as "mill," "joint-stock company," "insurance office," or the proscription or rupture, in Hemingway, of "glory," "sacred," and "in vain." These words (and the authority behind their representational usage) must be taken to have an existential and historical correlative which, while it may or may not establish some mimetic dimension in the text, is permanently informed by those circumstantial con ditions in history which are vital for the appropriation and communication of certain means and forms and aims of representation.

In this connection, "appropriation" (and appropriation, as we shall see, conceptually involves alienation and/or self-projection) needs to be defined more closely, if a historicizing counterperspective on the problem of representation in modern narrative is to be projected. As against both the view of the text as the purely referential activity of some "reflecting" subject and the (seemingly opposite) view of the text as some completely autonomous locus of self-determining differentials or discursive epistemes, the concept of appropriation may, I submit, help us to move beyond the subjectivism of the former and the formalism of the latter. It may do so in an effort to historicize the changeful constellations of the contradiction itself between whatever extralinguistic activity and whatever intralinguistic difference engage in the process of representation. Although, ultimately, this contradiction may turn out to be quite irreducible, the links as well as the gaps between historical activity and the use of signs in representational discourse are far from having been satisfactorily explored.

In attempting to make a contribution to the historicity of representation, a theory of appropriation would, however, have to confront at least three or four major theoretical problems (and it must, correspondingly, submit to the test of being able to meet the following questions and requirements): First, how to historicize the gaps as well as the links between what is representing and what is represented? If, as I have suggested, the moments of rupture and those of closure themselves must be defined in relation to some historical activity within the representational process, how is it possible, then, historically to account for this space as a locus of appropriation? Second, once differential predeterminations in the signifying process are acknowledged and once the activity of some (individual or collective) subject is equally conceded, the question must be faced:

How, and to what effect, can a concept of appropriation assist in establishing some conceptual frame of reference in accordance with which discursive and nondiscursive activities must be correlated in relation to what, linguistically as well as socially, is and what is not representing? Third, once historical-structural activities are postulated not only on the level of what is representing, not only in the collision of signifying signs and signifying interests but also in the signified, in the sense that the signified constitutes itself through the changeful contradiction between its semantic differential and its referential dimension of mimesis, the question must at least be formulated: To what extent may the changing effects of representation be functionally associated with appropriating activities? Finally, although in all these questions "appropriation" can at best *contribute* to a historicizing projection of representational activities (it must not be expected to provide some methodological master key), yet the problem must be acknowledged: How to relate appropriating activities to representation without defining their historymaking dimension as in any way teleological. If appropriation is, as it were, a producer of history, it is also and at the same time its product. In other words, "appropriation" can serve to historicize representation only insofar as it is itself being radically historicized, in the sense that its progress (especially when viewed culturally or ecologically) always involves painful contradiction rather than plenitude, that its outcome today remains precariously undecided, not to be subsumed under any particular form of representation as the ends, let alone the prophecy of the end (blissful or blightful) of history.[9]

As even these few questions (they are, heaven knows, formidable enough) indicate, my own use of the concept of appropriation[10] is not identical with that in recent post-structuralist parlance. As, for instance, against René Girard's definition of "appropriation" as some primordial impulse in mimesis, it seems helpful to insist that the appropriating functions of mimesis cannot be reduced to some prehistoric pattern of violence and victimage, to the conflict of those instincts which—

in Girard's scheme—stop short of the most powerful existential challenge of primitive existence. Instead, to think of appropriation at this level is impossible without taking into account the sheer need, in primitive society, for physical survival, the socializing need for safety and sustenance—which need releases energies that, I think, ultimately point beyond the prehistoric world to the temporal world of changeful social reproduction in ancient and modern history.[11] Similarly, while reconsidering Foucault's important position, according to which "discourses are objects of appropriation," so that "there exist properties or relationships peculiar to discourse (not reducible to the rules of grammar and logic),"[12] I have suggested that the study of discourses as juridical "*objects* of appropriation" must be complemented by their study as *Subjekte* of appropriation, that is, as historical agencies of knowledge, pleasure, energy, and power. In other words, the question of appropriation must be studied not only in relation to the exchange value of an author's works, that is, their property status, but also, and at the same time, in terms of the use value of *his work*, that is, in reference to the changing functions and effects of his literary production as an appropriating agency.

In any historicizing approach to representation it is of course vital that "appropriation" be defined at the crossing-point of both text-appropriating and world-appropriating activities, so that the concept will, over and beyond its economic, juridical, and proprietary aspects, encompass noneconomical and nonjuridical activities. These activities will be conceived in terms of *Aneignung*, of making things (relations, books, texts, writings) one's own. Hence, it seems possible to say that both the world in the book and the book in the world are *appropriated* through acts of intellectual acquisition and imaginative assimilation on the levels of writing as well as reading. In this connection, the German term *Aneignung* has the advantage of not necessarily involving an ideologically preconceived idea of (private) ownership or (physical) property; instead, it allows for acquisitive behavior as well as for nonacquisitive acts of intellectual energy, possession, and assimilation. Since, there-

fore, the term is not limited by juridical ideas of private property, the sense of making things one's own can and, in fact, must
be used literally, not as a metaphor of some juridical action or
condition associated with a certain type of (bourgeois) society.

"Appropriation" so defined would provide us with a
concept denoting an activity which, even while it can precede
ideology and signification, is not closed to the acts of the historical consciousness of the signifying subject. Linking the world
of prehistoric with that of historical activities, "appropriation,"
then, provides a context where desire (Hegel's *Trieb*) enters the
world of history. It is at this juncture that Marx's contribution to
the theory of *Aneignung* is most consequential: Rejecting the
"speculative unity" of Hegel's "absolute subject-object,"[13]
Marx was the first to define "appropriation" in relation to
Arbeit (work, labor) as the most basic mode of mediation between subject and object. Defining *Aneignung* as a function of
work, and relating the varying modes of appropriation not only
to the changing conditions of production and ownership but to
the changing patterns of relationship between the individual
and his community, Marx provided a theoretical foundation on
which appropriation necessarily involves homogeneity as well
as heterogeneity, acquisition as well as expropriation. In this
view, the process of making certain things one's own becomes
inseparable from making other things (and persons) alien, so
that the act of appropriation must be seen always already to
involve not only self-projection and assimilation but alienation
through reification and expropriation.

To emphasize this contradiction, which is at the heart of
"appropriation," is especially important as soon as we return to
the task of historicizing the variegated uses of representation.
As for the first of the theoretical requirements (which I have
listed above), the nonidentity between what is representing and
what is represented deserves particular interest, since it so
obviously involves the historical (and historically changeful)
discontinuity between the process and the result of work, between what produces and what is produced, between the subject and the object of appropriation. It is enough to make this

connection (and to define the act of representation as an act of intellectual production, not repetition) in order to realize that between the process and the product of representation there can never be a status of absolute congruity, simultaneity, and completeness. The act of *representing* (as some bringing forth, producing) is radically different from what it results in, the *represented*.

From a historicizing point of view, however, it is not good enough to view the distance between process and product as simply given, as some synchronic structure of nonidentity;[14] rather, the area of discontinuity can be thought of as not at all invariable as soon as it is seen in relation to that appropriating function which is constitutive of both the activity of production and the uses of its products. In other words, the contradiction between what is representing and what is represented does not just exist on some synchronic level; the historicity of this contradiction resides in the fact that, and the degree to which, the means, the forms, the agents of production, inherent in the process of representation, can appropriate or alienate its products. The respective amount of (dis)integration varies according to the circumstantial context in which the assimilating and/or the alienating forces are operative; but no matter how large the contiguous space of either rupture or closure, the basic contradiction is such that what is represented never is identical with either the act of representation or, for that matter, its object. Therefore, it seems perfectly possible to say that representation can both enhance and undermine, revitalize and efface whatever it is that it represents,[15] and that these differing uses of rupture and closure can best be historicized in relation to the contradictory contexts and effects of appropriation.

Once the moment of rupture or closure is viewed as a locus of both linguistic difference and historical activity, this activity must be defined more closely in its systematic (synchronic) limitations but also—my second aspect—in its capacity for being related to nondiscursive modes of appropriation. To assume some *correlation* (rather than homology or causality) between material and intellectual modes of reproduction makes it impossible to view the re- in representation as denoting the replica of an activity given prior to the act of representation itself. Even more important, once the modes and effects of appropriation are correlated on the levels of both discursive and nondiscursive activity, the function and the extent of their relatedness itself will appear extremely changeful. As my reading of Emerson's text as against that of Ernest Hemingway's suggests, the potential amount of interaction between, say, economic, political, and discursive modes of appropriating the world varies considerably.

The need for historicizing the variable degrees of (in)congruity emerges even more clearly when we compare modern narrative with, say, the heroic or courtly epic. There, the distance between the appropriator and his (intellectual) properties is much smaller: the extent to which his *matière*, "sources," genre, plot patterns, topoi, are given is much greater. The amount of intellectual and verbal activity, the capacities for self-projection or alienation between what represents and what is represented are limited, in the sense that the extent of appropriation, of making things one's own, would necessarily be undeveloped where the individual's mode of production was deeply integrated into that of his community, and where the division of labor was so relative that concepts like *technè* or *artes* were used to designate the cohesion of productive activities material and intellectual. At that stage, the discursive and nondiscursive ways of appropriating the means and results of production were more intensely correlated. As long as the appropriator related to the means and modes of his production as largely communal, as some unquestionably given, shared property, there is very little that *he can make his own.* Hence, the epic poet tended to take previously inscribed authority, the validity of the work of his predecessors, more readily for granted; he accepted as part of his own work the labor (as it were) already invested in the invention of a great story with widely known events and characters. But in doing just that, he subscribed to a literary mode of production that was in many ways correlated to a socially dominant mode of appropriation, in which "the chief objective condition of labour does not itself appear as a *product* of labour, but is already there."[16] The contradiction (the rupture) between what produces and what is produced is not intensified through alienating conditions of ownership: the distance between the appropriator and his properties is small; the act of intellectual assimilation constitutes itself on the basis of the giveness of what is to be assimilated: The author's function is to assert known and publicly acknowledged ideals; it is not to appropriate any area of thought or experience that has not previously been appropriated in (early feudal or courtly) society itself.

It is in this connection that my third question may receive what here, again, is no more than a highly provisional answer. For to relate the changing uses of representation to appropriation as a mode of social reproduction is to perceive that the moment of relative closure between the appropriator and his property is, historically speaking, determined by a whole close context of relationships. In terms of representational strategies, this involved a situation where the need for representation as a deliberate act of self-projection through the assimilating of relatedness was strictly limited. It was limited as long as appropriation was characterized not by dynamic tensions between individual activities and given objects and relationships but by "the *reproduction* of *presupposed* relations."[17] As long as the appropriator related to his properties and appropriations as, in the words of Marx, some "inorganic part of his own subjectivity," the uses of representation were restricted and the contradiction, which is at the heart of representation in the modern period, remained undeveloped. This contradiction was associated with the emergence of relationships which allowed for a much greater amount of social mobility and individual choice, with a historical situation in which people began to live, to produce, to write and read under circumstances which—for a far greater number of individuals—were less "given." Hence the process of Aneignung assumes a more highly dynamic and unpredictable quality; being less predetermined by the given state of communal property, natural resources, cultural materials, and literary conventions and traditions, *Aneignung* becomes more and more attached to forms of existence which, far from being presupposed to the socializing activity, appear as its result. But once the individual tends to confront the conditions and means of production as something alien, as something which itself is produced, which he cannot unquestionably consider as part of the existence of his own intellectual self, the *representative* quality of his writing, the function of representativity becomes problematic: As the individual's distance from the means and modes of production (including the production of literary texts) grows, there develops new scope for his own choice of productive strategies vis-à-vis the increasing availability of those means, modes, and materials which, practically and imaginatively (though not necessarily juridically), he can make his own.

Thus, the historicity of representation cannot be dissociated from whatever social representativity is involved in the collision between signifying signs and signifying interests. But to establish this representativity involves more than a sociological or political definition of a writer's function, and it is (our final point) quite incompatible with some progressive concept of appropriation as involving the closure of history through a return to some utopian homogeneity in social relations. On the contrary, if any one formula can at all hope to anticipate our reading of the following texts and to suggest the historical complexity involved, it is both the irretrievable loss of homogeneity and the attempt to cope with and control its consequences, which appears to mobilize and sustain the greatest cultural energies informing the art of representation. In terms of a historicizing theory of appropriation, the element of nonidentity between what produces and what is produced, between the appropriator and his property appears to be decisive. If anything, it was the gulf between the two which—*after* it emerged, but *before* it became unbridgable—offered the greatest challenge and the widest space for the social functions of representation. This is not the place to anticipate the results of my textual analysis (nor do I have the space to examine how different functions of mimesis can revitalize or defeat certain uses of representation),[18] but this theoretical chart finds itself in at least partial agreement with some of the recent (and, I think, most cogent) criticism that we have on the whole question of representation. As, for instance, Stephen Greenblatt has noted, "most great representational art in our culture seems to be generated" out of "a healing of some loss or undoing."[19] Although representation, as I shall persist in arguing, may or may not emphasize closure in the functional sense of recuperation, yet to presuppose "some loss or undoing" seems vital: What, more than anything else, representational art presupposes and what it thrives on is, indeed, the loss, the undoing of the plenitude of that property in which the self and the social are mutually most productive and intensely interactive. It is this loss and the resulting gap between them which constitutes the necessary field or scenario of appropriation, even though in the domain of representational discourse, the linguistic system of differentials will always already preclude the full projection of identity and totality, just as the temporality of writing and reading will again destroy any simultaneity between the representing and the represented. Similarly, although from a different angle, David Carroll has noted that "all representation is constituted by both production and loss": for on the one hand, representation "derives its force . . . from a desire to solidify and unify the traces constituting experience, as if to constitute a unified image of oneself (or of an ideal self), a totalized image of what one was and did, and at the same time, on the other hand, from a desire . . . to produce not a metaphorical equivalent of oneself or the sense of one's existence but the irreducible and repetitive loss of this unity."[20] But the "I" can define and represent itself only in relation to what is not herself or himself; the "unified" and the "totalized image of what one was and did" achieves its hoped-for moment of unity and totality only through relationship. And since the self and the social can, despite considerable variability in their relationships in history, never achieve identity, the "loss" of (the illusion of) "unity" is the result just as much as the prerequisite of representation.

Finally, this historicizing approach to the appropriating

functions of "representation" needs to be complemented by some rudimentary graph in which the space, limited as it is, for the historicity of language uses itself is marked in at least the roughest and briefest possible manner. As a general point of departure, it seems helpful to start from Julia Kristeva's definition of discourse as "appropriated language," in the sense that, as Umberto Eco suggests, even the use of signs presupposes some kind of work, some existential expense of energy, time, and labor.[21] Even though Kristeva's concept of textual production (that of some *travail pré-sens*, according to which a text produces itself) would presumably resist any historicizing perspective, yet this whole emphasis seems important, when the postulated "incompatibility" between the order of language and the history of society is to be questioned in relation to that tertium quid which—through appropriation—may establish certain links (without obliterating the existing gaps) between the use of signs and the activity of individuals.

In this connection, as I have suggested, the communicative dimension of representational forms of discourse deserves particular attention. More than anything else, it is the reciprocal nature of the kind of activity inherent in discourse which, having been defined as some "Cooperative Principle,"[22] appears most significant in our context. If representation, any representational gesture in discourse, can be viewed as some speech act or, in a wider sense, some discursive activity, then the distinction, first developed by J. L. Austin, between constative and performative utterances is obviously relevant. It is particularly helpful where the constative content of linguistic activity on the level of the represented is viewed as interactive with the performative process and where, in Austin's words, "the parallel between statements and performative utterances" breaks down as soon as "we are *assimilating* the supposed constative utterance to the performative."[23] Now, although speech act theoreticians tend to minimize or ignore any historicizing perspective on linguistic performance, yet it would be possible from within their own premises to argue that the performative element in the act of representation implicates the existential or playful interests of the performing representer. In particular, if the supposed constative utterance on the level of the represented can at all be assimilated to the needs, the energies, the context of the performative, then, obviously, there are differing degrees of assimilation, and some of these can vary, in the sense that historically the distance or otherwise between what represents and what is represented reflects varying degrees of assimilation, varying states of identity or alienation between the appropriator and his properties, physical and intellectual.

Again, once the synchronic classification of illocutionary acts, which John R. Searle has undertaken, is moved from the timeless table of typology to the diachronic dance of rule-governed behavior, similarly historicizing perspectives can be opened. Here, it must suffice to suggest that among the five basic categories of illocutionary action,[24] at least three, the representatives, the directives, and the expressive are, in the functional order and quantity of their occurrence, subjected to changing circumstances. Thus, illocutionary acts that undertake to reproduce a state of affairs and those that are designed to influence or teach the addressee would probably find themselves more frequently used, differently rated, and also interrelated in, say, early eighteenth- and late twentieth-century writing. This, of course, says very little about the changeful quality of the social content inherent in illocutionary acts, but perhaps it can suggest that the communicative dimension in the uses of language always already presupposes social relationships and appropriating activities which collide with the differential, preordained system of signification and, through this collision, inform whatever limited historicity the linguistic forms of representational discourse can be claimed to possess.

For our present purpose, the best way historically to study the problem of representation is to introduce two or three representational texts in which I propose to read changeful correlations between the performative and the constative levels

of representation and in which the assimilations and/or aliena-
tions between statement and performance can be traced on the
level of both what represents and what is represented. Since I
continue to be concerned with the function as well as the
disfunction of representation, with its changeful uses and ideologies, it will not, I hope, come as a surprise when my first text
is the two series of Emerson's essays, published in 1841 and
1844 respectively. Transcendentalism, the worship of the soul
and over-soul, "that great nature in which we rest"[25] would
naturally and organically favor a representational understanding of "the office of art" as one that, romantically, points beyond the mimetic premises of neoclassical aesthetics to the
more ambitious project "to educate the perception of beauty"
(307) itself. In this sense Emerson emphasizes "not imitation,
but creation" as "the aim" in "our fine arts" (305), and yet "the
poet is the sayer, the namer, and represents beauty" (331).
Since "Beauty" itself (now spelled with capital "B") is taken to
be "the creator of the universe," the poet's representation of
beauty would on the surface of this argument leave no room for
any tension between the representer and the represented: the
beauti-ful creation of the universe of things inspires the beautifying creator of its representations. Between the performance
and the statement, between the "saying," the "naming" of the
created, and the universal creation itself the state of identity is
almost perfect; if it is not quite absolute, the only reason is that
"the abridgment and selection we observe in all spiritual activity" is "itself the creative impulse" (306), which, then, is at
the heart of both the natural performance of beauty and the
beautiful statement of nature: central to both the activities and
the products of representation.

In the transcendentalist poetics, the social uses of homogeneity appear immense, and what they ultimately involve is
some projected form of concurrence among the poetic and the
economic modes of appropriation. For Emerson the intellectual
production of the poet and the material productions of society
appear to be so close to one another and can theoretically be so
integrated, that they all obey the law of nature, where "all is

useful, all is beautiful." Thus, the material appropriation of the natural world through "the useful arts" and the appropriation of the beautiful world of nature in the finer language of the poet are profoundly interrelated in Emerson's scheme of things. It is not that the sage of Concord does not perceive a threatening state of division between the mechanical arts and the fine arts; but the point that he makes is that precisely this division ought to be healed: "Beauty must come back to the useful arts, and the distinction between the fine and the useful arts be forgotten. If history were truly told, if life were nobly spent, it would be no longer easy or possible to distinguish the one from the other" (314).

Thus, the varying social modes of production and appropriation in early mid-nineteenth-century society can be subsumed under one naturalizing authority in the light of which the beautiful can represent the useful and the useful arts serve the same cause of culture as the fine arts. The scope of representation is as wide as the degree of representativity, which the poetry enjoys, is high, and the link between the scope of representation and the degree of representativity is extremely close. In fact, it is essential for Emerson's argument; as he puts it: "the breadth of the problem is great, for the poet is representative. He stands among partial men for the complete man, and apprises us not of his wealth, but of the common wealth" (320). The poetic appropriation of the world is one in which the appropriator is still believed to be close to some universal property, which is the common wealth. The performative qualities of his verbal action, the civility, morality, the patriotism, are richly representative, in that they correspond to the historical reference of his constative utterance.

It is this concurrence which accounts for the high degree of his representativity and allows for the felicity and the assuredness with which the poet can both assimilate the reference through the performative and reintegrate the performative into the constative. If the poet "is a sovereign, and stands on the centre," if he more deeply "knows and tells" and is, in fact, "the only teller of news" (321), the reason is that his performatives

are so widely representative of the appropriating activities of
all sorts and conditions of men, of that "common wealth"
which, in Emerson's own words, includes "not only poets, and
men of leisure and cultivation, . . . but also hunters, farmers,
grooms, and butchers" (326). In other words, the social interests and the impulse which inform the authority of the representer and those which inform the authority of the represented
are claimed to be mutually supporting. And although the appropriations of the poet and the appropriations of "farmers,
grooms, and butchers" are far from being identical, the performative gesture and the constative reference are made to appear
so close that they engage in assimilations which deeply affect
the homogeneity of what represents and what is represented.

If "the office of art" is "to educate the perception of
beauty," the performance of the writer, including the graceful
virility and poignancy of Emerson's style, is again part and
parcel of that larger appropriation of a new world which includes the politics of representing free citizens in the realm of
the spirit. For Emerson, the mark of this representativity is
communal as well as communicative, and its strength is inseparable from the power to experience all, the power to receive
and the power to impart everything:

> The poet is the person in whom these powers are in bal-
> ance, the man without impediment, who sees and handles
> that which others dream of, traverses the whole scale of
> experience, and is representative of man, in virtue of being
> the largest power to receive and to impart. (321)

Here, the concept of "power" is suggestive in that it
helps us critically to trace the precariousness of this romantic
performative and, more generally, the sheer amount of idealism
contained in this theoretical construct. This is not to say that
the postulated traversal of the "whole scale of experience" can
simply be dismissed as the naturalizing language of universality and, of course, ideology. For the poet to dispose of "the
largest power to receive and to impart" is to acknowledge the
very real connection between appropriation and selfprojection,

and it is willingly and deliberately to shoulder a burden of representativity which, paradoxically, is both a concrete sociological potentiality and an ideological rationalization. It is a potentiality, because in early mid-nineteenth-century society the poet may well have been better equipped to traverse a larger scale of socially representative experience than, say, in a more highly compartmentalized society or in one which the forms of property and the division of labor have made the poet's existence even more marginal. Still, to view the poet as "the man without impediment" involved the kind of illusion, if not contradiction, that is revealed in Emerson's absolutely unselfconscious use of "power" as a mere metaphor of intellectual capacities for appropriating and communicating worldliness. It is not so much that, in the teeth of his own postulate, Emerson's use of such "power" is forgetful about reconciling the appropriations of the fine arts and the quite different ownership of the instruments of the useful arts. What this use of "power" or even "impediment" suppresses is some unresolved contradiction, the enormous gulf, in Emerson himself, between the defiant individualism of self-reliance ("the only right is what is after my constitution," 148) and the proposed service to the "common wealth." In his more famous essay, Emerson suggests at least part of the deeper problematic; he speaks about "Chaos and the Dark" (147) and even refers to "the unintelligent brute force that lies at the bottom of society" (which, when it "is made to growl and mow," "needs the habit of magnanimity and religion to treat it godlike as a trifle of no concernment" (151).

Obviously, Emerson thought "the habit of magnanimity and religion" to be no "impediment" if the poet was to traverse "the whole scale" of social experience. But to treat "the unintelligent brute force . . . at the bottom of society" "godlike as a trifle of no concernment" must have involved an astonishing capacity for oblivion which, as a matter of course, found important correlatives in the idealism of the aims of representation which Emerson advocated. As we look at them more critically, they emerge in an ideological context in which the theoretically presumed representativity appears in practice rather limited, and the fervently projected beautiful congruity between the representer and the represented reveals dark areas of silence and obliteration. The highest and most disinterested authority in representation, even in the 1830s and 40s, was less representative of the commonwealth at large than Emerson cared to admit and it constituted itself within some very powerful confines of the dominant ideology. It is within these, then, that the aims of representation are historically predetermined. For all the remarkably achieved harmony of the naturalizing impulse, it could never bridge the gulf between the finely balanced intellectual power of the poet and "the unintellectual brute force . . . at the bottom of society." It is this gulf which has a lot to do with the unresolved contradiction between what represents and what is or isn't represented. The high price of ideological homogeneity involves the godlike obliteration of "Chaos and the Dark" as "a trifle of no concernment." As this aesthetic wrestles with its inhibitions and vulnerabilities, the enormous claim on its representativity is, if not substantially surrendered, at least relegated to "the fine innuendo" of the soul. Says Emerson in his essay on "The Over-soul":

> We grant that human life is mean; but how did we find out that it was mean? What is the ground of this uneasiness of ours; of this old discontent? What is the universal sense of want and ignorance, but the fine innuendo by which the soul makes its enormous claim? (261)

The rationalization is obvious, and painfully so. The "universal sense of want and ignorance" is unrepresentable in terms of the romantic naturalization of the signified. For a brief, almost speechless moment, the signifying energies of the beautifying representer and the signified hardness in the nature of the represented confront each other, and the depth of the contradiction between performative and constative appears unfathomable. At this point, the mean world of want and ignorance explodes the performer's claim on representativity, only to be relegated to the fine innuendo of the suffering soul. But it would be a private and highly ambiguous path for the romantic aesthetic to cope with its own enormous claim. What Emerson here calls "the authority of the soul" is both repressive and liberating. It was in this same context that Emerson noted: "but from some alien energy the visions come" (262). His poetic appropriation of the world is neither complete nor triumphant; the unacknowledged moment of alienation persists as that which is unrepresented and nonrepresentable by the more privileged standards of the authority of the highly cultivated soul.

The aims of such representation can easily be equated with recuperation, with the healing of a painful division between nature and society, the reconstitution of the social "Whole" at a time when this "Whole," although deeply flawed, can serve as an ideologically usable illusion still. But in studying the romantic aims of representation the point is not simply to see through the theoretical illusions of the subject and to discover that the hidden constraints of power have a way of predetermining one of the finest intellects and some of the most charmingly pithy prose that we have in mid-nineteenth-century English. The point that equally deserves to be made is that representation, at the flowering of the romantic movement in America, is a project full of both insight and ideology. At the heart of what is perhaps its most central contradiction there is the question of legitimation, the authority to decide what is to be represented and what is not, and the solution of this contradiction, especially in fiction, is inspired by alien energies which, pushing back the frontiers of the unrepresentable, collide with preconceived postulates of harmony and presuppositions of homogeneity. And although the recuperating functions of representation appear to be firmly installed, yet the appearance of harmony and the presumption of homogeneity are deceptive in that the relationship between what was representing and what was or was not represented foreshadowed the beginning of a contradiction at whose provisional, unresolved end the present crisis of representation finds itself.

In Emerson, this contradiction is pervasive in that repeatedly the representer recoils from what he is yet compelled to apprehend. In finally coming to confront the "dislocation and detachment from the life of God that makes things ugly," the writing of poetry is unambiguously summoned to recuperate the sense of wholeness and of beauty. This, then, is the most problematic power of romantic representation that it (in the words of Emerson himself) "reattaches things to nature and the Whole" and, thus, "disposes very easily of the most disagreeable facts." In its full context:

> For, as it is dislocation and detachment from the life of God that makes things ugly, the poet, who re-attaches things to nature and the Whole—re-attaching even artificial things, and violation of nature, to nature, by a deeper insight—disposes very easily of the most disagreeable facts. Readers of poetry see the factory-village and the railway, and fancy that the poetry of the landscape is broken up by these; for these works of art are not yet consecrated in their reading; but the poet sees them fall within the great Order not less than the beehive or the spider's geometrical web. (328)

This is a central theme in Emerson's view of the aims of representation. "The great Order," once it is installed in what he in the same context calls "a centred mind" (328), has such truly naturalizing power that it manages to bridge the widening gulf between the poet-appropriator and his unpoetic appropriations (in the form of prosaic property), between what healing faculties represent and what wounding circumstances are hardly representable. The chasm between the hard means of material appropriation and the lofty aims of aesthetic appropriation has finally become so deep that Emerson's beautiful synthesis shows painful signs of strain. The political economy of bourgeois appropriation was one of domination, the politics in Emerson's prose was designed to be one of liberation, at least for the individual.

But as Emerson's writings follow the course of nineteenthcentury history, the actual uses, as opposed to the aims, of this type of representation are deeply compromised. The true mark of "genius," as Emerson concluded in his essay on "Art," its unfailing "instinct," is

to find beauty and holiness in new and necessary facts, in
the field and road-side, in the shop and mill. Proceeding
from a religious heart it will raise to a divine use the
railroad, the insurance office, the joint-stock company; our
law, our primary assemblies, our commerce, the galvanic
battery, the electric jar, the prism, and the chemist's retort;
in which we seek now only an economical use. Is not the
selfish and even cruel aspect which belongs to our great
mechanical works—to mills, railways, and machinery—
the effect of the mercenary impulses which these works
obey? When its errands are noble and adequate, a steam-
boat bridging the Atlantic . . . is a step of man into harmony
with nature. . . . When science is learned in love, and its
powers are wielded by love, they will appear the supplements and continuations of the material creation. (210)

Poetry and science as "supplements and continuations
of the material creation"—the really noteworthy thing is that,
for once at this unexpected ending, the material modes of
appropriation have priority over poetry as it was summoned
"to raise to a divine use the railroad, the insurance office, the
joint-stock company." But if, again, the performative of transcendentalism founders, the reason is not wholly one of ideology, and it is not because the "errands" of industry may not, in a
thoroughly humanizing context, be both "noble and adequate."
The ideology is there, quite clearly, and almost outrageously so:
To represent the ugly world of shops and mills and commerce
so as to "find beauty and holiness in new and necessary facts" is
to provide, through representation, sorely needed legitimation.
But these authorizing aims of representation are themselves far
from being uniform, and they are not throughout subservient to
the dominating interests of economic ownership. As Emerson
reaches out to fathom the full heterogeneity between the performance of the romantic subject and the achievements of its
industrial subject matter, his endeavor, although deeply flawed
by ideology, also contains intimations of insight and necessity,
which only a few years later were to inspire the poetry of Walt
Whitman. So the question must be faced: Is there not, despite
the obvious idealism, an element of validity in this text which,

paradoxically, results out of the very depth of the discontinuity between what this text seeks to represent and what in reality is represented by it?

What this text finally articulates is not the closure but the rupture between its image of the useful arts and their actual function in history, the contradiction itself between the useful arts as world-appropriating agencies and their property function as objects of appropriation and commercial exploitation. If, at this point, the fine arts and the useful arts appear more deeply and, it seems, irretrievably divided, it is because the appropriator relates to the respective means and modes of his production so differently that the appropriations of the one have, in any sense of the word, ceased to be representative of the other. The inevitable crisis in the poet's representativity has a lot to do with his difficulty in assimilating the "new and necessary facts" in a society where the material, proprietary interests and those behind the productions of poetry will diverge much further than, say, in the times of Daniel Defoe and Benjamin Franklin. In this situation, when the "new and necessary facts" of living, including the machine in the American landscape, appear juridically alienated from the common wealth, the uses of poetic representations, just as the burdensome status of the poet's representativity, are about to undergo significant and far-reaching changes.

Even before Emerson, the links between the verbal representations and the social representativity of the poet had become much more tenuous in France, where the poetry of Baudelaire, Verlaine, Mallarmé, and Rimbaud, and even the more highly mimetic forms of the novel, especially Flaubert and the brothers Goncourt, reveal early inroads into the traditional authorities of representation. But in England and America (if we except a unique position like that of Edgar Allan Poe), it is only in the last decades of the century and shortly after that intellectual activity can no longer quite take for granted its customary spectrum of social representativity and that the concept of the artist as representative man enters a state of crisis. This weakening of the claim on representativity is of course a gradual and highly contradictory process which has important correlations in the circumstantial history of intellectual production. In particular, it is "the estrangement of intellectuals, as a class, from the dominant values of American culture,"[26] especially that of the middle class, which plays an important role. This "estrangement from the middle class," which Christopher Lasch has traced in connection with the emergence of *The Intellectual as a Social Type* (the subtitle to his book on *The New Radicalism in America: 1889–1963*), is of course part of that larger historical process in the course of which capitalist society loses its earlier cohesive influences and "tends to break up into smaller communities, autonomous, self-contained, and having no viable connection with the whole."[27] Needless to say, the loss of these cohesive forces, as it involves the division of interests and perspectives between the intellectual and the middle class, also and primarily implicates whatever links remained, in theory and ideology, between the economic and juridical forms of appropriation and those involved in the intellectual and artistic modes of production.

As far as the changing scope and function of fictional representation are concerned, the interesting point is that, in its early phase, the crisis in representativity does not at all preclude the continuity, in the major novel writing of the time, of traditional representational forms and functions. Paradoxically, but not without a certain consistency, it can be said that the erosion of representativity itself is *represented* in its most immediate individual and psychological form: in the figure of the artist himself, in his loss of social integration and bourgeois respectability, in the diminishing range of his participation in the moral and political consensus. The crisis of representativity is turned into a theme, into a novelistic representation itself, and its most consistently mimetic form is, of course, the biographical *Darstellung* of such characters as Tonio Kröger, Gustav Aschenbach, and Adrian Leverkühn in Thomas Mann, or Neil Paraday (in "The Death of the Lion"), Paul Overt ("The

Lesson of the Master"), Ray Linbert ("The Next Time"), and of course Nick Dormer (*The Tragic Muse*) in Henry James.

In these fictional representations, the artist, far from being representative man, either renounces the claims of middle-class life or is already an outsider, standing (in the words of Thomas Mann) in "a queer aloof relationship to our humanity," out of harmony with some of the most broadly received middle-class values and attitudes. Although on the surface, in the reduced scope of novelistic subject matter, the gulf between what represents and what is represented appears at least in part to be bridged once more, yet the underlying tensions between self-identification and relationship, between self-projection and appropriation have vastly increased. This becomes obvious as soon as the Emersonian conception of the poet as the "sayer" and "namer" of the "common wealth," as "the only teller" of the news of the world is critically, not to say sarcastically, redefined in relation to such public forms of activity as, for instance, a career in politics involve.

As in Henry James' *The Tragic Muse*, the new perspective on the diminishing social representativity of art is exemplified in the antagonism between the status of the artist and the role of the politician—which conflict leads to a defiant emphasis on the independence, the self-respect, and the uniqueness, if not the autonomy, of the function of art in society. In *The Princess Casamassima*, there is a suggestion that, in the last resort, it is art which makes endurable the "bloody sell" of life. The concept of art, then, as the most intensely representative vessel of life gives way to a sense of its autonomous or redeeming function which, precisely, resides in its freedom from representativity. As Stephen Donadio has shown in his *Nietzsche, Henry James, and the Artistic Will*, this fiction shares "the impulse to achieve a self-definition independent of one's own national or class origins, the impulse to be free of the limitations imposed by a particular time."[28] Since the traditional forms of mimetic self-definition all involved the exploration of relationships and relatedness, this new sense of identity is launched on the precarious ground of the separateness or "independence" of the artistic will. In fact, it is this separation which, for all its brave and defiant spirit, constitutes a note of tragedy in the decline of art's representativity. Such independence characterizes Nick Dormer, the central figure in *The Tragic Muse*, a promising politician, who begins to conceive of his future career as a liberal Member of Parliament as "talking a lot of rot" which "has nothing to do with the truth or the search for it; nothing to do with intelligence, or candour, or honour."[29] In the context of the book such rejection of a well-prepared political career appears as symptomatic: as a break with the illusion that the late nineteenth-century liberal political ideology can in any respect serve as a valid vessel or a viable source of consciousness. Nick Dormer forsakes his politically influential fiancée; he rejects "the old false measure of success" and chooses to become an artist so as to be able to enjoy "the beauty of having been disinterested and independent; of having taken the world in the free, brave, personal way."[30]

The longing for a disinterested kind of independence, the preference for "the free, brave, personal way" must be read as symptomatic, not only of the changing position of the artist in bourgeois society but of the new foundations on which James sets out to redefine the function and the art of fiction. In that he comes close to the Nietzschean position (as formulated by Thomas Mann) "that life can be justified only as an aesthetic phenomenon."[31] In this connection, the American novelist as well as the German philosopher respond to the same late nineteenth-century crisis in social and ideological representativity which Christopher Lasch has traced in that related "estrangement . . . from the dominant values of American culture" in the writing of intellectuals like Randolph Bourne, Lincoln Colcord, Lincoln Steffens, and others.

If, up to a point, marked perhaps by the figure of Stephen Dedalus, the erosion of representativity is rendered in highly representational forms of novelistic mimesis, the reason is not of course simply that of their undoubted resiliency. There is, at the very moment of his social alienation, the artist's attempt (as Michael Fried has shown in the work of Courbet[32]) more resolutely than ever before to efface the distance between creator and art object and, in the teeth of its deepening contradiction, once more to fuse representation with what it represents. In this sense, these late endeavors in traditional forms of realism do attempt "a healing of the loss or undoing out of which . . . most great representational art in our culture seems to be generated."[33]

However, if it is the gap, the lack of identity between what appropriates and what is appropriated which, in the first place, made representation necessary, this gap, once it is turned into an abyss, begins to affect and put strains upon representational form itself. The most immediate modernist link between the deepening crisis in representativity and the nascent erosion in representational form can of course be traced on the level of fictional communications: As, in *The Bostonians,* James satirically recoiled from the vulgar forms of commercialized publishing and cheap journalism and as, not fortuitously, this major novel, just as *The Tragic Muse,* was ill-received and spitefully or, at best, indifferently reviewed, he began to experiment in the traditional forms of representational narration. The results are too well-known for me to specify them here, but what needs to be emphasized is that there is a connection between the represented artist's option for "the free, brave, personal way" and James' own redefinition of the representational strategy of the novel as a "direct, personal impression of life." The "direct" and "personal" quality of novelistic writing (just like the impressionism in contemporary painting) now serves as a distinguishing mark of the braveness with which the artist breaks away from that ideological authority which, in the form of a social and aesthetic consensus, had hitherto informed the standards of his representation. The "brave, personal way" helps secure a new freedom from representativity; the directness of the novel's impression guarantees the related freedom by which the signifying activity of the representer constitutes itself in relative independence of the given signified in the represented.

However, this performative component in novelist strategy seeks to revitalize rather than disrupt the representation of life itself: If the tension between what represents and what is represented has increased enormously, there is yet the attempt to use the contradiction in representational form itself. This involves a new selectiveness in choosing the kind of congenial subject matter in whose rendering "the beauty of having been disinterested and independent" can reassert itself. At the same time, there is the new and largely experimental emphasis on narrative technique which makes it possible for the novelist to meet the widening gap between the representing and the represented through a similar latitude between objectification and appropriation, between, say, the directness, "objectivity," and precision of a personalized point of view on the one hand and the depth of apprehending and comprehending the complexity of the "impression of life" so rendered. Thus, the loss in the artist's representativity is both redeemed and compensated for in terms of narrative technique: The emerging forms of narrative immediacy, the repudiation of omniscience, the stylized modes of point of view can all, in one important respect, be understood as a formally acknowledged relief from the burden of authorial representativity. It is the "direct, personal impression," the seemingly authentic flow of individual consciousness, the slice of life itself, which helps the author to leap over the crippling effects of the conventional public "acceptations"[34] in contemporary ideology, what James in *The Tragic Muse* calls the "ignorance," the "density," "the love of hollow, idiotic words, of shutting the eyes tight and making a noise" (p. 75).

While the later fiction of Henry James reveals the vulnerability and the precariousness of the links between the changing aims of representation and the eroding relations of representativity, the elements of crisis reach their full force only in the rise of modernist strategies of narrative. Although it is of course quite impossible here for me to project the modernist problematic of narrative representation, let me at least suggest some of the gaps and moments of transition between the Jamesian and the post-Jamesian situation in regard to either the possibilities or the impossibilities of appropriation. Whereas Emerson (or, for that matter, the Victorian novelists) had attempted to overcome, to obliterate, or at least to reduce incongruity and discontinuity in representation, Henry James' position already anticipates at least some of the modernist strategies of rupture. This is the case when the free, brave, personal language of Nick Dormer dissociates itself from the public language of liberal politics, as that "talking a lot of rot" which has "nothing to do with intelligence, or candour, or honour." Here, the performative (in narration) repudiates the possibility and, indeed, desirability of assimilating a given constative (in politics) as that which was representable in traditional, more highly homogeneous modes of representation, such as those associated with Anthony Trollope and earlier Victorian novelists.

If we translate this problematic from the plane of speech act theory to that of subject, text, history, the historical decision in the use of language must be defined at the point where both the author and his characters, the representing and the represented language reject the politically dominant ideology as a viable medium of appropriating the more highly complex world of the novel. While this rejection is of course far from being absolute (note the use, in this connection, of concepts such as "truth," "candour," and "honour"), yet the Emersonian belief in the ultimate correlation of the practical and the poetic modes of appropriation is quite shattered. This is one more reason, I suggest, why in Henry James there is no talk about "hunters, farmers, grooms, and butchers," who have literally become as unrepresentable as the public language of politicians which now appears categorically distinct from the Emersonian language of the representative poet which "apprizes us not of . . . wealth, but of the commonwealth."

In order to explore the impact of history on this rupture between what represents and what is represented (and representable) somewhat more closely, let me glance at Van Wyck

Brooks' *America's Coming-of-Age* (written in 1913/14) where, shortly before the outbreak of World War I, the language of the dominant culture is revealingly taken to task. What Brooks, in the following passage, articulates is his sense of a growing incongruity between "transcendental theory ('high ideals')" on the one hand and "a simultaneous acceptance of catchpenny realities."[35] Again, there is the complaint that the public language of politics ("Patriotism, Democracy, . . . Liberty") is both unrepresentable and unrepresentative in terms of "personal contacts" and the enrichment of life.

> Certainly ideals of this kind, in this way presented, in this way prepared for, cannot enrich life, because they are wanting in all the elements of personal contact. Wholly dreamlike and vaporous, they end by breeding nothing but cynicism and chagrin; and in becoming permanently catalogued in the mind as impracticable they lead to a belief in the essential unreality of ideas as well. (p. 23)

For Brooks to complain about "the essential unreality of ideas" is not to deny that "certain ideals of this kind" actually and really do exist in public communication. Their assumed "unreality," from the point of view of the intellectual's appropriation of the world, consists in the fact that they have ceased to function either as performative action or signifying strategy vis-à-vis their historical reference or fictional constative. What Brooks is concerned with is the depth of the gulf between what represents personal consciousness and what is represented in public ideology, and the fact that in view of this gulf the traditional public representations have become problematic, in the sense that they are no longer respected as "genuine or adequate" and that they no longer serve the discursive process of discussion, insight, and consensus.

> The recognized divisions of opinion, the recognized issues, the recognized causes in American society are extinct. And although Patriotism, Democracy, the Future, Liberty are still the undefined, unexamined, unapplied catchwords over which the generality of our public men

dilate, enlarge themselves, and float (careful thought and intellectual contact still remaining on the level of engineering, finance, advertising, and trade)—while this remains true, everyone feels that the issues represented by them are no longer genuine or adequate.[36]

The failure, then, in these signifying concepts of politics and morality was that "the issue represented by them" had ceased to communicate any intellectual authority: The traditional transcendental signified had exhausted its capacity for legitimation, and the representational function of these signs was gravely impaired. What emerges so clearly from the writings of Brooks and those radical intellectuals who disowned the progressivism of the politicians is that the crisis in the representational function of language was primarily related to the erosion of a certain type of social, cultural, and philosophical authority. Hence, "our public men dilate . . . and float"; the instability in the relation between what represents and what is represented in their language was vitally affected by this erosion of authority, in whose absence the traditional significations, far from being representative of the commonwealth, now appeared as "undefined, unexamined, unapplied." These words designate historical conditions of discursive usage which, on the level of fictional texts, are inducive to a higher degree of indeterminacy, in the sense that the increased use, in and after Henry James, of unreliable strategies of narration not only involves a greater "mobilisation" of the reader's activity,[37] but also and beyond that transcribes changing historical relations in which the act of writing had to come to terms with the instability and precariousness of the signifying process. In the nonfictional language of Van Wyck Brooks, such indeterminacy was strictly limited still. If the underlying crisis in the legitimacy of the public uses of language was diagnosed as mainly a rupture "between university ethics and business ethics,"[38] the latter still seemed to retain an element of representability: Language on the "level of engineering, finance, advertising, and trade" still appeared intact and was not viewed as subjugated to that

crisis in appropriation which the public language of culture
and politics had succumbed to.

In early twentieth-century fictional discourse, the
changing constellations of crisis can best be traced where, during or shortly after World War I, the erosion of authority so
deeply affected narrative strategies of representation that traditional modes of interaction between the performative and the
constative were seriously impaired. As an illustration let me, in
conclusion, look at a well-known passage in Hemingway's *A
Farewell to Arms* which is revealing and perhaps unique because, paradoxically, what it represents is a crisis of representativity in the novelist's language itself. The first person
singular is of course Frederic Henry's:

> I was always embarrassed by the words sacred, glorious,
> and sacrifice and the expression in vain. We had heard
> them, sometimes standing in the rain almost out of earshot,
> so that only the shouted words came through, and had read
> them, on proclamations that were slapped up by billpost-
> ers over other proclamations, now for a long time, and I had
> seen nothing sacred, and the things that were glorious had
> no glory and the sacrifices were like the stockyards at
> Chicago if nothing was done with the meat except to bury
> it. There were many words that you could not stand to hear
> and finally only the names of places had dignity. Certain
> numbers were the same way and certain dates and these
> with the names of the places were all you could say and
> have them mean anything. Abstract words such as glory,
> honour, courage, or hallow were obscene beside the con-
> crete names of villages, the numbers of roads, the names of
> rivers, the numbers of regiments and the dates.[39]

Hemingway's hero is embarrassed by the collapse of any representational function on the part of some of his signifiers. Once
we understand the "I" (in "I was always embarrassed by . . .")
as an iconic sign which, on the fictional level of the first person
singular hero, symbolizes some difficulties in the discursive
practice of the novelist in history, the crisis in representation is

both representing and represented at the same time. Since the problem is articulated so self-consciously, on the level of both iconic sign and novelistic discourse, representational product and representational process, this text can be read on at least two levels. First, although my interests now do not point this way, it can be read in terms of the iconic constraints of the fictional product of representation which, most immediately, are revealed in the language and characterization of the Hemingway hero, his muteness, his modernist inability to assert himself anywhere except in the barroom, the bedroom, the arena, and on safari.[40] Second, the crisis in representation can be studied on the level of discursive strategies in reality, in terms of novelistic rhetoric and ideological practice. On this level, our text appears historically predetermined by a considerable amount of incongruity between the given spectrum of public signification and the actually usable, much more limited range of the novelist's signifier. When this signifier appears conditioned by its increasingly tenuous relation to any "abstract words," i.e., to any generalizing mode of signification, the consequences are of course more complex than a naively referential understanding of fictional discourse can ascertain. If here we follow Wolfgang Iser's position, according to which the fictional organization of signifiers does "not serve to designate a signified object, but instead designate[s] *instructions* for the *production* of the signified,"[41] then it seems safe to suggest that the novelist's mode of appropriating language in the world of history and the reader's mode of appropriating the world of history through the production of a novelistic signified are implicated even more deeply.

The noteworthy thing about this twofold burden on representation, iconic and discursive,[42] is that representational action on the level of its fictional images and figurations persists almost unbroken. In *A Farewell to Arms* as in other fictions of this period, the mimetically structured narrative of individual experience, especially in the love story, continues virtually unchallenged. As opposed to the as yet unbroken representational forms of fictional figuration, the representational action on the level of discursive practice and novelistic methods is so much more deeply affected. What we have in this text is not only, as in Van Wyck Brooks', a singular transcription of the erosion of authority; rather, let me suggest, the erosion of the conditions for the novelistic production of a socially relevant signified is itself so represented that it is turned into the narrative of its unrepresentability.

In this sense, this text goes out of its way to transcribe the troublesome distance between what represents and what is represented in terms of the image of a spatial situation where the physical isolation of the impossible signified, through the rain and the sheer distance (from those who stood there and were told to listen), is strongly underlined. In this image, just as in that of "proclamations . . . slapped up . . . over other proclamations," the imperfectly achieved or redundantly handled process of communication serves as some metaphor of the inefficacy of the authority transported therein. When Frederic Henry heard these words, "sometimes standing in the rain almost out of earshot, so that only the shouted words came through," any claim of representativity is refuted, precisely because, in Van Wyck Brooks' language, "ideals of this kind, in this way presented . . . are wanting in all the elements of personal contact."

For Hemingway, "intellectual contact" still remained, if not "on the level of . . . finance, advertising, and trade," at least perhaps on that of "engineering," geography, and statistics. In *A Farewell to Arms*, "only the names of places" had "dignity," and the irony in the use of a concept like "dignity" must not detract from the fact that place names did retain their representational function and authority, so that "dignity" here, presumably, was associated with a simple, unbroken sense of continuity between signifier and signified. Hence, it was "the concrete names of villages, the numbers of roads, the names of rivers, the numbers of regiments and the dates" which allowed for what Van Wyck Brooks called "careful thought and intellectual contact," and which did not sound "obscene" as against the real obscenity in taking for granted continuity in the representational function of transcendental signifieds with so heavy an ideological liability.

Notes

1. David Carroll, *The Subject in Question: The Languages of Theory and the Strategies of Fiction* (Chicago: University of Chicago Press, 1982), p. 18.

2. This, of course, is the ultimate projection in Michel Foucault, *The Order of Things*, Alan Sheridan, tr. (London and New York: Pantheon, 1970), envisioning "the disappearance of man" (p. 385) as part of the process by which language emancipates itself from a constellation where men, in biology, political economy, and philology, represent to themselves their activities as living, laboring, and speaking beings. But even though the advent of psychoanalysis may indeed be said to "leap over representation" (p. 374), the stipulated suspension of representation in sociology and literary criticism appears as questionable as "the disappearance of Discourse" (p. 385).

3. *Allegory and Representation: Selected Papers from the English Institute 1979–80*, Stephen J. Greenblatt, ed. (Baltimore and London: Johns Hopkins University Press, 1981), p. ix.

4. Foucault, *The Order of Things*, p. 386.

5. *Ibid.*, p. 384.

6. *Ibid.*, p. 387. This, in fact, involves the claim that now, at long last, "language regains its unity."

7. *Ibid.*, p. 209.

8. Jacques Derrida, *Of Grammatology*, Gayatri C. Spivak, tr. (Baltimore and London: Johns Hopkins University Press, 1974), pp. 285ff.

9. See my article, "Appropriation and Modern History in Renaissance Prose Narrative," *New Literary History* (1982–83), 14:492: "The price of appropriation can be alienation, 'ends' undesired or beyond control."

10. As first proposed and developed at some length in my introduction to *Realismus in der Renaissance: Aneignung der Welt in der erzählenden Prosa*, Robert Weimann, ed. (Berlin and Weimar: Aufbau-Verlag, 1977), pp. 5–182.

11. See my critique of post-structuralist uses of "appropriation" in the Epilogue to *Structure and Society in Literary History*, expanded edition (Baltimore: Johns Hopkins University Press, 1984), pp. 267–323.

12. Michel Foucault, "What is an Author?" *Textual Strategies: Perspectives in Post-Structuralist Criticism*, Josué V. Harari, ed. (Ithaca: Cornell University Press, 1979), p. 157.

13. Karl Marx and Friedrich Engels, *Die heilige Familie*, in *Werke* (Berlin: Dietz Verlag, 1962), 2:177.

14. See Pierre Trotignon, "Réflexions métaphysiques sur le concept de représentation," *Revue des Sciences Humaines* (1974), 34:195.

15. As an almost random example, take "the moral perspective on sadism" in *Salò*, where "Pasolini duplicates that from which he wants to separate himself"; see Leo Bersani, "Representation and Its Discontents," *Allegory and Representation*, Greenblatt, ed., p. 152 ff. In literature, even the most solidly mimetic forms of realism.

as, for instance, George Eliot's *Felix Holt,* can "derive their own value from their devaluation, their unmasking, of the thing they represent." Catherine Gallagher, "The Politics of Culture and the Debate Over Representation," *Representations* (Winter 1984), 5:145.

16. Karl Marx, *Grundrisse: Foundations of the Critique of Political Economy,* Martin Nicolaus, tr. (New York: Vintage Books, 1973), p. 485.

17. *Ibid.,* p. 487.

18. See my "Mimesis in *Hamlet,*" *Shakespeare and the Question of Theory,* Patricia Parker and Geoffrey Hartman, eds. (London and New York: Methuen, 1985).

19. *Allegory and Representation,* p. x.

20. Carroll, *The Subject in Question,* p. 116.

21. Umberto Eco, *Zeichen: Einführung in einen Begriff und seine Geschichte,* Günter Memmert, tr. (Frankfurt a. M.: Suhrkamp, 1981), pp. 15, 186.

22. Mary Louise Pratt, *Toward a Speech Act Theory of Literary Discourse* (Bloomington and London: Indiana University Press, 1977), pp. 125 ff., 153 ff. This corresponds with Bakhtin's "dialogic" conception of language, according to which the word is "a two-sided act": the "product of the reciprocal relationship between speaker and listener, addresser and addressee." V. N. Voloshinov (M. Bakhtin), *Marxism and Philosophy of Language,* Ladislav Matejka and J. R. Titunik, trs. (New York: Seminar Press, 1973), p. 86. On Bakhtin's position, see Michael Holquist, "The Politics of Representation," *Allegory and Representation,* Greenblatt, ed., pp. 163–183, where the above quotation is discussed in a different context (p. 170).

23. J. L. Austin, *How To Do Things With Words,* 2d ed. (Cambridge: Harvard University Press, 1975), p. 52.

24. As first outlined in John R. Searle, *Speech Acts* (Cambridge: Cambridge University Press, 1969), ch. 1. By *Expression and Meaning* (1979) Searle had opted for "assertives" to replace "representatives" since, as he noted, every speech act with a propositional utterance is in some sense a representation; see John R. Searle, *Ausdruck und Bedeutung: Untersuchungen zur Sprechakttheorie,* Andreas Kemmerling, tr. (Frankfurt a. M.: Suhrkamp, 1982), pp. 31f., 40f., 207.

25. *The Complete Essays and Other Writings of Ralph Waldo Emerson,* Brooks Atkinson, ed. (New York: Modern Library, 1950), p. 262; page references to this edition are inserted in the text. Since, in the text itself, there is no space to refer my reading of the essays to the literature on the subject, let me at least note in parenthesis the gradually emerging complexity of the context in which, for Emerson, the ways of representation were affected by poetic as well as practical and, of course, theological ideas of appropriation. According to Emerson's symbolistic design, which Charles Feidelson first explored in *Symbolism and American Literature* (Chicago: University of Chicago Press, 1953), pp. 119–161, the material world itself, even before it is represented in discourse, is viewed as a "symbol," i.e., "representatively," through "the perception of the symbolic character of things" (p. 121). It is easy today to criticize the idealism in Emerson's universe of symbols, where all becomes poetry because the disjunctions between man and nature, subject and object are sublimely reconciled. Once the distinctions between the knower and the known are surrendered, once "the identity of the observer with the observed" (p. 146) is positively asserted, everything becomes representable as well as representing. Given the identity of "I mean" and "it means," man can be said to be permanently representing as well as universally represented in a discourse which, knowing no alienation, serves mutually supporting acts of

appropriating the world in the "I" and self-projecting the "I" into the world. As Feidelson notes: "To symbolize is man's function, but to symbolize is to *become* a symbol" (p. 145). However, Emerson's transcendental design does involve practical issues and cultural demands on the poet, among which, as Michael H. Cowan, *City of the West: Emerson, America, and Urban Metaphor* (New Haven and London: Yale University Press, 1967), p. 203, notes, the "assimilation of the modern city" is not the least important. But there were other factors and traditions which informed Emerson's belief "that the test or measure of poetic genius" was its ability to transform the circumstances of the nineteenth century into literary material (p. 3). As R. A. Yoder has shown in *Emerson and the Orphic Poet in America* (Berkeley, Los Angeles, London: University of California Press, 1978), pp. 7ff., the Orphic aspiration, the humanizing or taming of nature, is close to Emerson's vision of the Universal Man, especially when the representativeness of the poet's voice is related to his success in restoring the complete cycle of Orphic words. If, then, "nothing engaged Emerson more throughout his whole life than the search for a truly representative man"—Joel Porte, *Representative Man: Ralph Waldo Emerson in His Time* (New York: Oxford University Press, 1979), p. 314—the reasons and the results cannot be dismissed simply because their idealism did not correspond to the actual "experience" of his time. Although, as Barbara Packer has recently pointed out in *Emerson's Fall: A New Interpretation of the Major Essays* (New York: Continuum, 1982), Emerson's desire to evade temporality is strong and informs, among other things, his use of spatial images, such as the circle and the eye, yet his metaphorical language can be seen to collide with a humanistic rhetoric which joins poetry and science in a natural historiography of human culture. As Joseph G. Kronick, following Harold Bloom, has suggested, Emerson's is the historical language of reading and quotation, a humanistic rhetoric, "a 'language of desire and possession' and, hence, a voicing," in *American Poetics of History: From Emerson to the Moderns* (Baton Rouge and London: Louisiana State University Press, 1984), pp. 4, 15, 87.

26. Christopher Lasch, *The New Radicalism in America (1889–1963): The Intellectual as a Social Type* (New York: Knopf, 1965), p. xv.

27. *Ibid.*, p. 69. From an altogether different point of view, the growing area of dissociation between cultural and economic, political, and other activities has been emphasized by Daniel Bell, *The Cultural Contradictions of Capitalism* (New York: Basic Books, 1976).

28. Stephen Donadio, *Nietzsche, Henry James, and the Artistic Will* (New York: Oxford, 1978), p. 90.

29. Henry James, *The Tragic Muse* (New York: Penguin Modern Classics), pp. 74f.

30. *Ibid.*, p. 125.

31. Cit. Donadio, p. 61.

32. Michael Fried, "Representing Representation: On the Central Group in Courbet's *Studio*," *Allegory and Representation*, Greenblatt, ed., pp. 94–127.

33. *Ibid.*, p. x.

34. William Dean Howells, *Harper's Magazine* (May 1906), 112:959; cit. H. Wayne Morgan, *American Writers in Rebellion: From Mark Twain to Dreiser* (New York: Hill and Wang, 1965), p. 62.

35. Van Wyck Brooks, *America's Coming-of-Age* (New York: B. W. Huebsch, 1915), p. 7.

36. *Ibid.*, pp. 166f.

37. Wolfgang Iser, "Indeterminacy and the Reader's Response in Prose Fiction;" *Aspects of Narrative: Selected Papers from the English Institute*, J. Hillis Miller, ed. (New York: Columbia University Press, 1971), p. 41.

38. Brooks, *America's Coming-of-Age*, p. 7.

39. Ernest Hemingway, *A Farewell to Arms* (London, Toronto: Scribner, 1977), p. 133.

40. See Stanley Cooperman, *World War I and the American Novel* (Baltimore and London: Johns Hopkins University Press, 1967), p. 185. This echoes a critical revaluation, as perhaps most stringently formulated by Brom Weber, "Ernest Hemingway's Genteel Bullfight," *The American Novel and the Nineteen Twenties*, Stratford-upon-Avon Studies 13 (London: Edward Arnold, 1971), pp. 151–163.

41. Wolfgang Iser, *The Act of Reading: A Theory of Aesthetic Response* (Baltimore and London: Johns Hopkins University Press, 1978), p. 65.

42. The distinction that I have made (between the iconic product of novelistic representation, which is fictional, and the "dialogic" process in discourse, which is real in that it involves the expense of energy, time, etc. in actual writing and reading) may perhaps be said to be complementary of Felix Martinez-Bonati's position on the "essential duality of representations," as set forth in "Representation and Fiction," *Dispositio* (1981), vol. 5, esp. pp. 21 ff.

7

REPRESENTATION: A PERFORMATIVE ACT

Wolfgang Iser

THE following is an attempt to develop an implication of my essay "Feigning in Fiction."[1] I shall try to give a rough outline of how representation in literature is to be conceived, but the ideas put forward are of a tentative nature and could at best be called work in progress. The presentation will therefore be rather abstract and at times foreshortened.

The English term "representation" causes problems because it is so loaded. It entails or at least suggests a given which the act of representation duplicates in one way or another. Representation and mimesis have therefore become interchangeable notions in literary criticism, thus concealing the performative qualities through which the act of representation brings about something that hitherto did not exist as a given object. For this reason I am tempted to replace the English term "representation" with the German *Darstellung*, which is more neutral and does not necessarily drag all the mimetic connotations in its wake. In order to avoid macaronic language, however, I shall retain representation, which should always be read in the sense of *Darstellung*, i.e., as not referring to any object given prior to the act of representation.

To conceive of representation not in terms of mimesis but in terms of performance makes it necessary to dig into the structure of the literary text, laying bare the levels and conditions out of which the performative quality arises. This archaeology of the act of representation begins at a layer which I shall call the doubling structure of fictionality, produced by the fictionalizing acts of the literary text. This doubling is the implication of the essay mentioned above, and I shall take it as a point of departure. The argument to be developed, then, is not cast in current linguistic, tropological, or deconstructivist terms, but rather in terms of our anthropological makeup, aiming to answer the question: what does representation—arising out of the doubling structure of fictionality—tell us about ourselves? In view of the rather common practice of equating literature with fictionality, a caveat must be made right at the beginning. Fictionality is not to be identified with the literary text, although it is a basic constituent of it. For this reason I refrain from using the word "fiction" whenever I can and speak instead of fictionalizing acts. These do not refer to an ontologically given, but to an operation, and therefore cannot be identical to what they produce. An archaeology of representation in literature could not dispense with these fictionalizing acts which, in turn, gain their objective in the performative quality of representation into which they merge.

The act of selection which is integral to fictionality is a form of doubling. Each text makes inroads into extratextual fields of reference and by disrupting them creates an eventful disorder, in consequence of which both structure and semantics of these fields are subject to certain deformations and their respective constituents are differently weighted according to the various deletions and supplementations. Thus each one is being reshuffled in the text, and takes on a new form—a form which nevertheless includes, and indeed depends on, the function of that field in our interpreted world.

This function now becomes virtual and provides a background against which the operation of restructuring may stand out in relief, thus featuring the intention underlying the "coherent deformation.''[2] In addition, the act of selection splits up each field of reference, since the chosen elements can only take on their significance through the exclusion of others—this being the precondition for the eventful disorder, the resolution of which demands the assembly of a new meaning.

The act of selection also culls elements from other texts, but the resultant intertextuality should not be thought of in terms of blurring distinctions, let alone transcending the text to which reference has been made. On the contrary, the doubling process becomes even more complex, for the texts alluded to and the segments quoted begin to unfold unforeseeably shifting relationships both in respect to their own contexts and to the new ones into which they have been transplanted. Whatever the relationships may be like, two different types of discourse are ever present, and their simultaneity triggers a mutual revealing and concealing of their respective contextual references. From this interplay there emerges semantic instability, which is exacerbated by the fact that the two sets of discourse are also contexts for each other, so that each in turn is constantly switching from background to foreground. The one discourse becomes the theme viewed from the standpoint of the other, and vice versa. The resultant dynamic oscillation between the two ensures that their old meanings now become potential sources for new ones. It is such transformations that give rise to the aesthetic dimension of the text, for what had long seemed closed is now opened up again. The more one text incorporates other texts, the more intensified will be the process of doubling induced by the act of selection. The text itself becomes a kind of junction, where other texts, norms, and values meet and work upon each other; as a point of intersection its core is virtual, and only when actualized—by the potential recipient—does it explode into its plurivocity.

The structure pinpointed in the act of selection also underlies the act of combination. Here the boundaries that are crossed are intratextual, ranging from lexical meanings to the constellation of characters. Once again the process should not be mistaken for an act of transcendence, because the various clusters—whether they be words with outstripped meanings or semantic enclosures exceeded or infringed by the characters—are inseparably linked together and thus mutually inscribe themselves into one another. Every word becomes dialogic, and every semantic field is doubled by another. Through this double-voiced discourse every utterance carries something else in its wake, so that the act of combination gives rise to a duplication of what is present by that which is absent—a process that often results in the balance being reversed and the present serving only to spotlight the absent. Thus what is said ceases to mean itself, but instead enables what is not said to become present. The double meaning engendered by the act of combination opens up a multifariousness of interconnections within the text.

The act of selection brings about a network of relationships by invoking and simultaneously deforming extratextual fields of reference, thereby giving rise to the aesthetic quality, while the act of combination—by inscribing the absent into the present—becomes the matrix of that aesthetic quality.

A further and similar doubling effect comes about through the literary text's disclosure of itself as fiction. This takes place on two different levels: that of the attitude to be imposed on the reader, and that of what the text is meant to represent. If the literary text reveals itself to be a staged discourse, asking only that the world it represents should be taken *as if* it were a real world, then the recipient has to suspend his or her natural attitude to the thing represented (i.e., the real world). This does not mean that his or her natural attitude is transcended, for it is still present as a virtualized background, against which comparisons may be made and new attitudes may take their shape.

If we regard the world of the text as being bracketed off from the world it represents, it follows that what is within the brackets is separated from the reality in which it is normally embedded. Thus the bracketed world of the novel is not only to be seen as if it were a world, but it is also to be seen as a world that does not exist empirically. Consequently there will be a continual oscillation between the bracketed world and that from which it has been separated. The former therefore becomes a medium for revealing what has remained concealed in the empirical world, and whatever may be the relation between the two, it is the "as if" world that brings about the interplay between them. Thus self-disclosed fictionality as an act of boundary-crossing causes the recipient's natural attitude to be doubled by the new attitude demanded of him, and the world of the text to be doubled by the world from which it has been bracketed off and whose reverse side is thus brought to the fore.

The various acts of fictionalizing carry with them whatever has been outstripped, and the resultant doubleness might therefore be defined as the simultaneity of the mutually exclusive. This formula may help us to describe the structure of the fictional component of literature. It also allows for certain distinctions to be made, which are pertinent to the literary text. As the simultaneity of the mutually exclusive, the literary text can be clearly set off from structures which govern our everyday world but are outstripped by the coexistence of what is mutually incompatible. Even more importantly, fictionality also overshoots what psychoanalysis has come to describe as the "ego-rhythm," by inscribing the latent into the manifest or absence into presence. Primary and secondary processes are not usually telescoped into each other as, in the words of Anton Ehrenzweig, "structured focusing" and "oceanic undifferentiation" tend to interlink rhythmically, thereby establishing what he calls the "ego-rhythm."[3] It is therefore interesting to note that Ehrenzweig considers the coexistence of structured focusing and oceanic undifferentiation/dedifferentiation as a basic condition for art.

Furthermore, only in dreams does a coexistence between primary and secondary processes occur, which poses the question, to what extent does finctionality as the simultaneity of the mutually exclusive have its anthropological roots in the dream pattern, and to what extent can its various manifestations be conceived as a form of rehearsing such patterns. Fictionality, then, might be viewed as a staging of that which only the dream allows.

If fictionality in literature exceeds both the structures of our everyday reality and our psychic patterning, it produces a specifically aesthetic quality. The coexistence of the mutually exclusive gives rise to a dynamic oscillation resulting in a constant interpenetration of things which are set off from one another without ever losing their difference. The tension ensuing from the attempt to resolve this ineradicable difference creates an aesthetic potential which, as a source of meaning, can never be substituted by anything else. This does not imply that the fictional component of literature is the actual work of art; it implies that the fictional component is what makes the work of art possible.

If our simultaneity formula allows us to pinpoint the aesthetic nature of fictionality in literature in its contrast to empirical reality, it also enables us to distinguish literary fiction from that concept of fiction that has arisen from a logocentric way of thinking. Vaihinger defined fiction as a contradiction, because in order to represent reality it posits something that does not exist. He introduced into the discussion of fiction what he termed the law of shifts of ideas, implying that according to its use fiction assumes three different shapes: (1) If equated with that which it is meant to represent, fiction turns into dogmatism. (2) If used in order to investigate given realities, it turns into a hypothesis. (3) If its true nature is laid bare, it turns into a way of positing something which in itself is totally unreal yet serves as a means of ordering, measuring, and computing things that are real.[4] Therefore, Vaihinger maintains that all assumptions and presuppositions put forward in the history of epistemology are nothing but useful fictions which posit something as real in order to constitute reality or make given realities manageable. Whatever use fictions are put to, basically they are "consciously false"[5] and hence have to be unmasked. But if fiction is understood as a posited reality—no matter how necessary such a positing may be—in philosophic discourse it will lose the all-important qualities that characterize it in literature: its self-disclosure, its doubleness, and its simultaneity of the mutually exclusive.

When these features of fictionality are eclipsed in philosophic discourse, an irreconcilable dichotomy is bound to open up: What appears to be useful is something in disguise. The necessary unmasking, however, so painstakingly executed by Vaihinger, puts the usefulness into jeopardy. If this is to be preserved, epistemology, then, has to turn a blind eye to what it has seen through. Thus in philosophic discourse—particularly that of the empiricists—at one moment fiction is being unmasked as an invention, and the next it is being elevated to the status of a necessity. Small wonder that it turned into a burden for epistemology, which could not come to grips with the dual nature of the fact that make-believe is indispensable for organizing that which appears to be given.

So long as the vision of duality remains blinkered in this way, the particularity of literary fiction will remain hidden from view. What distinguishes fiction in philosophic discourse from fiction in literary discourse is the fact that in the former it remains veiled whereas in the latter it discloses its own fictional nature; therefore it is not discourse, but staged discourse, which, unlike fiction in philosophic discourse, cannot be falsified. It is not subject to any rules of practical application, as it is not designed for any specific use but is basically an enabling structure generating an aesthetic potential.

The doubling effect as the hallmark of literary fictionality comes about because the mutually exclusive realms that are bracketed together nevertheless retain their difference. If they did not, that which appears as doubled would instead merge into one. But while difference is a precondition for doubling, it is also the driving force behind its own removal. From this counter-movement arises the act of representation (*Darstellung*), for whatever is opened up by the simultaneity of the mutually exclusive demands to be closed again, so that representation might be described as the third dimension, in which whatever emerges from the doubling effect seeks to be united in a meaningful form.

Elementary operations of representation are inevitable simply because of the fact that boundary-crossing accentuates difference, and difference requires reconciliation of what now appears as separated. Since every representation is to be conceived as a bridging of what has been split apart by difference, the question arises as to whether difference can ever be removed. The answer is that it cannot, for if the removal of difference is the origin of representation, it follows that the origin will always be present in the product.

We shall now try to pinpoint the modes of interrelation. The fictionalizing acts simultaneously separate and encompass the extratextual fields and their intratextual deformation (selection), the intratextual semantic enclosures and their mutual telescoping (combination), and finally a bracketed world and its suspension of the empirical world; the difference is bridged by such modes of connections as overlap, condensation, disfigurement, displacement, mirroring, and dramatization. In all cases, the fields, positions, and worlds marked in the text undergo a change. However, all the modes of difference-removal bear the mark of their origin, out of which arise forms of representation articulating both the connection and the separation of the elements they encompass. The difference simultaneously appears to be overcome and present. Again a close resemblance suggests itself between these basic forms of representation and the world of dreams, in which occurs an interpenetration of what defies combination according to the terms set by the "symbolic order" of our conscious life.

It is the versatility of this structure that gives rise to the variety of representational forms. The presence of difference within the modes of its removal can be intensified through duality, subversion, or negation of the interlinked though mutually exclusive positions. It can also be weakened through correspondence, equivalence, affirmation, confirmation, or reconciliation, though even at this end of the scale the apparent absence of difference cannot be absolute, because otherwise correspondence, affirmation, etc. could not signal anything. If difference is removed, representation appears only to be serving pragmatic ends, with a resultant loss of aesthetic tension, and indeed of truthfulness, as evinced in a good deal of light literature. The elimination of difference therefore makes representation seem deficient, so that even the attempt at total removal of difference spotlights the impossibility of such an endeavor. But perhaps the most interesting points on the scale are those in the middle, especially where difference is present as ambivalence or duplicity in the forms of its removal.

Representation, then, might be classified as "fact from fiction,"[6] in that it arises out of the difference characteristic of fictionality in literature which, as a form of boundary-crossing, leads to the simultaneity of mutually exclusive positions. It is the elucidation of difference that makes representation necessary, but the elementary forms of representation already show clearly that in the last analysis difference can never be eradicated, because as the origin of representation it can never be pinpointed by or equated with its product. Thus difference defies determination by any form of representation. As representation, however, arises out of the attempt to remove difference, what is to be removed appears to be something which does not have the nature of an object and cannot be qualified as actually "being" in the Heideggerian sense of the term *seiend*. It is intangible, and this fact cannot be concealed by any forms of representation—on the contrary, this intangibility inscribes itself into every form of representation, thus suffusing all of them with aesthetic semblance.

Semblance, then, appears to be a basic ingredient of representation, as it gives form to the otherwise inaccessible, for although difference (or the attempt to remove it) is the driving force behind representation, it is so only because it perpetually defers its own removal. The semblance is therefore the result of the resistance put up by difference against any form of mediation, and in turn this resistance ensures that no conceptualization of the inaccessible can ever be authentic. This apparent lack of authenticity, however, makes the semblance into a critical instrument to be applied against all explanations which claim to have fathomed origins, and so we may say that difference is present in the aesthetic semblance as a simultaneous conceptualization and inaccessibility of origins. But although difference downgrades representation to the level of semblance, it also needs this semblance in order to manifest itself.

The semblance is aesthetic insofar as something is represented that has no given reality of its own, and is therefore only the condition for the production of an imaginary object. Representation can only unfold itself in the recipient's mind, and it is through his active imaginings alone that the intangible can become an image. It follows, then, that representation, by bridging difference and thus making the intangible conceivable, is an act of performing and not—as Western tradition has reiterated time and again—an act of mimesis, since mimesis presupposes a given reality that is to be portrayed in one way or another.

Similarly, this performative element distinguishes the aesthetic semblance from Schiller's "beautiful semblance" and from Hegel's "sensuous appearance of the idea." The beautiful semblance always presupposed a reality on which it depended, but which it was meant to transcend. The sensual appearance of the idea presupposes the existence of a truth, with an inseparable unity between its abstract notion and its tangible manifestation; thus "the idea is not only true but also beautiful."[7] Aesthetic semblance, on the other hand, neither transcends a given reality nor mediates between idea and manifestation; it is an indication that the inaccessible can only be approached by being staged. Representation is therefore both performance and semblance. It conjures up an image of the unseeable, but being a semblance, it also denies it the status of a copy of reality. The aesthetic semblance can only take on its form by way of the recipient's ideational, performative activity, and so representation can only come to full fruition in the recipient's imagination; it is the recipient's performance that endows the semblance with its sense of reality. And so representation causes the recipient to repeat the very same performance out of which it arose, and it is the repeat of this performance that initiates and ensures the transfer from text to reader of that which is to be represented.

Now the fact that the aesthetic semblance brings about

this transfer from text to reader does not mean that the recipient's status advances to that of "a sovereign of understanding" or "the hero of the text."[8] If the aesthetic semblance is to take on its tone of reality, we must place our own thoughts and feelings at the disposal of that which representation seeks to make present in us.

In this respect the required activity of the recipient resembles that of an actor, who in order to perform his role must use his thoughts, his feelings, and even his body as an analogue for representing something he is not. In order to produce the determinate form of an unreal character, the actor must fade out his own reality. At the same time, however, he does not know precisely who, say, Hamlet is, for one cannot properly identify a character who has never existed. Thus role-playing endows a figment with a sense of reality in spite of its impenetrability which defies total determination. The reader finds himself in much the same situation. To imagine what has been simulated by aesthetic semblance entails placing our thoughts and feelings at the disposal of an unreality, bestowing on it a semblance of reality in proportion to a reducing of our own reality. For the duration of the performance we are both ourselves and someone else. Staging oneself as someone else is a source of aesthetic pleasure; it is also a means whereby representation is transferred from text to reader.

Representation as aesthetic semblance indicates the presence of the inaccessible. Literature reflects life under conditions that are either not available in the empirical world or are denied by it. Consequently literature turns life into a storehouse from which it draws its material in order to stage that which in life appeared to have been sealed off from access. The need for such a staging arises out of man's decentered position: we are, but do not have ourselves.[9] Wanting to have what we are, i.e., to step out of ourselves in order to grasp our own identity, would entail having final assurances as to our origins, but as these underlie what we are, we cannot "have" them. Beckett follows similar lines when he says that "live and invent" appears to be the alternative;[10] we know that we live, but we don't know what living is, and if we want to know, we have to invent what is denied us. Our unwillingness to accept this state of affairs is evinced by the multiplicity of our attempts to conceptualize life. Anthropologically speaking, these conceptualizations are motivated by our inherent drive to make accessible the inaccessible, and this holds true even of the pragmatic solutions offered by our many ideologies, which in the final analysis are meant to determine what eludes our grasp. It is therefore little wonder that one set of concepts is frequently rejected and subsequently replaced by another, which in turn has to be exposed as a fiction merely designed to compensate for what has been withheld from us. Whatever shape or form these various conceptualizations may have, their common denominator is the attempt to explain origins. In this respect they close off those very potentialities that literature holds open. Of course literature also springs from the same anthropological need, since it stages what is inaccessible, thus compensating for the impossibility of knowing what it is to be. But literature is not an explanation of origins; it is a staging of the constant deferment of explanation, which makes the origin explode into its multifariousness.

It is at this point that aesthetic semblance makes its full impact. Representation arises out of and thus entails the removal of difference, whose irremovability transforms representation into a performative act of staging something. This staging is almost infinitely variable, for in contrast to explanations, no single staging could ever remove difference and so explain origin. On the contrary, its very multiplicity facilitates an unending mirroring of what man is, because no mirrored manifestation can ever coincide with our actual being. This may be viewed as a drawback for literature, in comparison to the temporary comfort provided by conceptualizations of life as an explanation of origins; but it is also an advantage—indeed a unique advantage, insofar as knowledge of what man is can only come about in the form of play. Play, however, is something which the global conceptualizations of life cannot afford to incorporate into their explanatory patterns; they have to be one-dimensional in view of the finality of the explanation to be achieved and the certainties to be provided by them. The ludic nature of literature is basically unlimited, and as the different moves in the game attempt to stage the inaccessible, so they simultaneously present an illusion of origin and defer explanation of it.

It is the play element in the removal of difference that distinguishes literature as a form of staging from all conceptualizations of life as forms of explanations, but even this infinite variety does not fully explain the fascination of the aesthetic semblance which gives presence to the inaccessible. Staging presupposes a given something that is to appear on stage. But this "something" cannot be totally incorporated into the process of staging, since this would make the staging its own given something. In other words, staging is an activity propelled by something other than itself. Whatever takes place on the stage is in the service of something absent which makes itself felt through what is present. Staging is therefore a basic form of doubling, not least because it entails an awareness of its own doubling being ineradicable.

This can even be traced in the literary use of language, where the denotative function is suspended in order to release a figurative function. This does not mean that denotation is totally eclipsed. However, what it designates is no longer meant to represent a something to which it refers, but serves as an analogue instead, through which a wordless desire may find expression or a response-inviting appeal may be signaled. The representative function of speech is faded out in order to give voice to an expressive or an appealing function evoking that which defies verbalization. Thus with literary language, which is staged discourse, what is staged is simultaneously present but also exceeded in the very act of staging. Out of this doubleness of staging arises its aesthetic character as opposed to the conceptualizations of life as explanations of origins which seek to exercise an interest-oriented and hence a pragmatic control over that which cannot be known. The determinacy of all the global conceptualizations makes the unknowable disappear, whereas staging enables us both to register and even experience it. This makes the aesthetic semblance into a source of satisfaction, but also endows it with an ineluctable sense of duplicity. Perhaps this form of doubling—having the unavailable through an image of make-believe—may help us to explore given items in our anthropological makeup.

What is meant by this exploration can be briefly illustrated by having a look at two of Shakespeare's greatest tragedies. In *King Lear* we have the co-presence of two mutually exclusive facts of life. On the one hand there is Lear's insight into the inevitability of endings, and on the other is his experience that things go on. Ending and continuing are basic forms of life, but when they are both present simultaneously in one man's consciousness, they begin to invalidate each other. Continuing robs the end of its uniqueness, which would otherwise be a consolation. But from the standpoint of a finite individual, endless continuation is both aimless and beyond his control. Thus at the beginning of the tragedy, Lear acts as if the end were unique. Therefore he is set to glorify this event by trading his kingdom for deliberately solicited flattery. But after a while he realizes that things go on, and so the end is robbed of its consoling pathos, and Lear is "left darkling" in the co-presence of ending and continuing.

There is a similar problem in *Macbeth*. Macbeth wishes that his blow might be the be-all and the end-all—in other words that being and the ending of being should coincide. Once again a co-presence of the mutually exclusive looms large in the play, although Macbeth's impossible desire seems quite plausible from a human point of view.[11]

The simultaneity of the mutually exclusive, as it variously appears in Lear and Macbeth, is not even to be viewed in terms of a conflict, as the co-presence allows neither a real conflict nor an imaginable solution. Such basic facts of life as ending/continuing, or being/ simultaneously ending, are clearly beyond conflict, as there is no direction for unfolding this mutual cancellation. Thus we are given the impression that great literature is characterized by its presentation of insoluble human predicaments. If this is indeed so, then the decentered position of man, as staged by literature, appears in a somewhat unexpected light. Given his deep-rooted desire to be and at the same time to have himself in order that he might know what it is to be, literature—as the staging of this inaccessibility—would seem to offer two ways of meeting that need: either it can fulfill the desire by providing an image of having the unavailable, or it can stage the desire by an inverted mirror image, thus providing a rear view of this desire. In the first instance, by staging the fulfillment of it, literature will come close to what conceptualizations of life intend to achieve, and consequently historical necessities will condition the form of this desired fulfillment. The greater emphasis on compensation, the more dated will the solution appear to future generations of readers. In the second instance, the inversion or nonfulfillment of the deeply entrenched desire to be and simultaneously to have oneself will, paradoxically, endow this kind of literature with far greater longevity and even enduring fascination, since what it stages is not an ephemeral compensation but a deferment of compensation. This staged deferment is indeed a reason for literature surviving beyond the context of its genesis, and from this fact we might draw two possible conclusions: (1) The staging of what eludes our grasp due to man's decentered position exercises greater impact if, instead of an illusory wish-fulfillment, it spotlights the illusory nature of wished-for compensations. (2) Such a staging will lead, not to a flight from that which is inaccessible, but to an awareness of the fact that we can never be identical to the countless possibilities we produce in our attempts to grasp the ungraspable.

It is precisely because we are the source of all these possibilities that we cannot be identical to any of them, but can only hang suspended, as it were, amid our own products. The kind of literature that exceeds its period of genesis by exercising an undiminished appeal stages this "hanging between," whose depicting does not compensate anything anymore. Yet the image it offers of this precarious state makes us endure the agonizing certainty that knowledge of our origin is withheld from us. Perhaps ultimately the fascination of the aesthetic quality in literature originates in providing an experience of what it is to hang between our achievements and our possibilities. It is a state of unending oscillation by means of which closed positions are opened up again and apparent finalities are outstripped. To provide conditions for this state to be imagined, its staging must simultaneously deprive these conditions of any claim to authenticity. Otherwise we would get a frozen image of the ever-oscillating state, thereby turning it into an untruth. If this state, however, can never take on the character of an authenticated object, its presence is always an aesthetic semblance, and representation is first and foremost an act of performance, bringing forth in the mode of staging something which in itself is not a given.

Notes

1. "Feigning in Fiction," in The Identity of the Text, Mario J. Valdés and Owen Miller, eds. (Toronto: University of Toronto Press, 1985), pp. 204–228.

2. For the significance of that concept, see Maurice Merleau-Ponty, Das Auge und der Geist, Hans Werner Arndt, tr. (Hamburg: Rowohlt, 1967), p. 84.

3. Anton Ehrenzweig, The Hidden Order of Art (Berkeley and Los Angeles: University of California Press, 1967), pp. 120 f.

4. See Hans Vaihinger, Die Philosophie des Als-Ob (Leipzig: F. Meiner, 1922), pp. 219–230. The Philosophy of "As If," C. K. Ogden, tr. (New York: Barnes and Noble, 1952).

5. Ibid., pp. xii and 290 ff.

6. Nelson Goodman, Ways of Worldmaking (Indianapolis: Hackett, 1978), p. 102.

7. G. W. F. Hegel, Ästhetik, Friedrich Bassenge, ed. (Berlin: Aufbau-Verlag, 1955), p. 146. Aesthetics: Lectures on Fine Art, T. M. Knox, tr. (Oxford: Clarendon Press, 1975).

8. As has been suggested by Odo Marquard, "Das Fiktive als Ens Realissimum," in Funktionen des Fiktiven (Poetik und Hermeneutik X), Dieter Henrich and Wolfgang Iser, eds. (Munich: Fink Verlag, 1983), p. 491.

9. See Helmut Plessner, "Die anthropologische Dimension der Geschichtlichkeit," in Sozialer Wandel. Zivilisation und Fortschritt als Kategorien der soziologischen Theorie, Hans Peter Dreitzel, ed. (Neuwied: Luchterhand, 1972), p. 160.

10. See Samuel Beckett, Malone Dies (New York: Grove, 1956), pp. 18 f.

11. See also Frank Kermode, The Sense of an Ending (New York: Oxford University Press, 1967), pp. 82 ff.

ESSAYS AFTER THE ESSAYS

8

CRITICISM TODAY

Dominick LaCapra

> James looked at the Lighthouse. He could see the white-
> washed rocks; the tower, stark and straight; he could see
> that it was barred with black and white; he could see
> windows in it; he could even see washing spread on the
> rocks to dry. So that was the Lighthouse, was it?
> No, the other was also the Lighthouse. For nothing
> was simply one thing.
>
> Virginia Woolf, *To the Lighthouse*

HOW can one present a paper that tries to account for critical
discourses today, even if one acknowledges that any attempt to
"do justice" to them can never attain metanarrative or "mega-
theoretical" mastery and must by contrast accept, indeed ac-
tively affirm, its own status as one discursive venture engaging
in dialogue with heterogeneous others? And where can one
begin except with a brief and inadequate evocation of the problematic nature—the frustrations and the hopes—of contemporary criticism?

Any assembly of "critics" today will have representatives of various established departments who are uneasy with
their own "representative" function and may find more to say,
listen to, or at least argue about with other "critics" than with

more securely "representative" members of their own department or field. Indeed contemporary critics are no longer content with interdisciplinary efforts that simply combine, compare, or synthetically unify the methods of existing academic disciplines. Their questioning of established disciplines both raises doubts about internal criteria of purity or autonomy and unsettles the boundaries and protocols of given fields. Criticism in this sense is a discursive agitation running across a variety of disciplines and having an uneasy relation to its own institutionalization. It seeks out threshold "positions" that cannot securely locate their own theoretical grounds, and it may even cultivate the risks of insistently hybridized discourses— discourses that may breed fruitful variants but may also prove to be sterile if not monstrous. At least in terms of academic politics, the strategy of "criticism" is thus transgressive, and it demands not a quarantined place in the margins of established discourses or disciplines but a generalized displacement and rearticulation of them.

Yet it is also the case that disconcertingly "liminal" criticism has proved more compelling in certain established fields than in others: in literary criticism, continental philosophy, interpretive social theory, and intellectual history, say, than in literary history, analytic philosophy, positivistic social science, and conventional historiography. And within the fields or disciplines in which it has made a difference, it has been most pronounced in already marginalized areas of the university, even if "mainstream" thought has subsequently accommodated it in more or less naturalized form. Hence it has appeared first in French or Comparative Literature before making significant inroads in English departments, and it has had a sporadic, uneven role in intellectual history sensitive to the exceptional voices and counter-discourses of the past before affecting social history attuned to representative discourses and collective "mentalities." Elsewhere "criticism" in the sense I have evoked makes its mark at best through the active resistance or renewed stimulus for self-definition it provokes as well as through the convenient image of the "radically other" it provides for those seeking a reaffirmation of their identity.

In these respects, criticism is itself a paradoxical genre that contests the limits of generic classification. It brings down on itself the ire and the irony of those with an interest in reasserting the conceptual and institutional "integrity" of "realms of discourse" and disciplines. The very discourses of critics speaking in hybridized or "undecidable" voices are difficult to classify, and they at most bear the marks of certain disciplinary inflections which give them a relative specificity. Yet signs of internal strain also appear, for disciplinary and professional bonds have their hold even on those who grow restive with their constraints, and one may tire of the repeated sounds of the new or the predictable discovery of the uncanny in every discursive nook and cranny. This strain may help to explain the reversions to type and the "god-that-failed" reactions of some critics who become disenchanted with their earlier "experimental" selves, but it may also induce reflection about what specifically ought to be changed and what preserved in a discipline one questions. It may also induce one to confront the general problem of how the relations among disciplines or fields should be rearticulated.

Especially for those critics who see continental thought as a reference point, the most imposing tradition of critical theory is represented by Marxism. And one of the tasks of recent criticism has been the attempt to sort out the elements of the Marxist tradition in an attempt to discern what is still relevant to contemporary sociopolitical and interpretive issues.[1] One current in Marx's texts that was further codified by Engels and the theorists of the Second International is, of course, positivism, and it has been subjected to a far-reaching attack in the recent past. One might define positivism as the isolation and autonomization of the constative dimension of discourse. It fosters a narrowly "social-scientific" delimitation of research in empirical and analytic terms, and it avoids or occludes the very problem of a critical theory of society and culture. Jürgen Habermas has been a foremost critic of Marx in this respect, and he has attempted to recast critical theory in a complex manner that includes a relativized "constative" dimension in a more complex hermeneutic and emancipatory paradigm for social research.[2] In Louis Althusser's powerful rereading of Marx, however, one may perhaps detect tendencies that lend themselves to a subtle rehabilitation of positivism. Althusser's important conception of ideology as centered on the subject seems to obviate the possibility of an objectivist or scientistic ideology, notably one that privileges science by presenting it as a "subjectless" discourse. Science seems to become a "realm of discourse" that unproblematically transcends ideology, and the very role of a "scientific" subject in constituting an object realm is itself occulted. Yet other aspects of Althusser's conception of ideology would imply that its wiles are many-sided, and the recurrent displacement of the necessary blindnesses it brings is a sign of the necessity of recurrent critique.[3]

A second tendency in Marx's texts has had a remarkable staying power in modern thought despite the criticism of Althusser and many others. I am of course referring to Hegelianism. At times in Marx, e.g., in the Afterword to the second German edition of *Capital*, it is amalgamated with positivism in a composite image of a positivist dialectic that is revealed as the inverted Hegelian "rational kernel in the mystic shell" of speculative idealism. But, whatever the precise form it takes, Hegelian Marxism provides the basis for a metanarrative or "dialectic" in which the proletariat becomes the "materialist" surrogate for *Geist* as the redemptive subject of history. Hegelian Marxism has recently received a new lease on life in Fredric Jameson's theory of the political unconscious which, through a disarming ruse, construes the vast metanarrative of class struggle leading to redemptive emancipation as itself the repressed content of contemporary thought.[4]

My condensed and truncated account thus far should at least indicate that I would stress the heterogeneous forces in Marx's texts that help to account for the divergences and inner strains in subsequent Marxism. I would like at this point to mention two further aspects of Marx's thought that I think remain highly relevant today—aspects that deserve to be defended, if need be against other aspects of Marx's thought itself.

One of them is general: it is the very understanding of critical theory in contrast to both narrowly positivistic and expansively metanarrative inclinations. The problem is of course that of the nature of the critical theory one would defend. I would argue for a displacement of totalizing dialectics in the direction of supplementarity and dialogism that raise the issue of articulating the relations between contestatory, indeed incommensurable, forces in thought and practice.[5] This displacement requires an investigation of language and signifying practices in general that Marx never provided and that he even tended to obscure in his binary opposition between base and superstructure.[6]

   A second aspect of Marx's thought is more specific. It is his critique of a commodity system, much of which remains applicable even to a transformed capitalism and may, furthermore, furnish a "model" for the critique of other developments in modern history. Crucial to Marx's analysis of the commodity form is his delineation of the process of reductive equalization or commensuration whereby qualitative differences are bracketed in the constitution of exchange value. A commodity as an exchange value can replace or be substituted for another commodity. Substitution implies that commodities have something in common beneath their appearances in phenomenal form. (Marx is here rendering and developing the metaphysical assumptions of classical economics in free indirect style.) This principle of identity is asserted by Marx to be abstract labor power—an identity implicit in the theories of classical economists but never made explicit by them. Abstract labor power is itself produced through a reduction of qualitatively different modes of living labor to a commensurable, equalized, homogeneous form—human labor in the abstract, which is then employed as a means in the production of exchange values. The process of equalization or commensuration reaches its reductive apogee in the designation of one commodity, ultimately in the money-form, as universal equivalent.

   Marx's crucial analysis of the commodity harbors internal difficulties. The very voice in which it is formulated is divided: it is both positivistic and critical. The analysis, even in its critical dimension, seems to accept the binary opposition between exchange and use value. Use value is related to qualitative differences between commodities and seems entirely transparent in nature. The culminating account of "commodity fetishism" itself seems to trace the mystified, fetishized character of the commodity to a simple reversal: "A commodity is therefore a mysterious thing, simply because in it the social character of men's labor appears to them as an objective character stamped upon the product of that labor." This statement has the virtue of calling into question the process of naturalization or normalization essential to ideological mystification.[7] Yet the difficulty is that the strategy of simple reversal invests the social with foundational powers, and it readily accords both with a redemptive rendition of class struggle and with a productivist image of the revolutionary goal. The unproblematic notion of the transparency of use value, moreover, obscures the more basic issue of the very opposition between use and exchange value as well as the implication of use value in utilitarian norms that are operative in the reduction of living labor to instrumentalized labor power. (But does "use value" also evoke an older idea of usufruct as well as function in a newer, utopian register?) The more forceful dimension of Marx's account, I think, lies in the critical delineation of the mechanism of equalization involving a reduction of labor to "the same unsubstantial reality in each [exchange value], a mere congelation of homogeneous labor power." This critique enables one to question the very division between the instrumentalized labor and autonomized symbolic meaning in the fetishized commodity, and it may be extrapolated into a more general displacement of what Marx saw as the "absurd" forms of relationship in a commodity system.

Equalization is itself a normalizing device, and it is crucial in the formation of pure binary oppositions insofar as each opposite is fully homogeneous, identical, or equal to itself and totally different from its other. The critique of normalization and of pure binary opposites has, of course, been pronounced in so-called post-structuralism, and it signals a way in which the critique of language and of signifying practices in general finds a point of contact with a critique of the commodity system as a crucial signifying practice in modern society. Here the investigation of processes of signification may be seen as a necessary supplement to Marxism understood as a critical theory of society and culture, but of course it is a supplement that takes Marxism in certain directions rather than others.

The three "post-structural" figures to whom I shall briefly allude in the attempt to indicate the relation of a critique of signifying practices to a critical theory of society are Jacques Derrida, Michel Foucault, and Jean-François Lyotard.[8] Except for certain facets of Foucault's work, all three may be seen as engaging in a critique of positivism, one of whose primary characteristics is a reductive equalization of all texts and artifacts into a homogeneous body of documentary "information" or constative statements. All three also elude the familiar charge that post-structuralism is a neoformalism, especially in its manifest avoidance of political and historical issues and its autonomization of texts as scenes for the narcissistic play of liberated (or what Derrida would call transcendental) signifiers. In addition, I would contend that their work suggests the project of a critical genealogy of both positivism and formalism as complementary, fetishized enterprises: one reducing texts or artifacts to their narrowly constative dimension as documents in the reconstitution of "contexts" or "social realities," while the other becomes fixated on the internal play of the performative dimension of texts isolated from the "external" (or externalized) contexts of their writing, reception, and critical reading. Indeed, the following passage from Hemingway's *A Farewell to Arms* discloses how the quest for formal purity, averse to any complicity with the contamination of language in the dominant society, may even have results indistinguishable from those of documentary positivism:

> I was always embarrassed by the words sacred, glorious, and sacrifice and the expression in vain. We had heard them, sometimes standing in the rain almost out of earshot,

so that only the shouted words came through, and had read them, on proclamations that were slapped up by billposters over other proclamations, now for a long time, and I had seen nothing sacred, and the things that were glorious had no glory and the sacrifices were like the stockyards at Chicago if nothing was done with the meat except to bury it. There were many words that you could not stand to hear and finally only the names of places had dignity. Certain numbers were the same way and certain dates and these with the names of the places were all you could say and have them mean anything. Abstract words such as glory, honour, courage, or hallow were obscene beside the concrete names of villages, the numbers of roads, the names of rivers, the numbers of regiments and the dates.[9]

Could one see here a bizarre convergence between a hard-nosed but pathos-ridden aestheticism and positivism? (One could, for example, read the passage as a prolegomenon to a certain kind of social history.)

In different ways, Derrida, Foucault, and Lyotard attempt to intensify a "legitimation crisis" in modern society as well as to suggest antidotes to it. Their variable modes of writing are strategic interventions in the linguistic institution that has often been taken as the bedrock of communication and community. At times they almost seem to engage in stylistic guerrilla warfare waged under a black sun. They may even carry to an explosion point the "crisis of representation" that artistic and intellectual elites have confronted at least since the end of the nineteenth century.[10] Indeed, the stylistic experimentation and "alienation effects" in the writing of modern cultural elites may be interpreted as a complex response to disorder and "alienation" in the larger society—a response that resists, however problematically, symbolic and contemplative solutions to these problems in either explanatory or narrative form.

One of the recurrent motifs of social theorists such as Marx or Durkheim is that the established modern order is in fundamental ways an established disorder. For Nietzsche the established disorder is the scene of both nihilistic "decadence" that had to be worked through and the setting for unheard-of creativity, at times played out on the edge of madness. The most potent modes of thought had to be the most radically ambivalent and dangerous, open both to the best uses and the worst abuses. One point on which Durkheim and Nietzsche, who are so different in many respects, might nonetheless agree is that modern society and culture posed with special urgency the problem of the relation between the exception and the rule or, in other terms, the relation between transgression and normative commitment. They both also advocated the careful study of mores, routines, and practices in everyday life.

It may well be true that a desirable goal of sociocultural life is to provide the institutional and ethical basis for strong commitment to practices and routines in daily life that create trust among members of society.[11] This context might both lessen the prevalence or the need of routine transgression and make "sublime" or "uncanny" overtures more engaging and less banalized. It may also be the case that certain tacit ties and practical commitments have retained greater resiliency in areas of everyday life, and it would be foolhardy to root them out on the pretext that a "cultural revolution" must be furthered in every conceivable manner. But it is, I think, self-deceptive to point to everyday practice and routine or to identify face-to-face conversation (in contrast with the written text) as a pragmatic origin or source for the generation of meaning and thus the answer to doubt and criticism. This gesture is suspiciously ideological in a number of ways. It is altogether unspecific in its characterization of routine and the everyday "life world," thereby generalizing and normalizing what may well be only partial realities. It also ignores the problem of the extent to which a "legitimation crisis" has affected the level of everyday routine itself, turning routine into empty ritual and making cliché the linguistic definition of ordinary social reality. (One need not recount the familiar catalogue of daily mishaps and routine horrors that have helped to make the "sitcom" and the disaster movie two of the most "representative" documents of contemporary life.) Indeed in proposing everyday *phronesis* or

practical consciousness as the "meaningful" way out, one oc-
cults the very role of ideology in creating routine complacency,
and one threatens to replicate its role in one's own analysis.
One also transfers to a common-sense level the metaphysic of
origins and of presence one believes one has transcended, and
one may even further a methodological populism that in recent
sociology and social history has at times taken a decidedly anti-
intellectual turn.[12]

It should no longer be necessary to observe that Derrida
does not privilege writing in the ordinary sense and that his
notion of the text is not to be identified with the discrete written
artifact (and certainly not with codes). The very propensity,
despite all evidence to the contrary, to see his work in this light
is instructive, however, for it testifies to the deep-seated nature
of the metaphysical desires Derrida "deconstructs." Derrida
has insisted that philosophy, despite its own desire for totality
and closure, is not a separate realm and that the "logocentric"
metaphysic of presence, which significant philosophical texts
stage in a powerful *Darstellung*, may be operative in a more off-
hand and routine manner in everyday life as well as in the
social sciences that study it. Derrida has also recently stressed
the need to rethink the very notion of the institution, and he has
made some attempt to connect his readings of written texts with
a critique of institutions and forms of everyday life, notably in
the cases of education, technology, mass media, and nuclear
power.[13] But it is initially plausible to argue that the effects of
Derrida's intervention have been most evident in the rereading
and rewriting of written texts and that the implications of his
work for institutional formations and everyday life need to be
further developed and made more accessible in sociopolitical
terms. What should be apparent, however, is that the oft-quoted
"maxim," "*il n'y a pas de hors-texte*" (there is no outside-the-
text), is not a charter for formalism, an invitation to "intratextual" narcissism, or an endorsement of the "free play" of liberated signifiers. It is a critique of the attempt to ground the work
and play of textuality in some totally extratextual foundation
or "context" that itself would escape involvement in a rela-

tional network or field. And the very strategy of "deconstruction" requires that one assume a necessary complicity with dubious discourses and attempt to work through them in the articulation of significantly different possibilities. The implication is that there is no "inside-the-text" either—no autonomous realm of signification of either "literary" or "documentary" language. In brief, formalism is as questionable as positivism. One has here, I think, an invitation to reformulate the entire problem of the relation between "texts" and "contexts" in terms that may take one further in directions Derrida has at least traced.

The interest of Foucault, as well as the inducement not to make too much of his polemic with Derrida, is that he has ostensibly gone further in precisely these directions. He has investigated discursive and social practices as they bear on the "mad," the imprisoned, and various other social groups, and he has construed the treatment of "transgressive" minorities as indicative of the processes operating in society at large. More generally, he has forged an alliance between history and criticism that poses a stylistic and substantive challenge to standard procedures in both conventional historiography and literary criticism. Indeed a closer articulation of the initiatives of Foucault and Derrida might reveal a way to work through certain limitations of established disciplines.

Yet, at least on a thematic level, Foucault has often treated specific texts as mere tokens or symptoms of larger epistemic or discursive structures rather than explicitly posing in a more complex and problematic way the issue of symptomatic, critical, and possibly transformative relations between texts and their contexts of writing and reception. (There is a parallel, allusory use of artifacts in the more lyrical dimension of Foucault's writing.) In addition, he has often created the impression of offering a massively "totalizing" account, one which paradoxically eliminates or plays down the forces of resistance in the past that are the analogues of forces Foucault would like to further in the present. Thus in his influential *Discipline and Punish* (*Surveiller et punir*), Foucault—especially toward the

end of the book—provides the image of a "carceral archipelago" or a panoptic society that conjures up the fantasia of a
totalitarian organization of societies in the nineteenth century
that is beyond the dreams of even recent regimes.[14] (In his
contribution to L'Impossible prison, Foucault specifies that his
object of analysis in Discipline and Punish was a normative
paradigm cutting across a number of institutions—one that
motivated thought and action but was not fully realized in
existing society.[15] This retrospective self-interpretation is pertinent and fruitful, but much in the book exceeds its modest
claim.) Foucault has also proposed a concept of power-knowledge that is critical in revealing the complicity of forces that are
often neatly separated, especially in defense of a value-neutral,
unworldly, contemplative idea of research. He has thus elicited
the multiple ways idle curiosity is not simply gratuitous but
directly or indirectly implicated in a regime from which its
advocates would like to disinculpate themselves. But, in the
guise of a kind of "black functionalism," the form Foucault's
notion of power-knowledge has taken threatens to revive an
indiscriminate, late 1960s idea of "the system" or "the dominant ideology" that necessarily "co-opts" everything it
touches, including all forms of resistance. This all-consuming
idea offers too simple a short-cut in interpretation, and it may
even be politically self-defeating. It does, however, accord with
another questionable feature of some of Foucault's writing—a
feature that is perhaps most pronounced in his famous "principal" texts. It is the comprehensive delegitimation of existing
phenomena as hopelessly complicit with the dominant "system" of power-knowledge and the confinement of political
response to faint apocalyptic tremors on the other side of disaster.

This entire frame of reference not only provides little
space for the "punctual" political interventions Foucault defends in his occasional pieces. It also obscures the workings of
hegemony. Hegemony cannot be identified with power in that
it articulates power and authority in a manner that is at least
partially internalized, even by critics of a "system" or an "ideology." Moreover, to present hegemony in overly hegemonic

terms is to pave over the fissures, heterogeneities, and uncertainties in the "dominant system" where forces of resistance may appear. Forces of resistance do face the threat of "cooptation" or recycling, which is quite pervasive in a commodity system, but this threat should not be automatically transformed into a foregone conclusion (for example, by reifying "the system" and attributing to it all sorts of mysterious powers). The various tendencies in Foucault I have briefly evoked may help to account for his "evasiveness" or at least his hesitancy to propose alternatives, especially in terms of institutional practices. The question with which Foucault leaves us, I would suggest, is not the traditional one of "reform or revolution" but rather that of the way a necessarily delegitimating critique should proceed if it is sensitive to the problem of alternative institutions.

In discussing recent French thinkers, it is difficult not to succumb to the "star" (if not the Caliban) syndrome and to herald the advent of the latest—or at least the most recently discovered—virtuoso from Paris. Jean-François Lyotard has been around for a long time, but he has recently attained a rather distinctive "voice" among contemporary critics. His is an especially attractive "voice" since it seems to convey the best of recent French thought but to transcend its internecine contentiousness. Instead polemic is directed at more clearly differentiated opponents, such as Jürgen Habermas in his rather dismissive reaction to recent French criticism.

Lyotard's emphases may justifiably be seen as converging with those of another recently discovered theorist of language and culture, Mikhail Bakhtin, and as providing the occasion for a critique of some of the arrested developments of Bakhtin's own work (its occasional myth of populistic origins and its phonocentric metaphysic, for example).[16] I would like simply to focus on a few features of Lyotard's thought that I find particularly suggestive or controversial, and I shall extend the discussion into areas that border on Bakhtin's concerns. In this manner, I shall be able to return to more general problems in "criticism" that I touched upon at the beginning of this paper.

The political and social import of Lyotard's work is

immediately apparent in his attempt to conjoin the motif of difference or heterogeneity with his insistence upon justice. He has associated a passionate *plaidoyer* for "postmodern" experimentalism with a critique of metanarratives that "totalize" their objects. His emphasis upon "difference" has taken two more or less related forms. One is the partial return to Kant, notably to the implications of an incommensurable gap between the "Idea" and its embodiment or exemplification. Not only does the Idea remain "unpresentable" in that it cannot be fully realized, for example, in institutions. The Idea cannot even be adequately conceptualized, and it cannot be figured in the form of totality. It remains a critical fiction or regulative idea that is contestable and open to the future. Thus any claim to have realized the just society, either in thought or in practice, is necessarily mystified. Here one has a rebuke to both Hegelian and Marxist "totalization"—to conceptual Absolute Knowledge as well as the redemptive dictatorship of the proletariat. In line with his critique of totalization and metanarrative, Lyotard has defended the importance of "little stories" and of the right to a narrative voice as itself a significant political right. Any account is a supplement to existing accounts, and it cannot claim full authority (or authorship) in appropriating or totalizing the others. The roles of speaker and listener, as well as those of writer and reader, become reversible, and the "just" context is an openly dialogized one in which obligations are mutual.

Even this brief sketch of Lyotard's recent views is enough to bring out their significance and appeal. I would like, however, to raise certain questions about the implications of these views. Lyotard is convincing in his argument that any Idea—let us say, any utopia or sovereign, indeed "sublime" principle—cannot be fully conceptualized much less realized in institutional practice. But this convincing argument about the nature and role of critical fictions or regulative ideas does not obviate the need for critical thought about institutions or the possible duality of certain notions as both critical fictions and institutional options. (Bakhtin's "carnivalization" is, I think, one of these dual, ambivalent, or "catachretic" notions.)

In fact one might insist that Lyotard's concerns require the rethinking of institutions in terms that resist the inclination of modern intellectuals to align themselves exclusively with the Idea and to relegate the institution to the sublunary realm of the hopelessly degraded or fallen. This inclination relies on a binary opposition between realms or spheres, and it may return criticism to an unworldly, noumenal realm of detached Ideas or perhaps of blind faith. The problem, as I intimated earlier, would rather be to displace the concept of totalization in the direction of a notion of articulation between *différends* or even incommensurables such as the critical fiction and the institution—an articulation that might allow for the spanning of gaps that cannot be closed. Here one need not assume that institutional proposals are necessarily dogmatic. On the contrary, if attempts to formulate a regulative idea are contestable, institutional proposals are doubly contestable in that they attempt to trace the import of a regulative idea for sociocultural life. But they are also necessary, for if one takes leave of this obligation, one can be reasonably certain that others will all-too-readily take it up.

The very desire to relate the "themes" of difference and justice would itself seem to require a reopening of thought about institutions. While justice may require the respect for certain differences, not all differences are just and worthy of respect. The difficulty is in thinking through and creating institutions that articulate "just" differences in sociocultural life. This difficulty is great, and it requires inquiry into the relation of hierarchy and equality. A total egalitarianism does not pose the problem of justice; it eliminates it. And it is dubious as a simple reversal of hierarchy. Indeed in the contemporary political and academic context, it readily becomes subservient to populistic modes of scapegoating and intolerance for exceptions.

One of the most potent institutional implications of the post-structuralist critique of binary oppositions is a critique of the scapegoat mechanism. Scapegoating on a discursive level is itself essential to the constitution of pure oppositions insofar as internal alterity, perceived as guilty or fallen, is purged, and all "otherness" is projected onto the discrete other. In social life, scapegoating provides instant purification and the ability to localize the source of contamination in an individual or group bearing the most recognizable differences from the in-group. It is also operative in the crucial conversion of absence into loss— in the assumption that what is missing in the present (identity, totality, plenitude) must have existed in the past and must be recaptured in the future. Scapegoating has of course had a blatant historical role in generating solidarity and sociocultural identity. It has also had more subtle connections with the complex of metaphorical identity, narrative closure, and di- alectical synthesis (all of which require the expulsion or reduc- tion of heterogeneities and remainders). The critical task is to work out alternatives to it. A different understanding of institu- tions as settings for the interaction of social individuals, marked by internal alterity yet committed or obligated to one another, is a necessary step in this respect. The very oxy- moronic notion of a social individual reveals how the individ- ual is "altered" from the beginning of anything that may be called cultural life by social relations; but it also counters a simplistic social metaphysic that postulates "society" (collec- tive routines or mentalities) as the origin of all meaning and value.

Institutions require limiting norms, but these norms need not stipulate a rigid definition of class, status, and power or demarcate unbreachable boundaries between groups or indi- viduals. The axial opposition between hierarchy and equality should itself be displaced in the direction of a finer network of similarities and differences in terms of which the exception need not be scapegoated and the less able seen as mere refuse of the system. And boundaries should be rethought as a function of problematic distinctions instead of hard and fast dichoto- mies. I am of course merely gesturing toward a range of difficult problems, but, without an awareness that these problems exist, there is the danger that the defense of the Idea may become escapist, and the advocacy of little heterogeneous stories may turn into a narrativist rendition of *On Liberty* with a comparable blindness to the institutional and "material" correlates of free speech or the right to narrate. In fact, in certain fields, such as historiography, the right to tell stories is quite secure. But they often take the form of ingratiating anecdotes that void historiography of a critical impetus and induce premature "anecdotage."

I have intimated that Bakhtin's notion of carnivalization—the high point of dialogism—is best interpreted as a liminal or threshold term that connects, and perforce transgresses the opposition between, the regulative idea and the institution. It is indeed a critical fiction, but it would lose its critical force if it had no institutional import. Carnival is a social institution, although carnivalization would be mystifyingly reified if it were simply identified or conflated with an institutional embodiment.

Bakhtin's argument (as I read it) is that the interaction between carnival as a social institution and carnivalization as a critical force in art and literature is itself a vital component of a viable society and culture. For him the decline or disfigurement of carnival as a social institution affects both art and the nature of social life. In modern culture, it may induce a hermetic appropriation of carnivalesque forces in artifacts of high culture that are used to protest the nature of the dominant society but that confront the problem of their own distance from popular culture and their "cooptation" by elites as status symbols or signs of membership in a *cénacle*.[17]

The larger issue in the modern Western context is the relation among elite, popular, and mass or commodified cultures. Work in this context tends to be effectively cut off from play on the level of production, thus eliminating any alternation of labor and carnivalesque activity in the general "economy" of social life. But play is recuperated on the level of consumption and confined within "leisure" or "free" time. In this reduced state, it may be serviced by culture industries that have their share in the system of production. Or it may be restricted to the nuclear family as the domestic, privatized space for the celebration of holidays or the enactment of the "sitcoms" of everyday, routine life. Mass or commodified culture affects both elite and popular culture. Indeed, in the modern West, popular culture is to a significant extent assimilated or appropriated by commodified culture, and this development is one reason for the heightened "alienation" of segments of elite culture. (How much wishful thinking is there in the emphasis upon the critical force of commodified culture?) But elite culture itself of course does not escape the "star" syndrome, the "talk show" variant of dialogism, or the temptation of cultural despair and apocalyptic exaltation.

Bakhtin himself did not view the carnivalesque as a total answer to modern problems. But this was not because the notion had no institutional bearing for him. It was rather because it referred to a dimension of sociocultural activity that had to be related to other activities in the more general movement of social life. One of these other activities was of course work. Bakhtin did not envision a simple suspension of work in a totally carnivalized utopia. Instead he tried to rethink the relations of work and play, for example, by seeing the carnivalesque consumption of food as the culmination of the labor process.

Carnival itself for Bakhtin is on the borderline between life and art: it is neither a purely social nor a purely aesthetic institution.[18] One might invoke other theorists to suggest that craft is also on the borderline between life and art—the "missing link" between them. The rearticulation of work and play might in this sense be understood in terms of the relation between craft and carnival, and the enormous problem in modern society would be how to make all jobs crafts and simultaneously to introduce carnival-type institutions that would interact with work in a viable rhythm of social life.

One may note that for Bakhtin narrowly functional analyses of carnival were misguided because they ignored the philosophical and existential significance of carnival itself. Indeed, the turn to narrowly functional analysis may be taken as a sign of one's distance from the "carnival spirit." In any event, it is worth noting that the function of carnival varies. It has neither a universally conservative nor a universally revolutionary role. It does convey at least the possibility of change and in this sense has a contestatory potential, but this potential is actualized in different forms from the relatively harmless "safety-valve" to highly disruptive insurgence. For Bakhtin, however, carnival is best when its function is itself deeply ambivalent—when it demonstrates that one can legitimately take seriously and joke about one's basic commitments.

With penultimate concision that scarcely serves to broach an important set of problems, I shall raise an issue that deserves further reflection. Bakhtin approached the festive through carnival and tended to play down the element of scapegoating that might appear in carnival itself. More generally, he turned his eyes from bloodletting and acknowledged the ambivalence of the carnivalesque in a manner that affirmed its joyful, life-enhancing side. He did not raise the question of the relation of the feast to tragedy, which is perhaps epitomized in sacrifice. The approach to festivity through a notion of ambivalence that stresses the tragic and sacrifice was developed of course by Georges Bataille, and it has been taken to an extreme pitch by René Girard. Bataille saw sacrifice as a ritualized form of violence that enabled a momentary collective outlet for the excess everyone harbors and must control in daily life. He thus situated sacrifice within a "general" economy open to deep play between life and death. The festive consumption of a surplus in this economy, which at its limit involved the sacrifice of life itself, countered the instrumental, profit-maximizing norms of a "restricted" economy such as capitalism where a surplus is continually reinvested. Implicit in my own account is a desire to distance carnival from scapegoating and to align it with a critique of the scapegoat mechanism that would also be a critique of sacrifice insofar as it resorts to scapegoating. Here one may perhaps distinguish between the "sacrifice" or gift of self that Bataille saw as essential to social life, on the one hand, and the victimization of others which depends upon a denial of internal alterity, on the other. Insofar as sacrifice relies on victimization and the achievement of purity for the self through a projection of guilt onto a separate "other," it should, I think, itself be seen as a type of restricted economy and related to the series I mentioned earlier: metaphoric identification, narrative closure, and dialectical synthesis. The critique of scapegoating and of totalization would not deny the significance of other dimensions of Bataille's understanding of festive *dépense*, notably his insistence on the risk of extreme loss in nonacquisitive expenditure or his specific sense of "totality" in existential commitment to a group or a way of being that is not subordinated in instrumental fashion to some delimited end. It might also reinforce Bataille's attempt to distinguish his views from those put forth by fascist ideologists. But it would leave open the difficult questions of the relation between the "elective" groups Bataille defended and egalitarian, democratic values as well as the interaction between tragic and carnivalesque *dépense*. (At least indirectly, *dépense* in Bataille's sense might in addition serve to bring up the issue of liberality or generosity beyond delimited forms of "justice.")

I would like to conclude with a few brief remarks about "criticism" in the academic institution—remarks that may help to specify the institutional implications of my opening words. In terms of a "minimal program," what I have said would imply the need for greater diversity in basic perspective among those housed in the same department. A department should be a place where fundamental issues in interpretation can be argued—hence a significantly contested place. In addition, any university should have a somewhat decentered center where critics who are seeking their way can encounter others with comparable concerns. These two rather minimal institutional proposals—which in the existing academic context might well appear to be enormities if not "howlers"—would at least be initial steps in the attempt to rethink the articulation of the university. "Articulation" is after all not totalization but the (often problematic) joining of differences, and it becomes effective in culture when the differences engage one another in controversy and play—indeed when difference is itself linked to obligation and solidarity.

Notes

1. This is Mark Poster's project in his stimulating paper in this collection.

2. See especially *Knowledge and Human Interests*, Jeremy J. Shapiro, tr. (Boston: Beacon, 1971).

3. Compare *For Marx*, Ben Brewster, tr. (1965; London: New Left Books, 1979); *Reading Capital*, Ben Brewster, tr. (1968; London: New Left Books, 1979); *Lenin and Philosophy*, Ben Brewster, tr. (New York: Verso, 1971); and *Essays in Self-Criticism*, Grahame Lock, tr. (London: New Left Books, 1976).

4. *The Political Unconscious* (Ithaca, N.Y.: Cornell University Press, 1981).

5. One might compare this proposal with Jean-François Lyotard's notion of *différends* as it is explored in David Carroll's excellent paper.

6. In their emphasis upon the need for this sort of investigation, one might see a convergence in the arguments of Mark Poster and David Carroll.

7. This process is examined critically by John Carlos Rowe in his provocative account of the "aestheticist" turn in Americanized deconstruction.

8. These three figures are of course important reference points in a number of the papers in this collection.

9. Here I misappropriate a quote from Robert Weimann's paper and place it in a different context, but I later return to Weimann's concerns.

10. This is the crisis addressed in the papers of John Carlos Rowe and Robert Weimann.

11. I here touch upon the arguments in Anthony Giddens' paper.

12. On these issues, see my *History & Criticism* (Ithaca, N.Y.: Cornell University Press, 1985).

13. See, for example, GREPH, *Qui a peur de la philosophie* (Paris: Flammarion, 1977); "Entre crochets," *Digraphe* (1976), vol. 8; *La Carte postale: De Socrate à Freud et au-delà* (Paris: Flammarion, 1981); "Philosophie des Etats Généraux" in *Etats Généraux de la Philosophie* (Paris: Flammarion, 1979); and "No Apocalypse, Not Now" in *Diacritics* (1984), vol. 14.

14. *Discipline and Punish*, Alan Sheridan, tr. (1977; New York: Pantheon, 1979).

15. *L'Impossible prison*, Michelle Perrot, ed. (Paris: Seuil, 1980).

16. David Carroll of course argues this point. The rest of my discussion is in good part a dialogue with his paper.

17. The hermetic appropriation of the carnivalesque and the process of commodification pose problems for the contact between high and popular culture that are elided in Gregory Ulmer's recent appeal for a post-deconstructive pedagogy in *Applied Grammatology* (Baltimore and London: Johns Hopkins University Press, 1985). I must confess that I was seized by two perverse images in reading this thought-provoking book. One involved a massive movement to rechristen the Arts and Sciences Quad as the AG ("Applied Grammatology") Quad. The other was that of Derrida on MTV, along with the Dissemination Boys, singing "I Wish They All Could Be Deconstructed Girls!"

18. Could one see here a different perspective on the problem of "doubling" that is discussed in Wolfgang Iser's paper?

9

CAPITALIST CULTURE
AND THE CIRCULATORY SYSTEM

Stephen Greenblatt

LET me begin by acknowledging that it is impossible to sum-
marize, let alone to respond adequately, to the diverse concerns
of the dense and complex papers written for the Focused Research Program in Contemporary Critical Theory at Irvine. All
that I can hope to do is to examine a single strand that runs
through many of these fine papers—the relation between the
discourse of art and the circumambient discourses of society—
and to add my own reflections. And even here I am acutely
aware of my limitations—I am not a philosopher nor can I
propose a comprehensive theory of aesthetic experience. Having blindly committed myself to this occasion, I would have
embarked in any case in a spirit of genial resignation, but I am
emboldened somewhat by the doubts that flicker through these
papers about the usefulness of an overarching theory or, in
David Carroll's term, a metanarrative that does not attach itself
to specific discursive practices and strategic occasions. For it is
only such an embedded theory, theory glimpsed lurking in the
thickets of narrative pragmatics,[1] that I am able to deploy.

Walter Michaels and Steven Knapp argue, in a controversial essay, that while theory always posits a privileged position outside of interpretation, no such position is possible, and

hence the project of theory always fails.[2] I am not at all certain that theory does necessarily and by definition claim such a position for itself; my own reservations in any case arise more from political than hermeneutical doubts. My work has its most insistent contiguities with Marxist theory, but I find myself deeply uneasy with many of the characteristic Marxist stances. (That I am still more uneasy with a politics and perspective untouched by Marxist thought does not lead me to endorse propositions or embrace a rhetoric *faute de mieux*.) Thus the crucial identifying gestures made by the most distinguished American Marxist aesthetic theorist, Fredric Jameson, seem to me highly problematical. Let us take, for example, the following eloquent passage from *The Political Unconscious*: "the convenient working distinction between cultural texts that are social and political and those that are not becomes something worse than an error: namely, a symptom and a reinforcement of the reification and privatization of contemporary life. Such a distinction reconfirms that structural, experiential, and conceptual gap between the public and the private, between the social and the psychological, or the political and the poetic, between history or society and the 'individual,' which—the tendential law of social life under capitalism—maims our existence as individual subjects and paralyzes our thinking about time and change just as surely as it alienates us from our speech itself."[3]

A working distinction between cultural texts that are social and political and those that are not—that is, an aesthetic domain that is in some way marked off from the discursive institutions that are operative elsewhere in a culture—becomes for Jameson a malignant symptom of "privatization." Why should the "private" immediately enter into this distinction at all? Does the term here refer to private property, that is, to the ownership of the means of production and the regulation of the mode of consumption? If so, what is the historical relation between this mode of economic organization and a working distinction between the political and the poetic? It would seem that in print, let alone in the electronic media, private ownership has led not to "privatization" but to the drastic communalization of all discourse, the constitution of an ever larger mass audience, the organization of a public sphere unimagined and certainly unattained by the comparatively modest attempts in precapitalist societies to organize public discourse. Moreover, is it not possible to have a communal sphere of art that is distinct from other communal spheres? Is this communal differentiation, sanctioned by the laws of property, not in fact the dominant practice in capitalist society, manifestly in the film and television industries but also since the invention of movable type in the production of poems and novels as well? Would we really find it less alienating to have no distinction at all between the political and the poetic—the situation, let us say, during China's Cultural Revolution? Or, for that matter, do we find it notably liberating to have our own country governed by a film actor who is either cunningly or pathologically indifferent to the traditional differentiation between fantasy and reality?

For Jameson any demarcation of the aesthetic must be aligned with the private which is in turn aligned with the psychological, the poetic, and the individual, as distinct from the public, the social, and the political. All of these interlocking distinctions, none of which seem to me philosophically or even historically bound up with the original "working distinction," are then laid at the door of capitalism with its power to "maim" and "paralyze" us as "individual subjects." Though we may find a differentiation between cultural discourses that are artistic and cultural discourses that are social or political well before the European seventeenth century and in cultures that seem far removed from the capitalist mode of production, Jameson insists that somehow the perpetrator and agent of the alleged maiming is capitalism. A shadowy opposition is assumed between the "individual" (bad) and the "individual subject" (good); indeed the maiming of the latter creates the former.

The whole passage has the resonance of an allegory of the fall of man: once we were whole, agile, integrated; we were individual subjects but not individuals, we had no psychology distinct from the shared life of the society; politics and poetry were one. Then capitalism arose and shattered this luminous, benign totality. The myth echoes throughout Jameson's book, though by the close it has been eschatologically reoriented so that the totality lies not in a past revealed to have always already fallen but in the classless future. A philosophical claim then appeals to an absent empirical event. And literature is invoked at once as the dark token of fallenness and the shimmering emblem of the absent transfiguration.

But, of course, as Mark Poster points out in "Foucault, Post-Structuralism, and the Mode of Information," post-structuralism has raised serious questions about such a vision, challenging both its underlying oppositions and the primal organic unity that it posits as either paradisal origin or utopian end. This challenge has already greatly modified, though by no means simply displaced, Marxist discourse. The complexity of the interaction between Marxism and post-structuralism is perfectly exemplified in Jean-François Lyotard's paper, "Judiciousness in Dispute, or Kant after Marx." Here, as in Jameson, the distinction between discursive fields is once again at stake: for Lyotard the existence of proper names makes possible "the coexistence of those worlds that Kant calls fields, territories, and domains—those worlds which of course present the same object, but which also make that object the stakes of heterogeneous (or incommensurable) expectations in universes of phrases, none of which can be transformed into any other" (p. 51).

Lyotard's model for these differentiated discourses is the existence of proper names. But now it is the role of capitalism not to demarcate discursive domains but, quite the opposite, to make such domains untenable. "Capital is that which wants a single language and a single network, and it never stops trying to present them" (p. 64). Lyotard's principle exhibit of this attempt by capital to institute a single language—what Bakhtin would call monologism—is Faurisson's denial of the Holocaust, and behind this denial, the Nazi's attempt to obliterate the existence of millions of Jews and other undesirables, an attempt Lyotard characterizes as the will "to strike from history and from the map entire worlds of names."

The immediate problem with this account is that the Nazis did not seem particularly interested in exterminating names along with the persons who possessed those names; on the contrary, they kept, insofar as was compatible with a campaign of mass murder, remarkably full records, and they looked forward to a time in which they could share their accomplishment with a grateful world by establishing a museum dedicated to the culture of the wretches they had destroyed. The Faurisson affair is at bottom not an epistemological dilemma, as Lyotard claims, but an attempt to wish away evidence that is both substantial and verifiable. The issue is not an Epicurean paradox—"if death is there, you are not there; if you are there, death is not there; hence it is impossible for you to prove that death is there"—but a historical problem: what is the evidence of mass murder? how reliable is this evidence? are there convincing grounds for denying or doubting the documented events? and if there are not such grounds, how may we interpret the motives of those who seek to cast doubt upon the historical record?

There is a further problem in Lyotard's use of the Faurisson affair as an instance of capitalist hostility to names: the conflation of Fascist apologetics and capitalism would seem to be itself an instance of monologism, since it suppresses all of the aspects of capitalism that are wedded to the generation and inscription of individual identities and to the demarcation of boundaries separating those identities. We may argue, of course, that the capitalist insistence upon individuality is fraudulent, but it is difficult, I think, to keep the principle of endlessly proliferated, irreducible individuality separate from the marketplace version against which it is set. For it is capitalism, as Marx suggested, that mounts the West's most powerful and sustained assault upon collective, communal values and identities. And it is in the marketplace and in the state apparatus linked to the circulation and accumulation of capital that names themselves are forged. Proper names, as distinct from common names, seem less the victims than the products of property—they are bound up not only with the property one has in oneself, that is, with the theory of possessive individualism, but quite literally with the property one possesses, for proper names are insisted upon in the early modern period precisely in order to register them in the official documents that enable the state to calculate and tax personal property.[4]

The difference between Jameson's capitalism, the perpetrator of separate discursive domains, the agent of privacy, psychology, and the individual, and Lyotard's capitalism, the enemy of such domains and the destroyer of privacy, psychology, and the individual, may in part be traced to a difference between the Marxist and post-structuralist projects. Jameson, seeking to expose the fallaciousness of a separate artistic sphere and to celebrate the materialist integration of all discourses, finds capitalism at the root of the false differentiation; Lyotard, seeking to celebrate the differentiation of all discourses and to expose the fallaciousness of monological unity, finds capitalism at the root of the false integration. History functions in both cases as a convenient anecdotal ornament upon a theoretical structure, and capitalism appears not as a complex social and economic development in the West but as a malign philosophical principle.

I propose that the general question addressed by Jameson and Lyotard and echoed in many of the papers written for the Irvine Focused Research Program—what is the historical relation between art and society or between one institutionally demarcated discursive practice and another?—does not lend itself to a single, theoretically satisfactory answer of the kind that Jameson and Lyotard are trying to provide. Or rather theoretical satisfaction here seems to depend upon a utopian vision that collapses the contradictions of history into a moral imperative. The problem is not simply the incompatibility of two theories—Marxist and post-structuralist—with one another, but the inability of either of the theories to come to terms with the apparently contradictory effects of capitalism. In principle, of course, both Marxism and post-structuralism seize upon contradictions: for the former they are signs of repressed class conflicts, for the latter they disclose hidden cracks in the spurious uncertainties of logocentrism. But in practice Jameson treats capitalism as the agent of repressive differentiation, while Lyotard treats it as the agent of monological totalization. And this effacement of contradiction is not the consequence of an accidental lapse but rather the logical outcome of theory's search for the obstacle that blocks the realization of its eschatological vision.

If capitalism is invoked not as a unitary demonic principle but as a complex, historical movement in a world without paradisal origins or chiliastic expectations, then an inquiry into the relation between art and society in capitalist cultures must address both the formation of the working distinction upon which Jameson remarks and the totalizing impulse upon which Lyotard remarks. For capitalism has characteristically generated neither regimes in which all discourses seem coordinated nor regimes in which they seem radically isolated or discontinuous but regimes in which the drive toward differentiation and the drive toward monological organization operate simultaneously or at least oscillate so rapidly as to create the impression of simultaneity.

In a brilliant paper that received unusual attention, elicited a response from a White House speechwriter, and most recently generated a segment of CBS's "Sixty Minutes," the political scientist and historian Michael Rogin recently observed the number of times in which President Reagan has, at critical moments in his career, quoted lines from his own or other popular films. The President is a man, Rogin remarks, "whose most spontaneous moments—('Where do we find such men?' about the American D-Day dead; 'I am paying for this microphone, Mr. Green,' during the 1980 New Hampshire primary debate)—are not only preserved and projected on film, but also turn out to be lines from old movies."[5] To a remarkable extent, Ronald Reagan, who made his final Hollywood film, *Hellcats of the Navy*, in 1957, continues to live within the movies; he has been shaped by them, draws much of his cold war rhetoric from them, cannot or will not distinguish between them and an external reality. Indeed his political career has depended upon an ability to project himself and his mass audience into a realm in which there is no distinction between simulation and reality.

The response from Anthony Dolan, a White House speechwriter who was asked to comment on Rogin's paper, was highly revealing. "What he's really saying," Dolan suggested, "is that all of us are deeply affected by a uniquely American art form: the movies."[6] Rogin had in fact argued that the presidential character "was produced from the convergence of two sets of substitutions which generated cold war countersubversion in the 1940s and underlie its 1980s revival—the political replacement of Nazism by Communism, from which the national security state was born; and the psychological shift from an embodied self to its simulacrum on film." Both the political and the psychological substitution were intimately bound up with Ronald Reagan's career in the movies. Dolan in response rewrites Rogin's thesis into a celebration of the power of "a uniquely American art form" to shape "all of us." Movies, Dolan told the New York Times reporter, "heighten reality rather than lessen it."

Such a statement appears to welcome the collapse of the working distinction between the aesthetic and the real; the aesthetic is not an alternative realm but a way of intensifying the single realm we all inhabit. But then the spokesman went on to assert that the President "usually credits the films whose lines he uses." That is, at the moment of appropriation, the President acknowledges that he is borrowing from the aesthetic and hence acknowledges the existence of a working distinction. In so doing he respects and even calls attention to the difference between his own presidential discourse and the fictions in which he himself at one time took part; they are differences upon which his own transition from actor to politician in part depends, and they are the signs of the legal and economic system that he represents. For the capitalist aesthetic demands acknowledgments—hence the various marks of property rights that are flashed on the screen or inscribed in a text—and the political arena insists that it is not a fiction. That without acknowledgment the President delivers speeches written by Anthony Dolan or others does not appear to concern anyone; this has long been the standard operating procedure of American politicians. But it would concern people if the President recited speeches that were lifted without acknowledgment from old movies. He would then seem not to know the difference between fantasy and reality. And that might be alarming.

The White House, of course, was not responding to a theoretical problem, but to the implication that somehow the President did not fully recognize that he was quoting or alternatively that he did realize it and chose to repress the fact in order to make a more powerful impression. In one version he is a kind of sleepwalker, in the other a plagiarist. To avoid these implications the White House spokesman needed in effect to invoke a difference that he had himself a moment before undermined.

The spokesman's remarks were hasty and ad hoc, but it did not take reflection to reproduce the complex dialectic of differentiation and identity that those remarks articulate. That dialectic is powerful precisely because it is by now virtually thoughtless; it takes a substantial intellectual effort to separate the boundaries of art from the subversion of those boundaries, an effort such as that exemplified in the work of Jameson or Lyotard. But the effect of such an effort is to remove itself from the very phenomenon it had proposed to analyze, the relation between art and surrounding discourses in capitalist culture. For the effortless invocation of two apparently contradictory accounts of art is characteristic of American capitalism in the late twentieth century and an outcome of long-term tendencies in the relationship of art and capital: in the same moment a working distinction between the aesthetic and reality is established and abrogated.

We could argue, following Jameson, that the establishment of the distinction is the principal effect, with a view toward alienating us from our own imaginations by isolating fantasies in a private, apolitical realm. Or we could argue, following Lyotard, that the abrogation of the distinction is the principal effect, with a view toward effacing or evading differences by establishing a single, monolithic ideological structure. But if we are asked to choose between these alternatives, we will be drawn away from an analysis of the relation between capitalism and aesthetic production. For from the sixteenth century, when the effects for art of joint-stock company organization first began to be felt, to the present, capitalism has produced a powerful and effective oscillation between the establishment of distinct discursive domains and the collapse of those domains into one another. It is this restless oscillation rather than the securing of a particular fixed position that constitutes the distinct power of capitalism. The individual elements—a range of discontinuous discourses, on the one hand, the monological unification of all discourses, on the other— may be found fully articulated in other economic and social systems; only capitalism has managed to generate a dizzying, seemingly inexhaustible circulation between the two.

My use of the term *circulation* here is influenced by the work of Derrida, but sensitivity to the practical strategies of negotiation and exchange depends less upon post-structuralist theory than upon the circulatory rhythms of American politics. And the crucial point is that it is not politics alone but the whole structure of production and consumption—the systematic organization of ordinary life and consciousness—that generates the pattern of boundary making and breaking, the oscillation between demarcated objects and monological totality, that I have sketched. If we restrict our focus to the zone of political institutions, we can easily fall into the illusion that everything depends upon the unique talents—if that is the word—of Ronald Reagan, that he alone has managed to generate the enormously effective shuttling between massive, universalizing fantasies and centerlessness that characterizes his administration. This illusion leads in turn to the humanist trivialization of power upon which John Carlos Rowe comments, a trivialization that finds its local political expression in the belief that the fantasmatics of current American politics are the product of a single man and will pass with him. On the contrary, Ronald Reagan is manifestly the product of a larger and more durable American structure—not only a structure of power, ideological extremism, and militarism but of pleasure, recreation, and interest, a structure that shapes the spaces we construct for ourselves, the way we present "the news," the fantasies we daily consume on television or in the movies, the entertainments that we characteristically make and take.

I am suggesting then that the oscillation between totalization and difference, uniformity and the diversity of names, unitary truth and a proliferation of distinct entities—in short between Lyotard's capitalism and Jameson's—is built into the poetics of everyday behavior in America.[7] Let us consider, for example, not the President's Hollywood career but a far more innocent California pastime, a trip to Yosemite National Park. One of the most popular walks at Yosemite is the Nevada Falls Trail. So popular, indeed, is this walk that the Park Service has had to pave the first miles of the trail in order to keep them from being dug into trenches by the heavy traffic. At a certain point the asphalt stops, and you encounter a sign that tells you that you are entering the wilderness. You have passed then from the National Forests that surround the park—forests that serve principally as state-subsidized nurseries for large timber companies and hence are not visibly distinguishable from the tracts of privately-owned forest with which they are contiguous—to the park itself, marked by the payment of admission to the uniformed ranger at the entrance kiosk, and finally to a third and privileged zone of publically demarcated Nature. This zone, called the wilderness, is marked by the abrupt termination of the asphalt and by a sign that lists the rules of behavior that you must now observe: no dogs, no littering, no fires, no camping without a permit, and so forth. The wilderness then is signalled by an intensification of the rules, an intensification that serves as the condition of an escape from the asphalt.

You continue on this trail then until you reach a steep cliff onto which the guardians of the wilderness have thoughtfully bolted a cast-iron stairway. The stairway leads to a bridge that spans a rushing torrent, and from the middle of the bridge you are rewarded with a splendid view of Nevada Falls. On the railing that keeps you from falling to your death as you enjoy your vision of the wilderness, there are signs—information about the dimensions of the falls, warnings against attempting to climb the treacherous, mist-slickened rocks, trail markers for those who wish to walk further—and an anodyzed aluminum plaque on which are inscribed inspirational, vaguely Wordsworthian sentiments by John Muir. The passage, as best I can recall, assures you that in years to come you will treasure the image you have before you. And next to these words, also etched into the aluminum, is precisely an image: a photograph of Nevada Falls taken from the very spot on which you stand.

The pleasure of this moment—beyond the pleasure of the mountain air and the waterfall and the great boulders and the deep forests of Lodgepole and Jeffrey pine—arises from the unusually candid glimpse of the process of circulation that shapes the whole experience of the park. The wilderness is at once secured and obliterated by the official gestures that establish its boundaries; the natural is set over against the artificial through means that render such an opposition meaningless. The eye passes from the "natural" image of the waterfall to the aluminum image, as if to secure a difference (for why else bother to go to the park at all? why not simply look at a book of pictures?), even as that difference is effaced. The effacement is by no means complete—on the contrary, parks like Yosemite are one of the ways in which the distinction between nature and artifice is constituted in our society—and yet the Park Service's plaque on the Nevada Falls bridge conveniently calls attention to the interpenetration of nature and artifice that makes the distinction possible.

What is missing from this exemplary fable of capitalist aesthetics is the question of property relations, since the National Parks exist precisely to suspend or marginalize that question through the ideology of protected public space. Everyone owns the parks. That ideology is somewhat bruised by the actual development of a park like Yosemite, with its expensive hotel, a restaurant that has a dress code, fancy gift shops, and the like, but it is not entirely emptied out: even the administration of James Watt stopped short of permitting a private golf course to be constructed on park grounds, and there was public outrage when a television production company that had contracted to film a series in Yosemite decided to paint the rocks to make them look more realistic. What we need is an example that combines recreation or entertainment, aesthetics, the public sphere, and private property. The example most compelling to a literary critic like myself is not a political career or a national park but a novel.

In 1976, a convict named Gary Gilmore was released from a federal penitentiary and moved to Provo, Utah. Several months later, he robbed and killed two men, was arrested for the crimes, and convicted of murder. The case became famous when Gilmore demanded that he be executed—a punishment that had not been inflicted in America for some years, due to legal protections—and, over the strenuous objections of the ACLU and NAACP, had his way. The legal maneuvers and the eventual firing-squad execution became national media events. Well before the denouement the proceedings had come to the attention of Norman Mailer and his publisher Warner Books which is, as it announces on its title pages, "a Warner Communications Company." Mailer's research assistant, Jere Herzenberg, and a hack writer and interviewer, Lawrence Schiller, conducted extensive interviews and acquired documents, records of court proceedings, and personal papers such as the intimate letters between Gilmore and his girlfriend. Some of these materials were in the public domain but many of them were not; they were purchased, and the details of the purchases themselves became part of the materials that were reworked by Mailer into The Executioner's Song,[8] a "true life novel" as it is called, that brilliantly combines documentary realism with Mailer's characteristic romance themes. The novel was a critical and popular success—a success signaled not only by the sheaves of admiring reviews but by the Universal Product Code printed on its paperback cover. It was subsequently made into an NBC-TV mini-series where on successive evenings it helped to sell cars, soap powder, and deodorant.

Mailer's book had further, and less predictable, ramifications. While he was working on *The Executioner's Song*, there was an article on Mailer in *People* magazine. The article caught the attention of a convict named Jack H. Abbott who wrote to offer Mailer first-hand instruction on the conditions of prison life. An exchange of letters began, and Mailer grew increasingly impressed not only with their detailed information but with what he calls their "literary measure." The letters were cut and arranged by a Random House editor, Erroll McDonald, and appeared as a book called *In the Belly of the Beast*. This book too was widely acclaimed and contributed, with Mailer's help, to win a parole for its author.

"As I am writing these words," Mailer wrote in the Introduction to Abbott's book, "it looks like Abbott will be released on parole this summer. It is certainly the time for him to get out."⁹ "I have never come into bodily contact with another human being in almost twenty years," wrote Abbott in his book, "except in combat; in acts of struggle, of violence" (63). Shortly after his release, Abbott, now a celebrity, approached a waiter in an all-night restaurant and asked to use the men's room. The waiter—Richard Adan, an aspiring actor and playwright—told Abbott that the restaurant had no men's room and asked him to step outside. When Adan followed him onto the sidewalk, Abbott, apparently thinking that he was being challenged, stabbed Adan in the heart with a kitchen knife. Abbott was arrested and convicted once again of murder. The events have themselves been made into a play, also called *In the Belly of the Beast*, that recently opened to very favorable reviews.

Literary criticism has a familiar set of terms for the relationship between a work of art and the historical events to which it refers: we speak of allusion, symbolization, allegorization, representation, and above all mimesis. Each of these terms has a rich history and is virtually indispensable, and yet they all seem curiously inadequate to the cultural phenomenon which Mailer's book and Abbott's and the television series and the play constitute. And their inadequacy extends to aspects not only of contemporary culture but of the culture of the past. We need to develop terms to describe the ways in which material—

here official documents, private papers, newspaper clippings, and so forth—is transferred from one discursive sphere to another and becomes aesthetic property. It would, I think, be a mistake to regard this process as uni-directional—from social discourse to aesthetic discourse—not only because the aesthetic discourse in this case is so entirely bound up with capitalist venture but because the social discourse is already charged with aesthetic energies. Not only was Gilmore explicitly and powerfully moved by the film version of *One Flew Over the Cuckoo's Nest*, but his entire pattern of behavior seems to have been shaped by the characteristic representations of American popular fiction, including Mailer's own.

Michael Baxandall has argued recently that "art and society are analytical concepts from two different kinds of categorisation of human experience. . . . unhomologous systematic constructions put upon interpenetrating subject-matters." In consequence, he suggests, any attempt to relate the two must first "modify one of the terms till it matches the other, but keeping note of what modification has been necessary since this is a necessary part of one's information."[10] It is imperative that we acknowledge the modification and find a way to measure its degree, for it is only in such measurements that we can hope to chart the relationship between art and society. Such an admonition is important—methodological self-consciousness is one of the distinguishing marks of the new historicism in cultural studies as opposed to a historicism based upon faith in the transparency of signs and interpretive procedures—but it must be supplemented by an understanding that the work of art is not itself a pure flame that lies at the source of our speculations. Rather the work of art is itself the product of a set of manipulations, some of them our own (most striking in the case of works that were not originally conceived as "art" at all but rather as something else—votive objects, propaganda, prayer, etc.), many others undertaken in the construction of the original work. That is, the work of art is the product of a negotiation between a creator or class of creators, equipped with a complex, communally shared repertoire of conventions, and the institu-

tions and practices of society. In order to achieve the negotiation, artists need to create a currency that is valid for a meaningful, mutually profitable exchange. It is important to emphasize
that the process involves not simply appropriation but exchange, since the existence of art always implies a return, a
return normally measured in pleasure and interest. I should
add that the society's dominant currencies, money and pres-
tige, are invariably involved, but I am here using the term
"currency" metaphorically to designate the systematic adjust-
ments, symbolizations, and lines of credit necessary to enable
an exchange to take place. The terms "currency" and "negotiation" are the signs of our own manipulation and adjustment of
the relative systems.

The papers written for the Focused Research Program in
Contemporary Critical Theory must, I think, be understood in
the context of a search for a new set of terms to understand the
cultural phenomenon that I have tried to describe. Hence, for
example, Wolfgang Iser writes of the creation of the aesthetic
dimension through the "dynamic oscillation" between two
discourses; Robert Weimann argues that "the process of making
certain things one's own becomes inseparable from making
other things (and persons) alien, so that the act of appropriation
must be seen always already to involve not only self-projection
and assimilation but alienation through reification and expropriation"; Anthony Giddens proposes that we substitute a concept of textual distanciation for that of the autonomy of the text,
so that we can fruitfully grasp the "recursive character" of
social life and of language. Each of these formulations—and, of
course, there are significant differences among them—pulls
away from a stable, mimetic theory of art and attempts to
construct in its stead an interpretive model that will more
adequately account for the unsettling circulation of materials
and discourses that is, I have argued, the heart of modern
aesthetic practice. It is in response to this practice that contemporary theory must situate itself: not outside of interpretation
but in the hidden places of negotiation and exchange.

Notes

1. See David Carroll, "Narrative, Heterogeneity, and the Question of the Political: Bakhtin and Lyotard," p. 69.

2. *Against Theory: Literary Studies and the New Pragmatism*, W. J. T. Mitchell, ed. (Chicago: University of Chicago Press, 1985), pp. 11–30.

3. Fredric Jameson, *The Political Unconscious: Narrative As a Socially Symbolic Act* (Ithaca, N.Y.: Cornell University Press, 1981), p. 20.

4. See, for example, William E. Tate, *The Parish Chest: A Study in the Records of Parochial Administration in England* (Cambridge: Cambridge University Press, 1946).

5. Michael Rogin, " 'Ronald Reagan': The Movie" (unpublished manuscript).

6. Quoted by reporter Michael Tolchin in the *New York Times* account of Rogin's paper, an account headlined "How Reagan Always Gets the Best Lines," *New York Times*, September 9, 1985, p. 10.

7. I borrow the phrase "the poetics of everyday behavior" from Iurii M. Lotman. See his essay in A. D. Nakhimovsky and A. S. Nakhimovsky, eds., *The Semiotics of Russian Cultural History* (Ithaca, N.Y.: Cornell University Press, 1985).

8. Norman Mailer, *The Executioner's Song* (New York: Warner Books, 1979).

9. "Introduction" to Jack Henry Abbott, *In the Belly of the Beast: Letters from Prison* (New York: Random House, 1981), p. xviii.

10. Michael Baxandall, "Art, Society, and the Bouger Principle," in *Representations* (1985), 12:40–41.

INDEX